FLOYD CLYMER - 2025 EDITION
HODAKA
WORKSHOP MANUAL
90cc - 100cc - 125cc 1964-1978

A Floyd Clymer Publication - 2025 VelocePress.com

PREFACE

TRADEMARKS & COPYRIGHT

Hodaka® is the registered trademark of Pabatco Inc. This publication is not sponsored by or endorsed by the trademark owner. We recognize that some words, model names and designations, for example, mentioned herein are the property of the trademark holder. We use them for identification purposes only. This is not an official publication however; it may include non-copyright works of the trademark holder.

INTRODUCTION

Welcome to the world of digital publishing ~ the book you now hold in your hand was printed using the latest state of the art digital technology. The advent of print-on-demand has forever changed the publishing process, never has information been so accessible and it is our hope that this book serves your informational needs for years to come. If this is your first exposure to digital publishing, we hope that you are pleased with the results. Many more titles of interest to the classic automobile and motorcycle enthusiast, collector and restorer are available via our website at www.VelocePress.com. We hope that you find this title as interesting as we do.

NOTE FROM THE PUBLISHER

The information presented is true and complete to the best of our knowledge. All recommendations are made without any guarantees on the part of the author or the publisher, who also disclaim all liability incurred with the use of this information.

INFORMATION ON THE USE OF THIS PUBLICATION

This manual is an invaluable resource for those interested in performing their own maintenance. However, in today's information age we are constantly subject to changes in common practice, new technology, availability of improved materials and increased awareness of chemical toxicity. As such, it is advised that the user consult with an experienced professional prior to undertaking any procedure described herein. While every care has been taken to ensure correctness of information, it is obviously not possible to guarantee complete freedom from errors or omissions or to accept liability arising from such errors or omissions. Therefore, any individual that uses the information contained within, or elects to perform or participate in do-it-yourself repairs or modifications acknowledges that there is a risk factor involved and that the publisher or its associates cannot be held responsible for personal injury or property damage resulting from the use of the information or the outcome of such procedures.

WARNING!

One final word of advice, this publication is intended to be used as a reference guide, and when in doubt the reader should consult with a qualified technician.

QUICK REFERENCE DATA

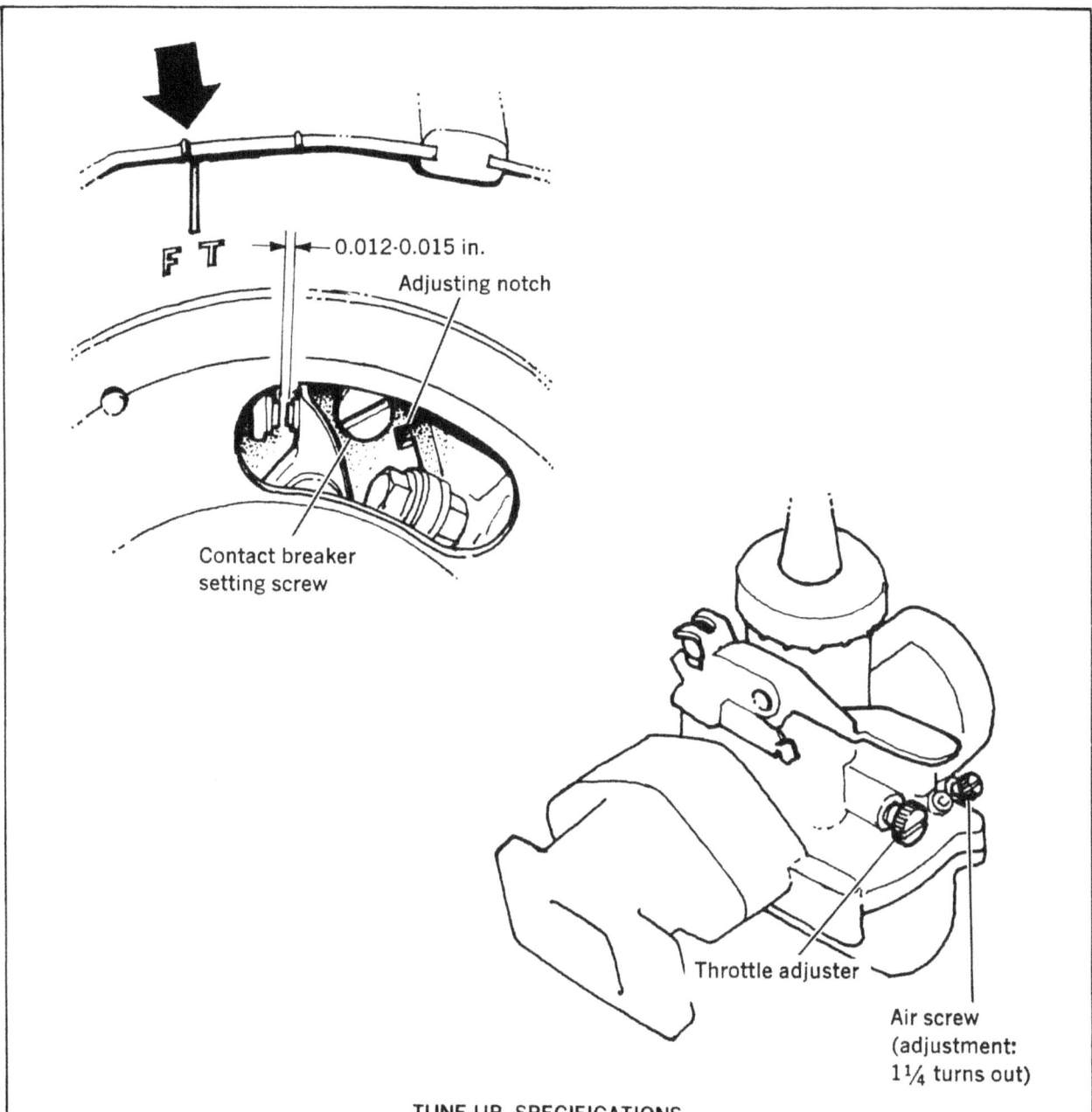

TUNE-UP SPECIFICATIONS

Item	Type, NGK	Gap
Spark plug		
Ace 90	B-7, B-8*	0.024-0.028 in. (0.6-0.7mm)
Ace 100, Ace 100B and Dirt Squirt	B-8, B-9*	0.024-0.028 in. (0.6-0.7mm)
Super Rat 100MX	B-10HN, B-11HN*	0.018-0.020 in. (0.45-0.50mm)
Wombat 125	B-8HS, B-9HS*	0.024-0.028 in. (0.6-0.7mm)
Combat 125	B-9HV, B-10V*	0.016-0.024 in. (0.4-0.6mm)
Point gap (all models)	0.012-0.014 in. (0.3-0.4mm)	
Firing point (measured as piston position)		
All 90 & 100 models	0.114 in. (2.90mm) BTDC	
Wombat 125	0.094 in. (2.4mm) BTDC	
Combat 125	0.155 in. (3.95mm) BTDC	

RECOMMENDED LUBRICANTS

Transmission oil
  Type (all models)   SAE 10W-40
  Quantity (all models)   1 ¼ pints (590cc)

Fork oil
  Type (all models)   SAE 20
  Quantity (each leg)
    Ace 90/100   4.5 ounces (135cc)
    Dirt Squirt 100   5.5 ounces (165cc)
    Ace 100B and Super Rat   5.5 ounces (165cc) with type 938750 and 938750A forks
                                               6 ounces (175cc) with type 938700 forks
    Wombat 125   5 ounces (148cc)
    Combat 125   6 ounces (175cc)

ADJUSTMENTS

Clutch lever free play	¼ in. measured at lever end
Drive chain free play	¾ in. measured midway on bottom run with rider seated
Front brake lever free play	¼ in. measured at lever end
Rear brake pedal free play	¾ in. at tip of pedal

TORQUE SPECIFICATIONS

Cylinder head nuts
  90/100 models   105 in.-lb. (1.2 mkg)
  125 models   170 in.-lb. (2 mkg)
Flywheel nut (all models)   170 in.-lb. (2 mkg)
Clutch nut (all models)   250 in.-lb. (2.9 mkg)

LIGHT BULBS

Headlight
  90/100 models   6V, 15/15W
  125 models   6V, 35/35W
Stop/taillight   6V, 20/5W
High-beam indicator   6V, 1.5W
Speedometer light   6V, 1.5W

TIRES

Ace 90	2.50 x 17" front, 2.75 x 17" rear, traction tread, 4-ply nylon cord IRC tires
Ace 100	2.75 x 17" front, 3.00 x 17" rear traction tread, 4-ply nylon cord Nitto tires
Ace 100B	2.75 x 19" front, 3.00 x 18" rear, trials tread, 4-ply nylon cord Nitto tires
Dirt Squirt 100	2.75 x 19" front, 3.25 x 17" rear, knobby tread, 4-ply nylon cord Nitto tires
100 Mx, Super Rat	3.00 x 19" front, 3.25 x 18" rear, knobby tread, 4-ply Nitto nylon cord tires
Wombat 125	2.75 x 21" front, 3.50 x 18" rear, trial tread, 4-ply nylon cord Nitto tires
Super Combat 125	3.00 x 21" front, 3.50 x 18" rear, motocross tread, 4-ply nylon cord Nitto tires

CHAPTER ONE

GENERAL INFORMATION

The successful Hodaka motorcycle is the result of a collaboration between Hodaka Industrial Company of Japan and an American marketing company, Pacific Basin Trading Company, commonly known as PABATCO.

Pabatco designed the motorcycle in 1963, with the aim of making it as simple and durable as possible. The original design was intended to be modified continually with bolt-on improvements that would allow the Hodaka owner to upgrade his older machine to the latest specifications. This design philosophy, along with the good performance, are the 2 major reasons for the success of this marque.

The original design was completed by Pabatco in 1963 and production began in Japan in early 1964 on the first model of the Ace 90. That model designation was continued until 1967. Displacement has since increased to 125cc.

MANUAL ORGANIZATION

This manual provides service information and procedures for all models to 1975. All dimensions and capacities are expressed in inch units familiar to U.S. mechanics as well as in metric units in most areas.

This chapter provides general information and specifications. It also discusses equipment and tools useful both for preventive maintenance and troubleshooting.

Chapter Two explains all periodic lubrication and routine maintenance necessary to keep your bike running well. Chapter Two also includes recommended tune-up procedures, eliminating the need to constantly consult chapters on the various subassemblies.

Chapter Three provides methods and suggestions for quick and accurate diagnosis and repair of problems. Troubleshooting procedures discuss typical symptoms and logical methods to pinpoint the trouble.

Subsequent chapters describe specific systems such as the engine, transmission, and electrical system. Each chapter provides disassembly, repair, and assembly procedures in simple step-by-step form. If a repair is impractical for a home mechanic, it is so indicated. It is usually faster and cheaper to take such repairs to a dealer or competent repair shop. Specifications concerning a particular system are included at the end of the appropriate chapter.

Some of the procedures in this manual specify special tools. In all cases, the tool is illustrated either in actual use or alone. A well-equipped mechanic may be able to substitute similar tools already on hand or can fabricate new ones.

The terms NOTE, CAUTION, and WARNING have specific meanings in this manual. A NOTE provides additional information to make a step or procedure easier or clearer. Disregarding a NOTE could cause inconvenience, but would not cause damage or personal injury.

A CAUTION emphasizes areas where equipment damage could result. Disregarding a CAUTION could cause permanent mechanical damage; however, personal injury is unlikely.

A WARNING emphasizes areas where personal injury or even death could result from negligence. Mechanical damage may also occur. WARNINGS are to be taken seriously. In some cases serious injury or death has been caused when mechanics have disregarded similar warnings.

Throughout this manual keep in mind 2 conventions. "Front" refers to the front of the bike. The front of any component such as the engine is that end which faces toward the front of the bike. The left and right side refer to a person sitting on the bike facing forward. For example, the shift lever is on the left side. These rules are simple, but even experienced mcehanics occasionally become disoriented.

SERVICE HINTS

Most of the service procedures covered are straightforward and can be performed by anyone reasonably handy with tools. It is suggested, however, that you consider your own capabilities carefully before attempting any operation involving major disassembly of the engine.

Some operations, for example, require the use of a press. It would be wiser to have these performed by a shop equipped for such work, rather than to try to do the job yourself with makeshift equipment. Other procedures require precision measurements. Unless you have the skills and equipment required, it would be better to have a qualified repair shop make the measurements for you.

Repairs go much faster and easier if your machine is clean before you begin work. There are special cleaners for washing the engine and related parts. Just brush or spray on the cleaning solution, let it stand, then rinse it away with a garden hose. Clean all oily or greasy parts with cleaning solvent as you remove them.

WARNING
Never use gasoline as a cleaning agent. It presents an extreme fire hazard. Be sure to work in a well-ventilated area when using cleaning solvent. Keep a fire extinguisher, rated for gasoline fires, handy in any case.

Special tools are required for some repair procedures. These may be purchased at a dealer (or borrowed if you're on good terms with the service department) or may be fabricated by a mechanic or machinist, often at considerable savings.

Much of the labor charge for repairs made by dealers is for the removal and disassembly of other parts to reach the defective unit. It is frequently possible to perform the preliminary operations yourself and then take the defective unit in to the dealer for repair at considerable savings.

Once you have decided to tackle the job yourself, read the entire section in this manual which pertains to it, making sure you have identified the proper one. Study the illustrations and text until you have a good idea of what is involved in completing the job satisfactorily. If special tools are required, make arrangements to get them before you start. It is frustrating and time-consuming to get partly into a job and then be unable to complete it.

Simple wiring checks are easily made at home; but knowledge of electronics is almost a necessity for performing tests with complicated electronic testing gear.

During disassembly of parts, keep a few general cautions in mind. Force is rarely needed to get things apart. If parts are a tight fit, like a magneto on a crankshaft, there is usually a tool designed to separate them. Never use a screwdriver to pry apart parts with machined surfaces such as crankcase halves and valve covers. You'll mar the surfaces and end up with leaks.

Make diagrams wherever similar-appearing parts are found. For instance, case cover screws are often not the same length. You may think you can remember where everything came from —but mistakes are costly. There is also the possibility you may be sidetracked and not return to work for days or even weeks—in which interval, carefully laid out parts may have become disturbed.

Tag all similar internal parts for location and mark all mating parts for position. Record number and thickness of any shims as they are removed. Small parts such as bolts can be identified by placing them in plastic sandwich bags. Seal and label the bags with masking tape.

Wiring should be tagged with masking tape and marked as each wire is removed. Again, don't rely on memory alone.

Disconnect battery ground cable before working near electrical connections and before disconnecting wires. Never run the engine with the battery disconnected; the alternator could be seriously damaged.

Protect finished surfaces from physical damage or corrosion. Keep gasoline and brake fluid off painted surfaces.

Frozen or very tight bolts and screws can often be loosened by soaking with penetrating oil, then sharply striking the bolt head a few times with a hammer and punch (or screwdriver for screws). Avoid heat unless absolutely necessary, since it may melt, warp, or remove the temper from many parts.

Avoid flames or sparks when working near a charging battery or flammable liquids such as brake fluid or gasoline.

No parts, except those assembled with a press fit, require unusual force during assembly. If a part is hard to remove or install, find out why before proceeding.

Cover all openings after removing parts to keep dirt, small tools, etc., from falling in.

When assembling 2 parts, start all fasteners, then tighten evenly.

Clutch plates, wiring connections, and brake shoes and drums should be kept clean and free of grease and oil.

When assembling parts, be sure all shims and washers are replaced exactly as they came out.

Whenever a rotating part butts against a stationary part, look for a shim or washer. Use new gaskets if there is any doubt about the condition of old ones. Generally you should apply gasket cement to one mating surface only so the parts may be easily disassembled in the future. A thin coat of oil on gaskets helps them seal effectively.

Heavy grease can be used to hold small parts in place if they tend to fall out during assembly. However, keep grease and oil away from electrical components or brake shoes and drums.

High spots may be sanded off a piston with sandpaper, but emery cloth and oil do a much more professional job.

Carburetors are best cleaned by disassembling them and soaking the parts in a commercial carburetor cleaner. Never soak gaskets and rubber parts in these cleaners. Never use wire to clean out jets and air passages; they are easily damaged. Use compressed air to blow out the carburetor only if the float has been removed first.

A baby bottle makes a good measuring device for adding oil to forks and transmissions. Get one that is graduated in ounces and cubic centimeters.

Take your time and do the job right. Don't forget that a newly rebuilt motorcycle engine must be broken in the same as a new one. Keep rpm's within the limits given in your owner's manual when you get back on the road.

SAFETY FIRST

Professional motorcycle mechanics can work for years and never sustain a serious injury. If you observe a few rules of common sense and safety, you can enjoy many safe hours servicing your own machine. You could hurt yourself or damage the bike if you ignore these rules.

1. Never use gasoline as a cleaning solvent.

2. Never smoke or use a torch in the vicinity of flammable liquids such as cleaning solvent in open containers or in an area where batteries are being charged. Highly explosive hydrogen gas is formed during the charging process.

3. If welding or brazing is required on the machine, remove the fuel tank to a safe distance, at least 50 feet away. Welding on gas tanks requires special safety procedures and must be performed only by someone skilled in the process.

4. Use the proper sized wrenches to avoid damage to nuts and injury to yourself.

5. When loosening a tight or stuck nut, be guided by what would happen if the wrench should slip. Protect yourself accordingly.

6. Keep your work area clean and uncluttered.
7. Wear safety goggles during all operations involving drilling, grinding, or use of a cold chisel.
8. Never use worn tools.
9. Keep a fire extinguisher handy and be sure it is rated for gasoline and electrical fires.

PARTS REPLACEMENT

When you order parts from the dealer or other parts distributor, always order by engine and chassis number. Write the numbers down and carry them in your wallet. Compare new parts to old before purchasing them. If they are not alike, have the parts person explain the difference to you.

TOOLS

Tool Kit

Most new models are equipped with fairly complete tool kits. The kit is located in a large compartment under the seat.

These tools are satisfactory for most small jobs and emergency roadside repairs. See **Figure 1**.

Shop Tools

For proper servicing, you will need an assortment of ordinary handtools. As a minimum, these include:

1. Metric combination wrenches
2. Metric sockets
3. Plastic mallet
4. Small hammer
5. Snap ring pliers
6. Pliers
7. Phillips screwdrivers
8. Slot (common) screwdrivers
9. Feeler gauges
10. Spark plug gauge
11. Spark plug wrench
12. Dial indicator

Special tools necessary are shown in the chapters covering the particular repair in which they are used. See **Figure 2**.

Electrical system servicing requires a voltmeter, ohmmeter or other device for determining continuity, and a hydrometer for battery equipped machines.

Advanced tune-up and troubleshooting procedures require a few more tools.

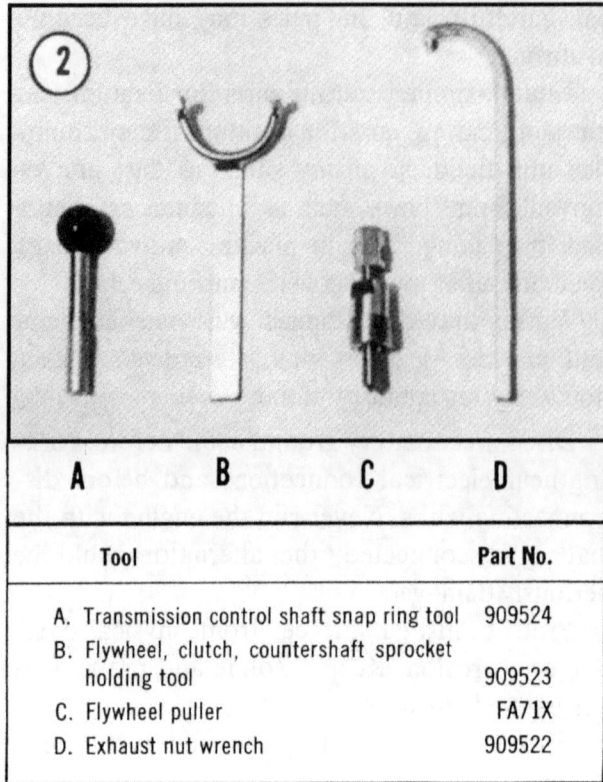

Tool	Part No.
A. Transmission control shaft snap ring tool	909524
B. Flywheel, clutch, countershaft sprocket holding tool	909523
C. Flywheel puller	FA71X
D. Exhaust nut wrench	909522

1. *Timing gauge* (**Figure 3**). By screwing this instrument into the spark plug hole, piston position may be determined. The tool shown costs about $20, and is available from larger dealers and mail order houses. Inexpensive ones, which utilize a vernier scale instead of a dial indicator, are also available. They are satisfactory, but are not quite so quick and easy to use.

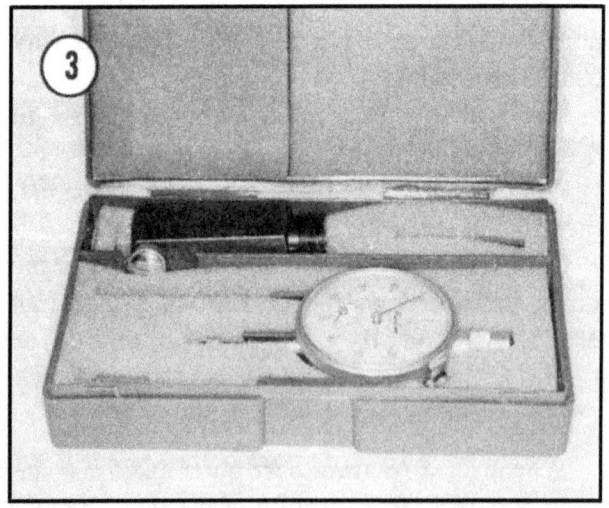

2. *Hydrometer* (**Figure 4**). This instrument measures state of charge of the battery, and tells much about battery condition. Such an instrument is available at any auto parts store and

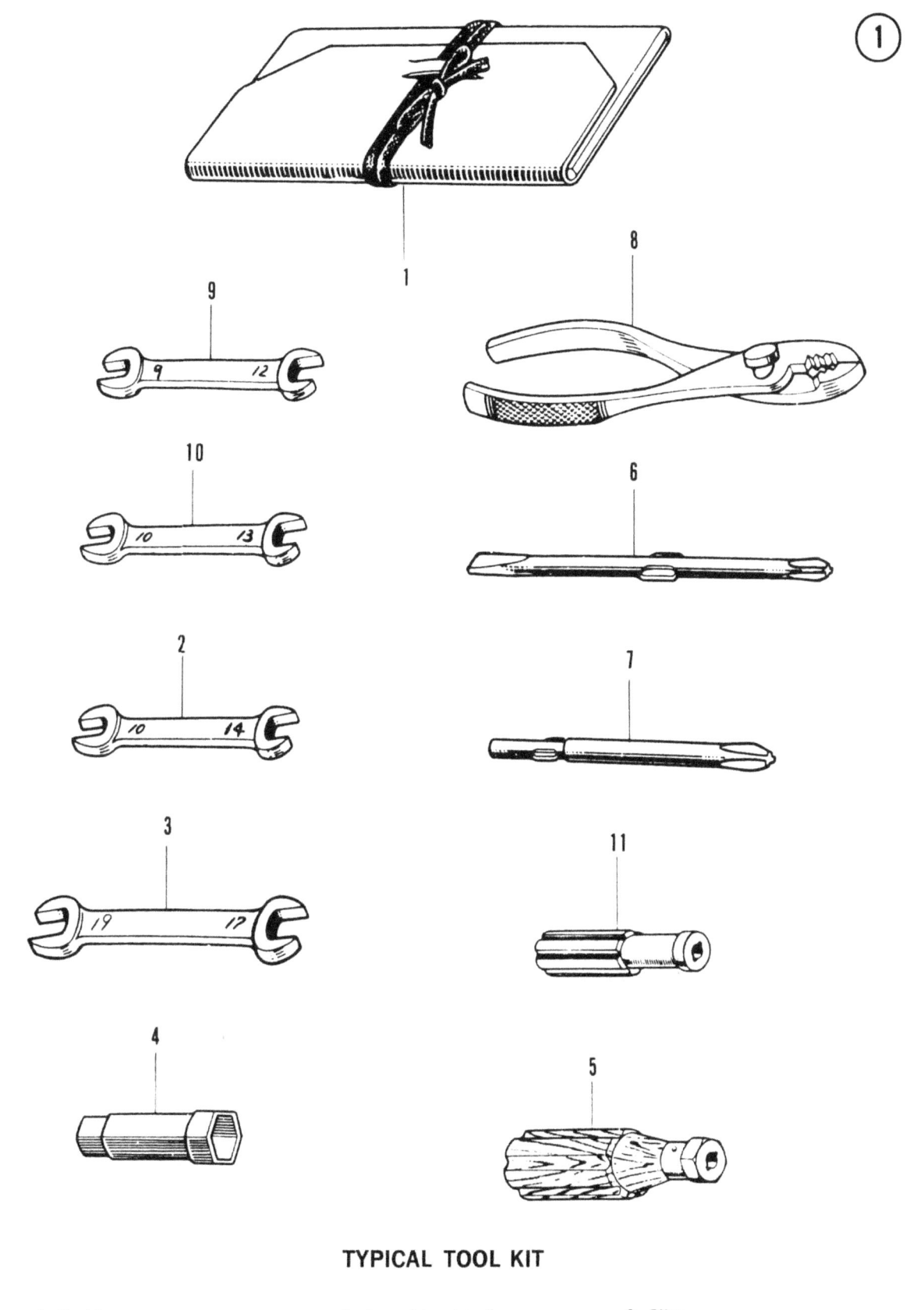

TYPICAL TOOL KIT

1. Tool bag
2. Open-end wrench 10 x 14mm
3. Open-end wrench 17 x 19mm
4. Spark plug wrench
5. Screwdriver handle
6. No. 2 Phillips and slotted screwdriver
7. No. 3 Phillips screwdriver
8. Pliers
9. Open-end wrench 9 x 12mm
10. Open-end wrench 10 x 13mm
11. Screwdriver handle

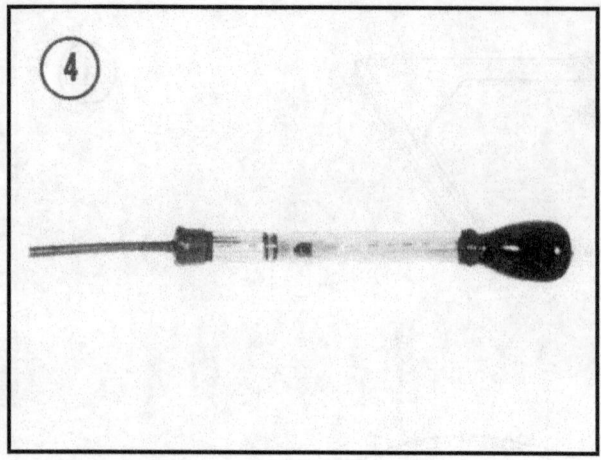

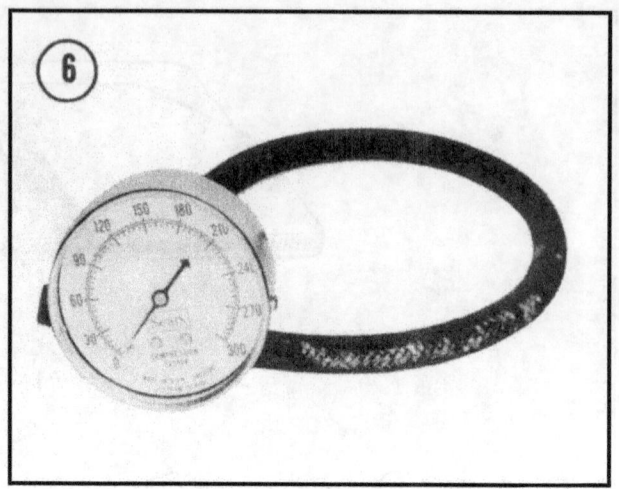

through most larger mail order outlets. A satisfactory one costs less than $3.

3. *Multimeter or VOM* (**Figure 5**). This instrument is invaluable for electrical system troubleshooting and service. A few of its functions may be duplicated by cheaper substitutes, but for the serious hobbyist, it is a must. Its uses are described in the applicable sections of this book. Prices start at around $10 at electronics hobbyist stores and mail order outlets.

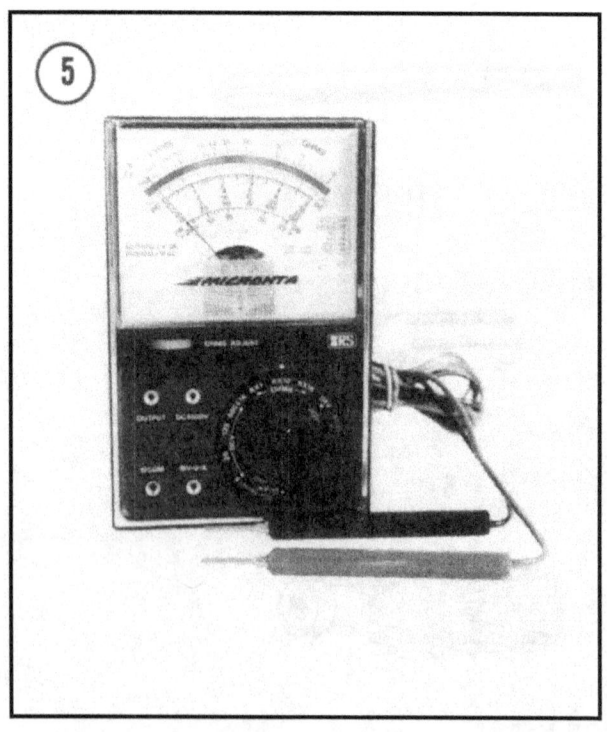

4. *Compression gauge* (**Figure 6**). An engine with low compression cannot be properly tuned and will not develop full power. A compression gauge measures engine compression. The one shown has a flexible stem, which enables it to reach cylinders where there is little clearance between the cylinder head and frame. Inexpensive ones start around $3, available at auto accessory stores or by mail order from large catalog order firms.

5. *Impact driver* (**Figure 7**). This tool must have been designed with the motorcyclist in mind. It makes removal of engine cover screws easy, and eliminates damaged screw slots. Good ones run about $12 at larger hardware stores.

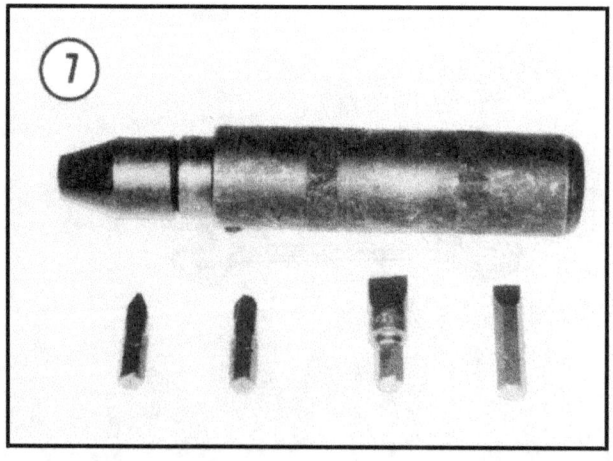

6. *Ignition gauge* (**Figure 8**). This tool measures point gap. It also has round wire gauges for measuring spark plug gap.

A few special tools may also be required for major engine service. They are available at dealers.

EXPENDABLE SUPPLIES

Certain expendable supplies are also required. These include grease, oil, gasket cement, wiping

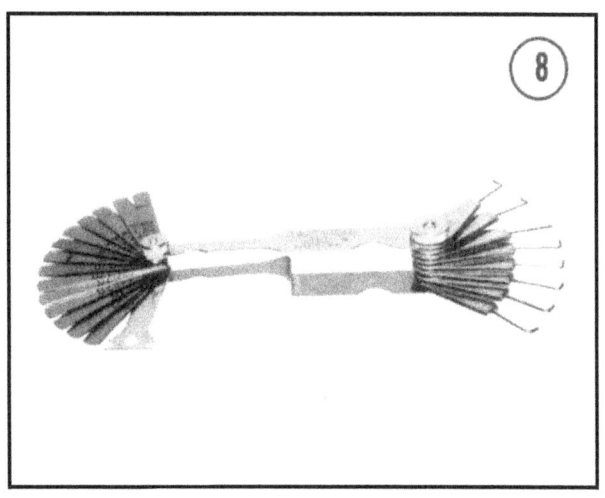

rags, cleaning solvent, and distilled water. Ask your dealer for the special locking compounds, silicone lubricants, and commercial chain lube products which make maintenance simpler and easier. Solvent is available at most service stations and distilled water for the battery is available at most supermarkets.

SERIAL NUMBERS

You must know the model serial number for the sake of registration and when ordering special parts. These identification numbers are located in the same general area on all models.

The engine number is located on the crankcase between the motor mount and frame.

The frame number is stamped on the steering head down-tube.

These numbers can be permanently recorded by placing a sheet of paper over the imprinted area and rubbing with the side of a pencil. Some motor vehicle registration offices will accept such evidence in lieu of inspecting the bike in person. This process is dubbed "finger printing."

CHAPTER TWO

PERIODIC MAINTENANCE

Be sure to perform general or preventive maintenance at regular intervals as recommended. To ignore this is one of the most expensive mistakes you can make. The difference can mean thousands of trouble free miles and hundreds of dollars saved in repair bills. **Figures 1 and 2** list required maintenance for all models, and should be followed faithfully by the owner.

TOOLS AND PARTS

You will need the basic tools suggested in the introduction to the manual. In addition, equipment required for a complete tune-up includes a static timing light, a strobe light, dwell tachometer, carburetor float gauge, sets of flat and round feeler gauges calibrated in millimeters, a spark plug, set of breaker points and condenser, and motor oil for a normal tune-up.

TUNE-UP

A complete tune-up should be performed every 2,000 miles or prior to each race or long trail ride. The procedures are presented in this chapter and the tune-up specifications are shown in the *Quick Reference Data* at the beginning of the book.

Different systems in an engine interact and the steps required for a tune-up must be considered in relationship to one another. Perform the steps in the following order:

1. Tighten cylinder head nuts.
2. Service and adjust ignition system.
3. Adjust the carburetor.

SPARK PLUGS

Spark plugs are available in various heat ranges hotter or colder than the plugs originally installed at the factory.

Select plugs of a heat range designed for the loads and temperature conditions under which the bike will run. Use of incorrect heat ranges can cause seized pistons, scored cylinder walls or damaged piston crowns.

In general, use a lower numbered plug for low speeds, low loads, and low temperatures. Use a higher numbered plug for high speeds, high engine loads, and high temperature.

> NOTE: *Use the highest numbered plug that will not foul. In areas where seasonal temperature variations are great, the factory recommends a "2-plug system" — a high numbered plug for hard summer riding and a low numbered plug for slower winter operation.*

The reach (length) of a plug is also important. A longer than normal plug could interfere with the piston causing permanent and severe damage. Refer to **Figures 3 and 4**.

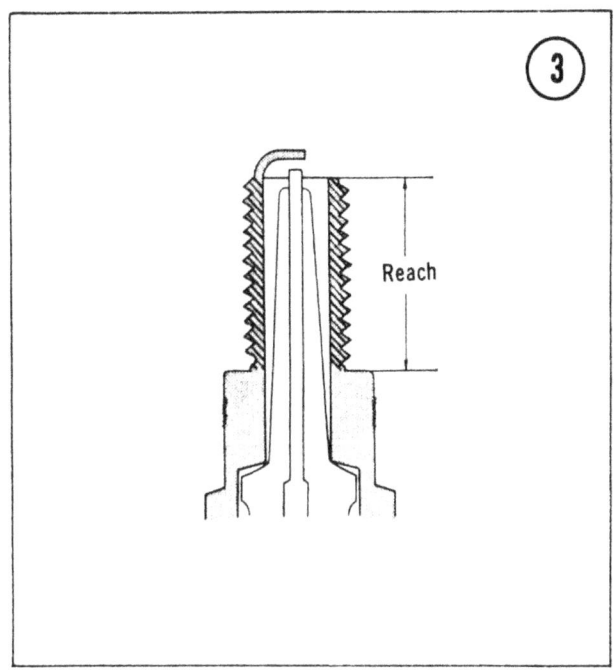

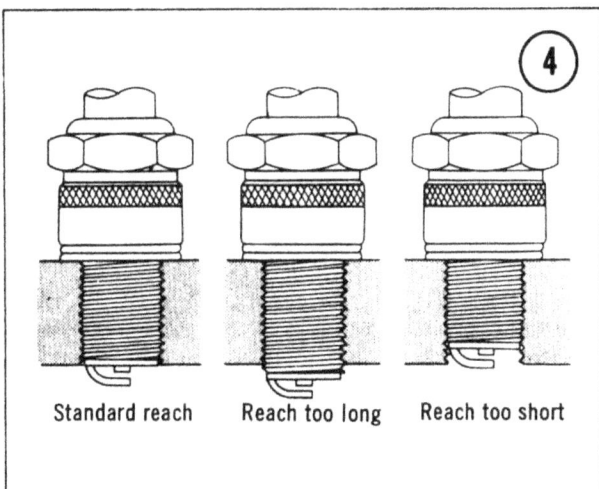

Standard reach | Reach too long | Reach too short

Testing Plugs

A quick and simple test can be made to determine if the plug is correct for your type of riding. Accelerate hard enough through the gears and maintain a high, steady speed. Shut the throttle off, and kill the engine at the same time, allowing the bike to slow, out of gear. Don't allow the engine to slow the bike. Remove the plug and check the condition of the electrode area. A spark plug of the correct heat range, with the engine in a proper state of tune, will appear light tan. See **Figure 5**, page 14.

If the insulator is white or burned, the plug is too hot and should be replaced with a cooler one. Also check the setting of the carburetor as it may be too lean.

A too cold plug will have sooty deposits ranging in color from dark brown to black. Replace with a hotter plug and check for too rich carburetion or evidence of oil blow-by at the piston rings.

If any one plug is found unsatisfactory, discard the set.

Removal/Installation

Remove and clean the spark plugs at least once every 1,000 miles of riding. Electrode gap should be measured with a round feeler gauge and set at 0.024 to 0.028 in. (6-7mm) as shown in **Figure 6**.

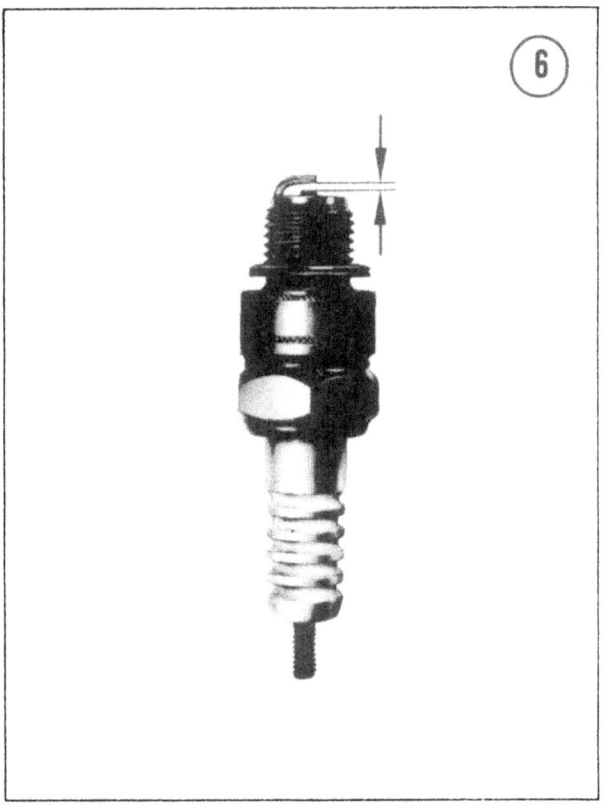

Often, heat and corrosion can cause the plug to bind in the head making removal difficult. Don't use force; the head is easily damaged.

Here is the proper way to replace a plug.

1. Blow out any debris which has collected in the spark plug wells. It could fall into the hole causing engine damage.

2. Gently remove the spark plug leads by pulling up and out. Don't jerk the wires or pull on the wire itself.

3. Apply penetrating oil to the base of the plug and allow it to work into the threads.

① PERIODIC MAINTENANCE (ENDURO MODELS)

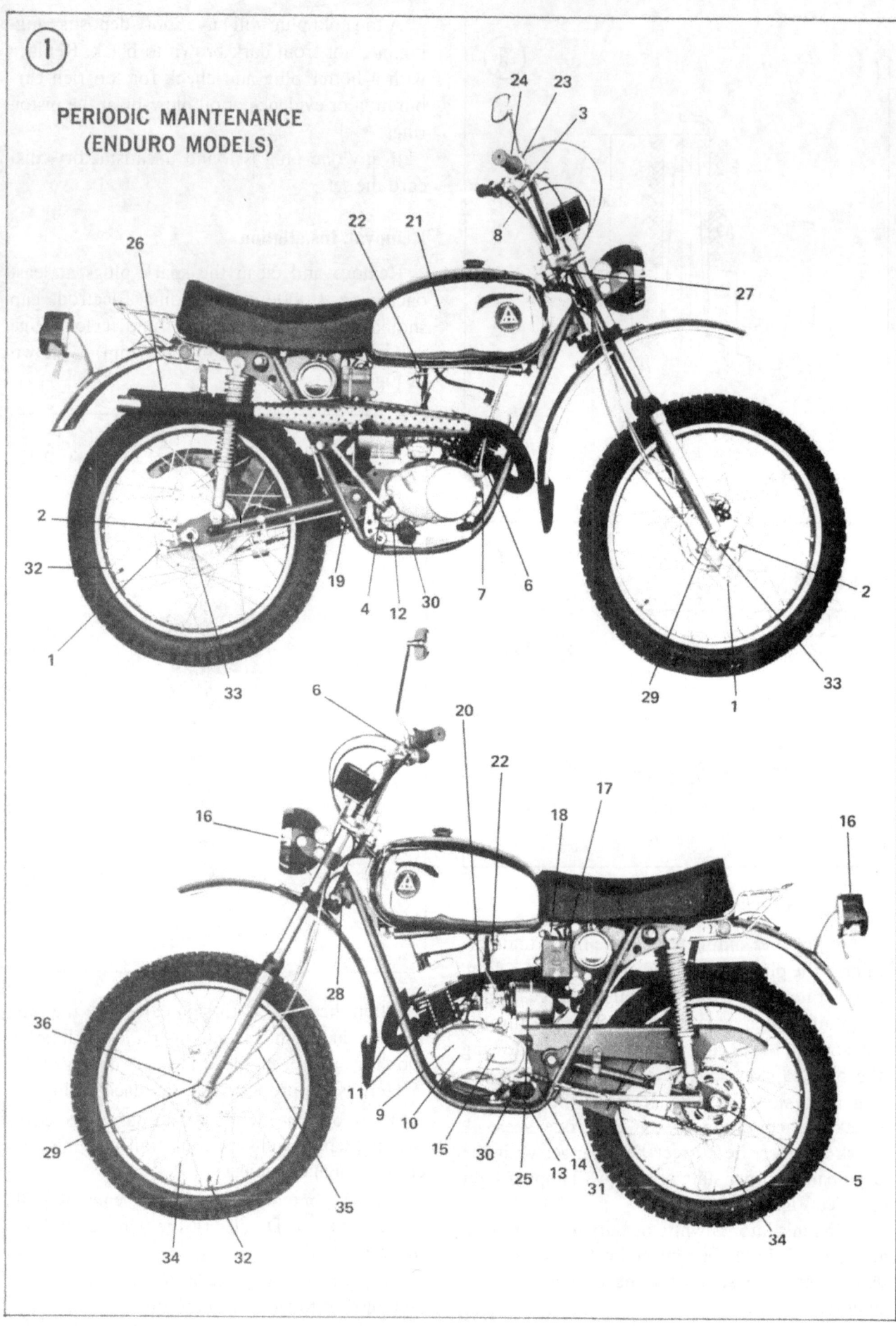

No.	Item	500	1,000	1,500	2,000	2,500	3,000	3,500	4,000	4,500	5,000
					Running Distance (Miles)						
1	Adjust brakes	X	X		X		X		X		X
2	Lubricate brake cam shafts		X		X		X		X		X
3	Lubricate front brake cable		X		X		X		X		X
4	Lubricate brake pedal pivot		X		X		X		X		X
5	Clean, oil and adjust chain	X	X		X		X		X		X
6	Adjust clutch cable free-play	X	X		X		X		X		X
7	Check clutch lever free-play	X		X			X			X	
8	Lubricate clutch cable		X		X		X		X		X
9	Clean and adjust breaker points	X	X			X				X	
10	Lubricate breaker point cam		X			X				X	
11	Decarbonize cylinder head—ports					X					X
12	Change gear box oil	X	X		X		X		X		X
13	Lubricate foot change shaft		X		X		X		X		X
14	Lubricate ratchet plunger		X		X		X		X		X
15	Repack shifter mechanism					X					X
16	Check light bulbs	X	X	X	X	X	X	X	X	X	X
17	Check electrical connections		X		X		X		X		X
18	Check battery water level		X		X		X		X		X
19	Lubricate stoplight switch shaft				X				X		
20	Clean carburetor/adjust float level					X					X
21	Clean fuel tank										X
22	Clean fuel tank petcock										X
23	Lubricate throttle cable		X		X		X		X		X
24	Lubricate twistgrip assembly		X		X		X		X		X
25	Clean air filter		X		X		X		X		X
26	Decarbonize exhaust system					X					X
27	Adjust steering head bearing play		X		X		X		X		X
28	Lubricate steering head bearing		X		X		X		X		X
29	Change fork oil	X									X
30	Lubricate footrest hinge points		X		X		X		X		X
31	Lubricate side stand hinge points		X		X		X		X		X
32	Check tire pressure	X	X	X	X	X	X	X	X	X	X
33	Repack wheel bearings										X
34	Inspect spokes (tighten, if needed)	X	X		X		X		X		X
35	Lubricate speedometer cable						X				X
36	Lubricate speedo drive unit								X		X
	Check for loose nuts/bolts	X	X	X	X	X	X	X	X	X	X

② PERIODIC MAINTENANCE (OFF-ROAD MODELS)

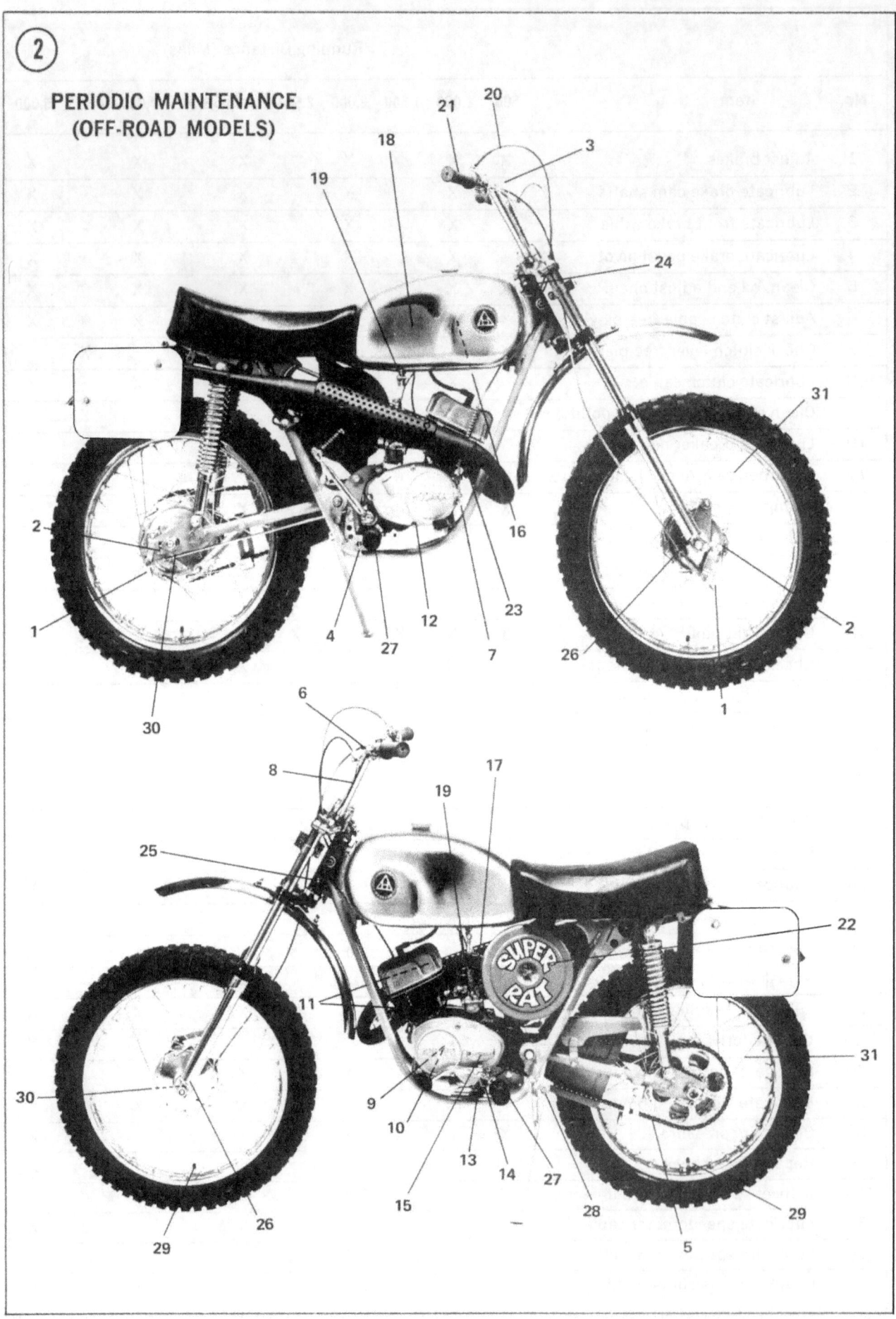

No.	Item	\ 500	1,000	1,500	2,000	2,500	3,000	3,500	4,000	4,500	5,000	After every Race	After every 3rd Race
		Running Distance (Miles)*											
1	Adjust brakes	X	X	X	X	X	X	X	X	X	X	X	
2	Lubricate brake cam shafts		X		X		X		X		X	X	
3	Lubricate front brake cable	X	X	X	X	X	X	X	X	X	X	X	
4	Lubricate brake pedal pivot		X		X		X		X		X	X	
5	Clean, oil and adjust chain	X	X	X	X	X	X	X	X	X	X	X	
6	Adjust clutch cable free-play	X	X		X		X		X		X	X	
7	Check clutch lever free-play	X	X	X	X	X	X	X	X	X	X	X	
8	Lubricate clutch cable	X	X	X	X	X	X	X	X	X	X	X	
9	Clean and adjust breaker points	X	X	X	X	X	X	X	X	X	X		X
10	Lubricate breaker point cam		X			X			X				X
11	Decarbonize cylinder head—ports					X					X		X
12	Change gear box oil	X	X	X	X	X	X	X	X	X	X		X
13	Lubricate foot change shaft	X	X	X	X	X	X	X	X	X	X	X	
14	Lubricate ratchet plunger	X	X	X	X	X	X	X	X	X	X	X	
15	Repack shifter mechanism					X					X		X
16	Check electrical connections		X		X		X		X		X	X	X
17	Clean carburetor/adjust float level			X		X			X		X	X	X
18	Clean fuel tank	X	X	X	X	X	X	X	X	X	X		
19	Clean fuel cock screens										X		X
20	Lubricate throttle cable	X	X	X	X	X	X	X	X	X	X	X	X
21	Lubricate twistgrip assembly		X		X		X		X		X	X	X
22	Clean air filter	X	X	X	X	X	X	X	X	X	X	X	
23	Decarbonize exhaust system					X					X		X
24	Adjust steering head bearing play		X		X		X		X		X	X	X
25	Lubricate steering head bearing		X		X		X		X		X	X	
26	Change fork oil	X				X					X		X
27	Lubricate footrest hinge points		X		X		X		X		X	X	
28	Lubricate side stand hinge points		X		X		X		X		X	X	
29	Check tire pressure	X	X	X	X	X	X	X	X	X	X	X	
30	Repack wheel bearings					X					X		X
31	Inspect spokes (tighten, if needed)	X	X	X	X	X	X	X	X	X	X	X	
	Check for loose nuts/bolts	X	X	X	X	X	X	X	X	X	X	X	

*The severity of conditions will determine running distance (Estimated miles).

Normal plug appearance noted by the brown to grayish-tan deposits and light electrode wear. This plug indicates the correct plug heat range and proper air/fuel ratio.

Red, brown, yellow, and white coatings caused by fuel and oil additives. Such additives should not be used or damage will result.

Carbon fouling distinguished by dry, fluffy black carbon deposits which may be caused by an over-rich air/fuel mixture, excessive hand choking, clogged air filter, or excessive idling.

Shiny yellow glaze on insulator cone is caused when the powdery deposits from fuel and oil additives melt. Melting occurs during hard acceleration after prolonged idling. This glaze conducts electricity and shorts out the plug. Avoid the use of additives at all times.

Oil fouling indicated by wet, oily deposits caused by too much oil in the mix. A hotter plug temporarily reduces oil deposits, but a plug that is too hot leads to preignition and possible engine damage.

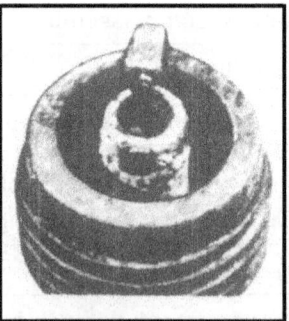

Overheated plug indicated by burned or blistered insulator tip and badly worn electrodes. This condition may be caused by preignition, cooling system defects, lean air/fuel ratios, low octane fuel, or over advanced ignition timing.

4. Back out the plugs with a socket that has a rubber insert designed to grip the insulator. Be careful not to drop the plug into the cooling fins where they could become lodged.

5. Clean the seating area after removal and apply graphite to the threads to simplify future removal.

6. Clean the tip of the plug with a sandblasting machine (some gas stations have them) or with a wire brush and solvent.

7. Always use a new gasket if the old plug is to be reused after cleaning.

8. Run the plug in finger-tight and tighten one-quarter of a turn more with a wrench. Further tightening will flatten the gasekt and cause binding.

> NOTE: *A short piece of fuel line can be used to install the plug initially in areas where space is a problem.*

CONDENSER (CAPACITOR)

The condenser (capacitor) is a sealed unit and requires no maintenance. Be sure the connections are clean and tight.

The only possible proper test is to measure the resistance of the insulation with an ohmmeter. The value should be 5,000 ohms. A make-do test is to charge the capacitor by hooking the leads, or case and lead, to a 6V battery. After a few seconds, touch the leads together, or lead to case, and check for a spark. A damaged capacitor won't store electricity or spark.

Most mechanics prefer to discard the condensers and replace them with new ones during engine tune-up.

IGNITION SYSTEM OPERATION

When the breaker points are closed, current flows from the battery through the primary winding of the ignition coil, thereby building a magnetic field around the coil. The breaker cam rotates with the crankshaft and is so adjusted that the breaker points open as the piston reaches the firing position.

As the points open, the magnetic field collapses. When this happens, a very high voltage (up to approximately 15,000 volts) is induced in the secondary winding of the ignition coil. This high voltage is sufficient to jump the gap at the spark plug.

The condenser serves primarily to protect the points. Inductance of the ignition coil primary tends to keep a surge of current flowing through the circuit even after the points have started to open. The condenser stores this surge and thus prevents arcing at the points.

BREAKER POINTS

Normal use of the motorcycle causes the breaker points to gradually become pitted and worn. To maintain peak ignition efficiency, breaker points must be serviced regularly. Check and adjust breaker points every 2,000 miles (3,000 kilometers), and replace them every 8,000 miles (12,000 kilometers).

Checking and Adjusting Points

There is one set of points. Normal use of the motorcycle causes the points to burn and pit gradually. If the points are not too pitted, they can be dressed with a few strokes of a clean point file. Do not use emery cloth or sandpaper, as particles can remain on the points and cause arcing and burning. If a few strokes of the file don't smooth the points completely, they should be replaced.

Oil or dirt may get on the points, resulting in premature failure. Common causes for this condition are defective crankshaft seals, improper lubrication of the breaker cam, or lack of care when the crankcase cover is removed.

If the point spring is weak, the points will bounce and cause misfiring at high speeds.

Clean and regap the points every 2,000 miles (3,000 kilometers). To clean the points, dress them lightly with a point file, then remove all residue with lacquer thinner. Close the points on a piece of clean white paper such as a business card. Continue to pull the card through the closed points until no particles or discoloration remains on the card. Finally, rotate the engine as you observe the points while they open and close. If they do not meet squarely, replace them (**Figure 7**).

After the points have been dressed and cleaned, they must be adjusted.

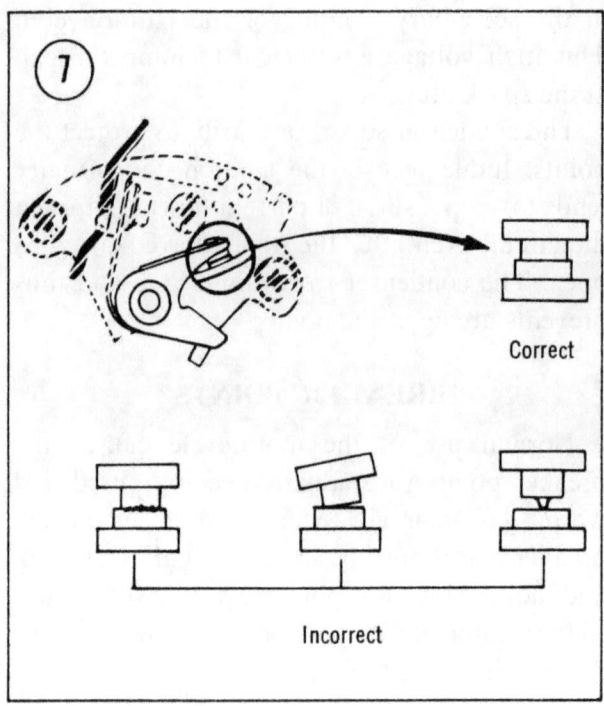

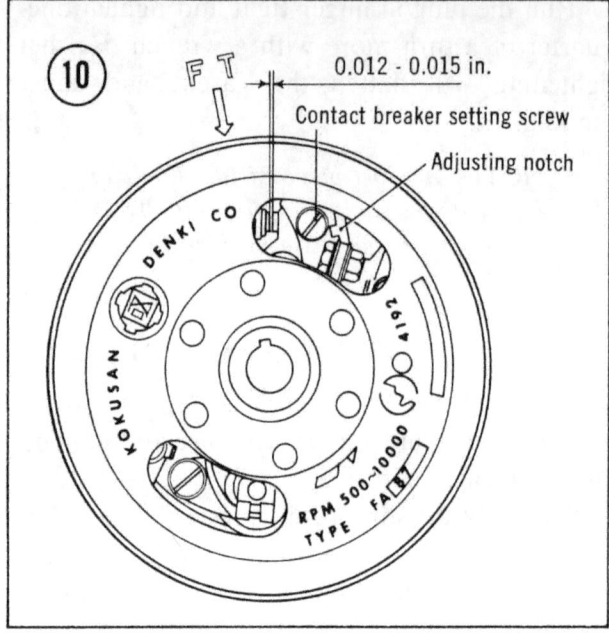

IGNITION TIMING

1. Use a Phillips screwdriver to remove the shifter cover.

2. Shift the transmission into top gear.

3. Use an impact-type Phillips tool to remove magneto cover screws.

4. Look through the shifter cover opening and tilt the magneto cover to free the shifter sliding pin (see **Figure 8**) from the control shaft. Then remove the magneto cover.

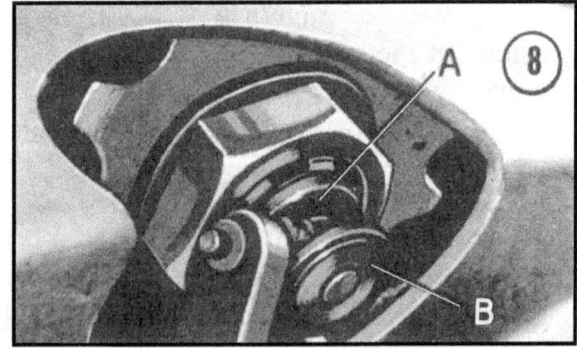

A. Shifter   B. Control shaft spool

5. Rotate the flywheel until the FT mark aligns with the left-hand mark on the engine case (see **Figure 9**).

6. Use a flat-bladed screwdriver through the top inspection window on the flywheel face to loosen the contact breaker setting screw (see **Figure 10**).

7. Insert the screwdriver between the magneto frame breaker point bracket to adjust the point gap to 0.012-0.015 in.

8. Measure the gap with a feeler gauge before and after the screw is tightened.

9. This service has an accelerated schedule, as detailed in this chapter for dirt models.

Alternative Timing Methods

1. Disconnect the blue and black wires of the magneto harness at the battery box junction. Connect one wire of a continuity light or ohmmeter to the black magneto wire. Connect the other wire to the blue magneto wire or to the engine case.

2. Rotate the flywheel counterclockwise until the light dims or the meter needle shows the points are opening.

3. Adjust the point gap setting so the flywheel mark aligns with the right-hand mark on the case just as the points open. The piston is now 25 degrees before top dead center. With the flywheel mark aligned with the left-hand mark on the engine case, the piston is at top dead center.

4. For the degree wheel method of engine timing, set breaker points to open at 25 degrees BTDC. For extremely accurate timing, it should be 25 degrees and 15 minutes.

5. For the dial indicator method, set the point opening at 0.114 in. BTDC.

6. When reconnecting magneto wires, be sure to connect matching colors.

7. Clean the points with a point file and clean paper before setting gap.

8. Use alcohol or acetone to remove polishing wax on new points installed.

Lubrication

1. Remove the flywheel from the engine as detailed in Chapter Four.

2. Clean the magneto components with compressed air.

3. Wipe the flywheel cam with a clean cloth and smear a thin coat of SAE 10W oil on the cam.

4. Put 2 to 4 drops of oil on the felt pad that rides on the cam (see **Figure 11**).

CARBURETOR

1. Carefully screw in the air mixture screw until it seats, and then turn it out 1¼ turns. Start the engine and set the idle with the throttle stop screw at about 1,500 rpm.

2. Slowly turn the air screw in until the engine speed begins to drop. Then, slowly turn it out (the speed will increase) until it drops once again.

3. Again turn the screw in until the engine speed increases to the highest point when controlled by the air screw; the air screw setting is now correct. With the throttle stop screw, set the idle so that the engine does not falter and does not race.

BATTERY

The battery is the heart of the electrical system. Its condition should be checked regularly.

Battery charging procedures are covered in the electrical system chapter (Chapter Six).

Inspection

1. Remove the battery cover.

2. Check the electrolyte level. If necessary, top up with distilled water only. Do not overfill.

> **CAUTION**
> *Painted surfaces will be damaged if corrosive battery electrolyte is spilled on them. Flush away all spills with water, and neutralize with baking soda if necessary.*

3. Inspect the terminals for corrosion. Flush off any oxidation with a solution of baking soda and water. Coat the terminals lightly with Vaseline or a silicone grease to retard new corrosion.

Periodic Maintenance

1. Trickle charge the battery at 0.4Ah rate if discharged.

2. Refill the fluid to the upper level with distilled water only.

3. Trickle charge the battery once a month when not in service.

4. Do not add extra acid after initial filling. Refill only with distilled water.

FUSE

1. The 5 amp fuse is located next to battery box.

2. The fuse can be checked visually.

C. Felt lubricating pad   D. Frame mounting screws

3. Always replace a blown fuse with one having the same capacity.

4. Chronically blown fuses indicate a short circuit in the wiring or a defective component. Correct the problem before replacing fuse.

HEADLIGHT

Adjustment

1. Start engine and shine high beam on wall 25 feet away with an assistant on the motorcycle. The beam should be at the same height on the wall as on the motorcycle.

2. Loosen the 2 body mounting bolts to adjust the headlight.

3. All models adjust essentially the same way.

4. Side-to-side adjusts with a screw in the rim.

GEAR SELECTOR ADJUSTMENT

Trial and Error Method

1. Jack up the machine so the rear wheel is clear of the ground.

2. Shift transmission into low gear.

3. Remove shifter cover from magneto cover.

4. Scribe a line with a metal stylus from the head of the shifter arm adjusting bolt down and across the shifter guide (see **Figure 12**).

5. Loosen the locknut on the shifter arm adjusting bolt one turn.

6. Turn the adjuster bolt ¼ turn counterclockwise from the scribed line and tighten locknut.

7. Move the rear wheel to test for low gear engagement.

8. Repeat the test for the other gears.

9. Test ride the machine if engagement seems satisfactory in all gears.

10. If gear engagement is not satisfactory, loosen the locknut and turn adjuster bolt ¼ turn clockwise from the scribed line, and test again.

11. The transmission should not skip a gear or come out of gear under hard acceleration. Double check locknut and replace the shifter cover.

Measurement Method

1. Remove the magneto cover assembly as detailed in Chapter Six.

2. Measure from the inside surface of the magneto cover to the leading edge of the shifter sliding pin (see **Figure 13**).

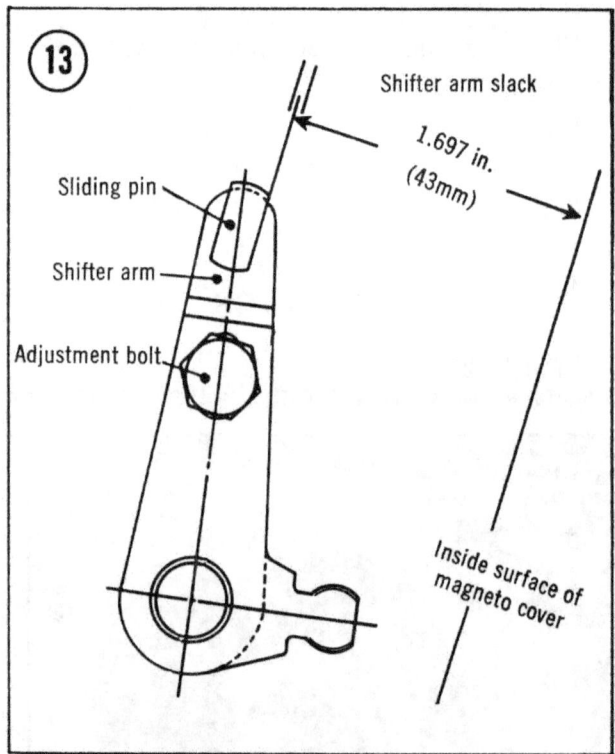

3. The correct distance for the Ace 90 model is 1.697 in. at the center of the shifter arm slack.

4. On other models, the correct measurement is 1.382 in. (see **Figure 14**).

5. Adjust as required with the adjuster bolt as detailed above.

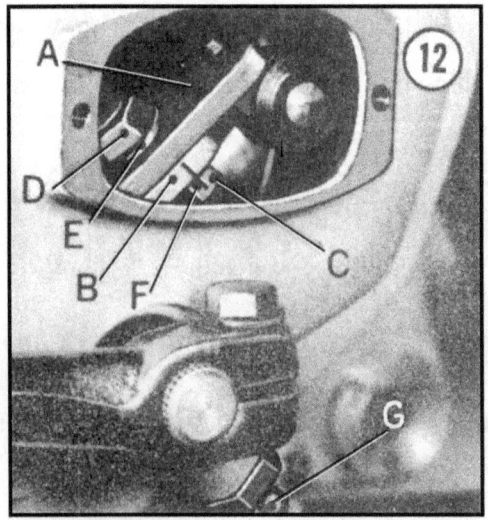

A. Shifter arm
B. Shifter guide
C. Adjust bolt
D. Locknut
E. Lockwasher
F. Scribed line
G. Grease nipple

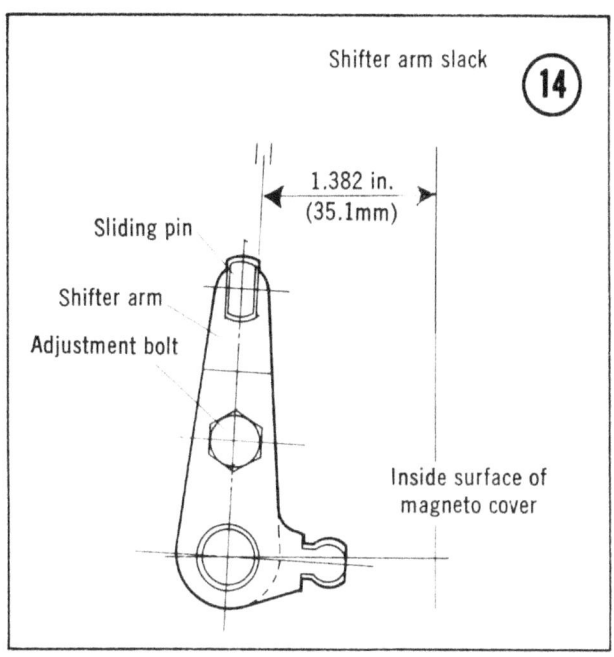

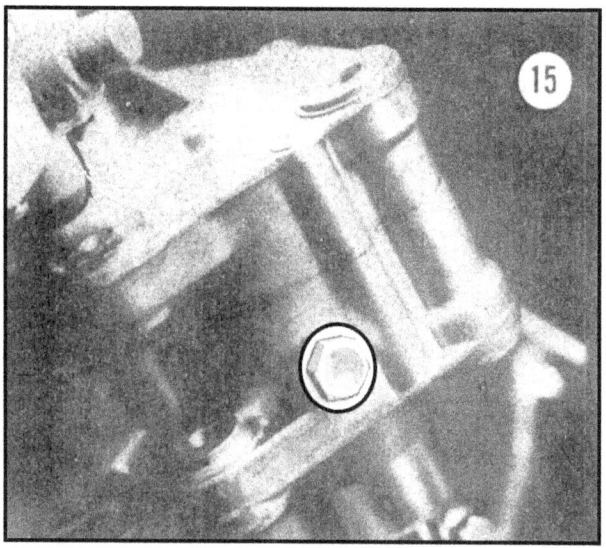

LUBRICATION

Engine

1. Use 2-stroke SAE 30W oil mixed 16:1 for the first 500 miles, and 20:1 after that. The exceptions are the new special oils that recommend mixing as high as 40:1. Follow the recommendations, except in the case of the competition models when the mix should be no higher than 32:1.

2. Never use 4-stroke oils, as they form excessive carbon deposits.

Transmission

1. Use only recommended oils. Any additives may cause the clutch to slip, as it uses the same oil supply.

2. Change the oil every 200 miles for the first 1,000 miles, to remove the metal particles resulting from the engine seating in.

3. Lay the machine on its side for a moment when draining the crankcase to enable drainage of the oil from the clutch side cover (**Figure 15**).

4. Flush the transmission case after draining oil. Fill with 1¼ pints of solvent and run the engine at low rpm for 3 or 4 minutes. Then drain the solvent and refill with oil. Do not ride with the solvent in the machine.

5. Refill with 1¼ pints of oil. Check oil level in screwing down the filler plug and then removing it to read the gauge level.

6. On Model 100-MX, the oil must be changed more often.

CHAIN ADJUSTMENT

1. Loosen the rear axle nut 3 turns.

2. Turn the chain adjuster nuts (see **Figure 16**) equally until the chain has ¾ in. slack on the bottom run with the rider on the machine (see **Figure 17**).

3. Tighten the axle nut and recheck the chain adjustment.

4. A major adjustment is required if any of the following occurs: if the sprockets are not parallel, if a new chain is installed, if the wheel has been removed from the frame, or if the sprockets are being changed.

5. Turn the chain adjuster nuts until the sprockets are aligned. Sight along the top run of the chain to check the alignment (**Figure 18**). A straight chain is readily visible from the rear sprocket.

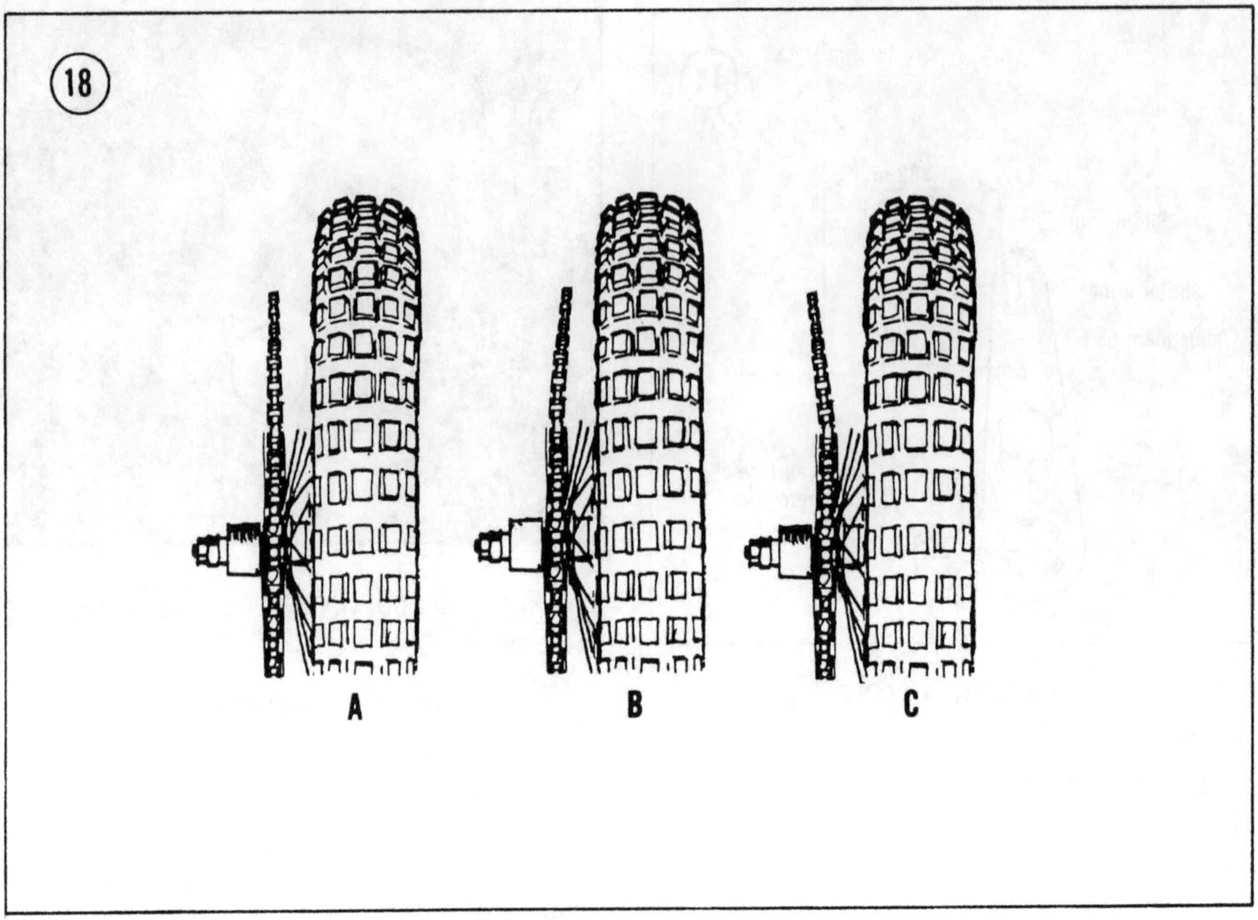

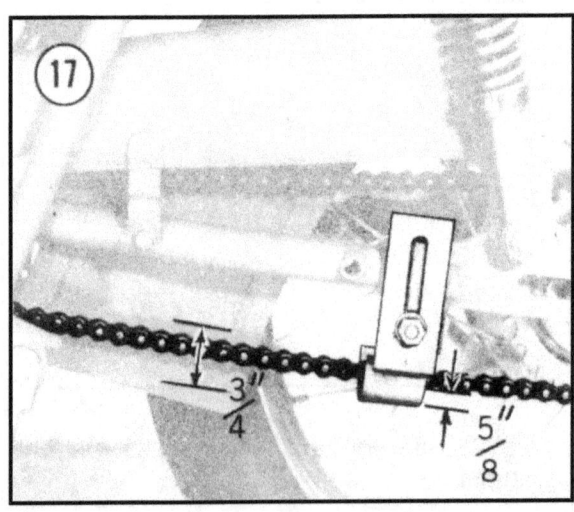

6. Tighten the axle nut and recheck alignment and adjustment for slack.
7. Tighten the brake anchor bolt and use a new cotter pin for the nut.
8. Adjust brake pedal and brake light switch.
9. Be sure to do this job right. A chain out of alignment or too tight can cause chain and sprocket wear as well as engine damage.

Chain Guide Adjustment

Loosen the nut and adjust the guide so there is 5/8 in. clearance between it and the chain's bottom run.

CHAIN LUBRICATION

1. Remove the chain and clean with solvent and a stiff brush.
2. Rinse thoroughly in clean solvent and dry with a clean rag or compressed air.
3. Put the chain in a pail of melted grease or motor oil and then hang it to drain excess lubricant. As an alternate, use one of the chain lubes sold by most motorcycle dealers.
4. Failure to clean the chain regularly will result in faster chain wear.
5. Follow the recommended service intervals listed in this chapter. Note that the MX model requires chain service more often. More frequent attention is obviously required when any machine has been in competition or ridden over dusty or muddy terrain.

MASTER LINK SERVICE

1. Use pliers to remove or install the master link spring clip (see **Figure 19**). Be sure the spring clip is in good condition.

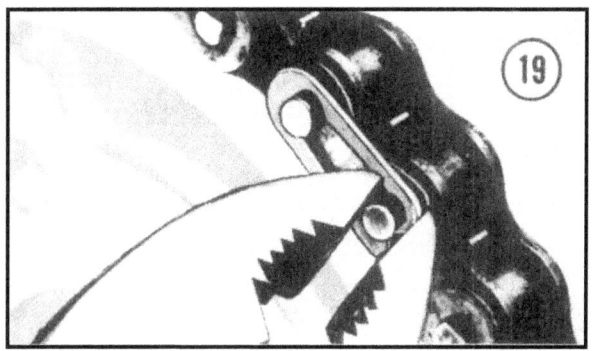

2. Install the spring clip so the closed end is in the direction of chain travel (see **Figure 20**).

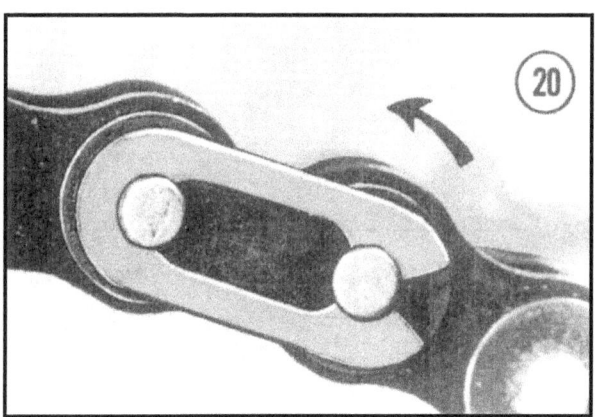

CHAIN INSPECTION

1. After cleaning the chain, examine it carefully. If any signs of wear or damage are visible, replace the chain.
2. Lay the chain alongside a ruler (**Figure 21**) and compress the links together. Then stretch them apart. If more than ¼ in. of movement is possible, replace the chain; it's too worn to be used again.
3. Never replace the chain with bargain chain sold as "motorcycle quality." This is often industrial chain with a strength too low for motorcycle use.
4. Always check both sprockets every time the chain is removed. If any wear is visible on the teeth, replace the sprocket. Never install a new chain over worn sprockets or a worn chain over new sprockets.

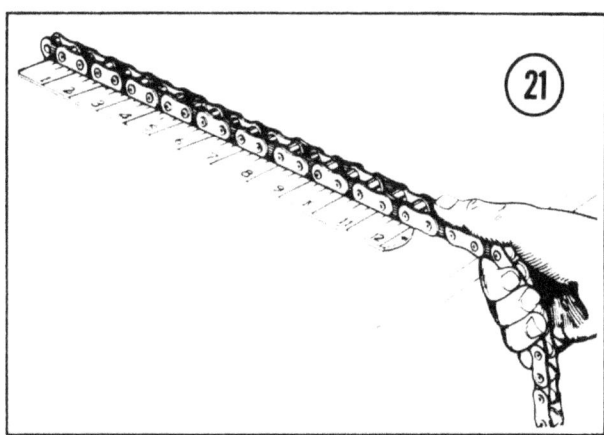

5. See **Figure 22** for a comparison of dished and non-dished sprockets. Non-dished sprockets must only be used with cushion hubs.

BRAKE ADJUSTMENT

Front Brake

1. Adjust the knurled knob on the brake hub cam lever (see **Figure 23**).

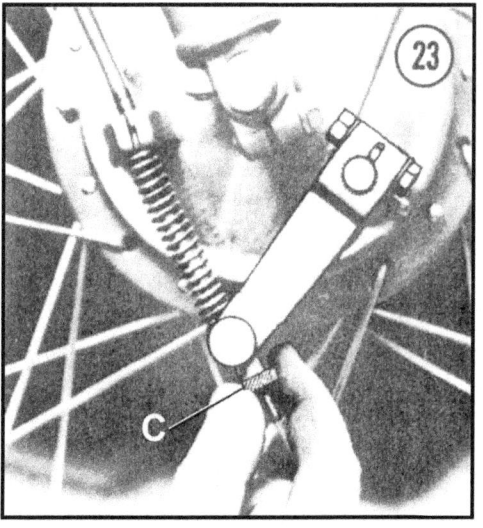

C. Knurled adjuster knob

2. Complete adjustment with the handlebar adjuster (see **Figure 24**) until there is ¼ in. of play at the end of the lever.

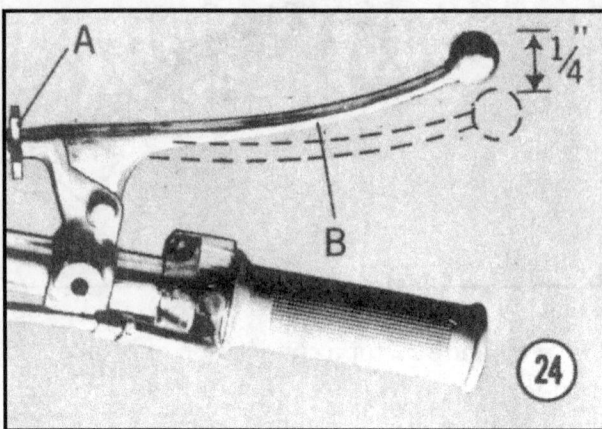

A. Cable adjuster   B. Brake lever

3. Rotate the front wheel after adjusting to be sure there is no brake drag.

Rear Brake

1. Adjust the knurled knob at the brake hub cam lever (see **Figure 25**) until there is ¾ to 1⅛ in. of play at the tip of the pedal.

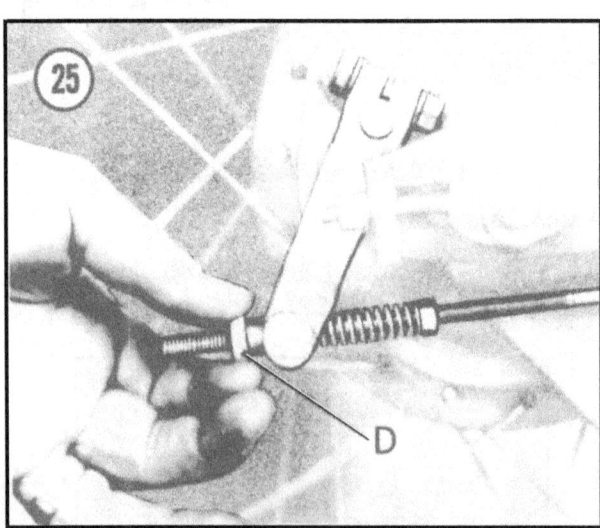

D. Knurled adjuster knob

2. Rotate the rear wheel after adjusting to be sure there is no brake drag.

3. Always adjust the rear brake after chain adjustment or alignment.

Brake Cam Lever Adjustment

1. The splined end of the lever fits over the splined end of the shaft.

2. Adjust the lever so it cannot swing past a 90 degree angle to either the front brake cable or the rear brake rod.

3. Draw the shaft out and push the lever in against the backing plate before tightening the pinch bolt.

STOPLIGHT SWITCH

Adjustment

1. Use a Phillips head screwdriver to loosen the mounting screws (see **Figure 26**).

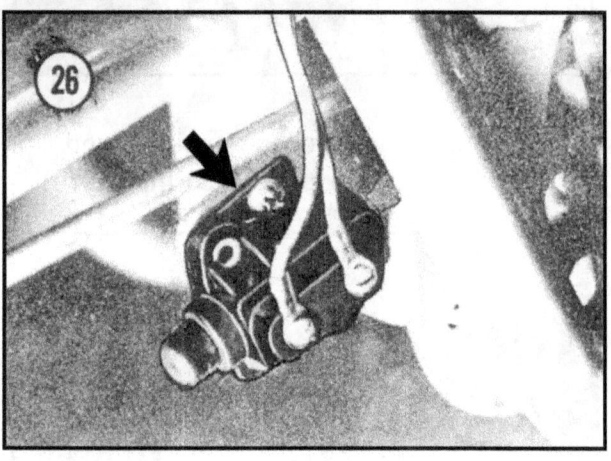

2. Adjust the switch location by moving it in the slotted holes in the switch base, so the brake light comes on when the pedal is depressed ½ in.

3. Tighten the mounting screws. Be sure the lockwashers are in good condition so the switch remains in position.

4. Always adjust switch after adjusting brake.

5. The procedure for adjusting the front switch is the same as the rear (see **Figure 27**). Adjust so the light comes on as the brake is applied.

22

BRAKE LUBRICATION

1. Use a hand operated grease gun to give *one* stroke to the grease fitting on the front and rear backing plates, every 1,000 miles.

2. Remove the front brake cable and oil the inner cable with an oil can while working the housing up and down, every 1,000 miles.

3. Put one or two drops of oil on the 3 friction points of the rear brake pedal, rod, and cam lever, every 1,000 miles.

CLUTCH

Clutch Cable Lubrication

1. Remove the clutch cable from the machine.

2. Oil the inner cable with an oil can while working the housing up and down so the oil flows to the bottom. Lubricate every 1,000 miles.

3. Install clutch cable on the machine.

Clutch Oil

1. The clutch assembly and lever are lubricated by the transmission oil supply. Change the oil every 1,000 miles.

2. Use only recommended oils, or the clutch may slip or stick.

3. Drain and replace the original oil in a new machine before riding. This is a factory lubricant for shipping purposes only.

4. Recommended oil for transmission: above 32°F, SAE 30W-Service MM; below 32°F, SAE 20W-Service MM.

Clutch Cable Adjustment

1. Loosen the locknut on the crankcase end of the clutch cable (see **Figure 28**).

2. Adjust the cable with the adjuster nut.

3. Tighten the locknut securely.

4. Complete cable adjustment with the handlebar adjuster (see **Figure 29**).

5. Allow ¼ in. of play at the end of the clutch hand lever.

AIR CLEANER

A clogged air cleaner can decrease the efficiency and the life of the engine. It should be

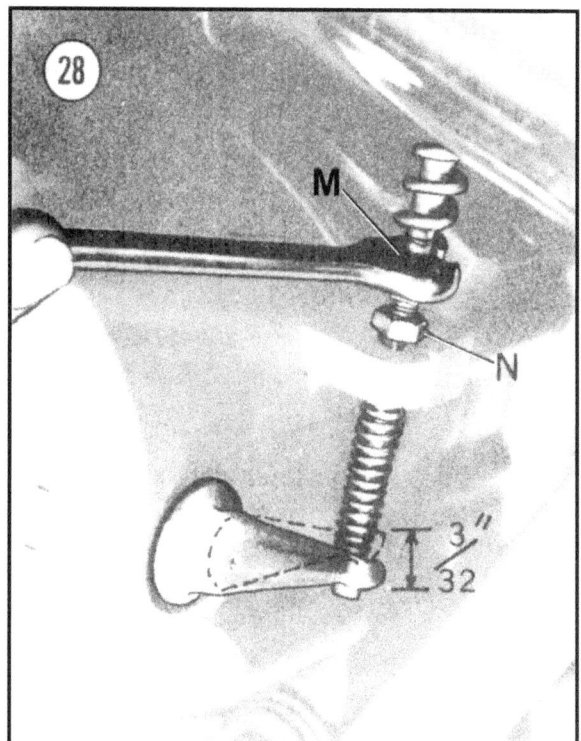

M. Cable adjuster   N. Locknut

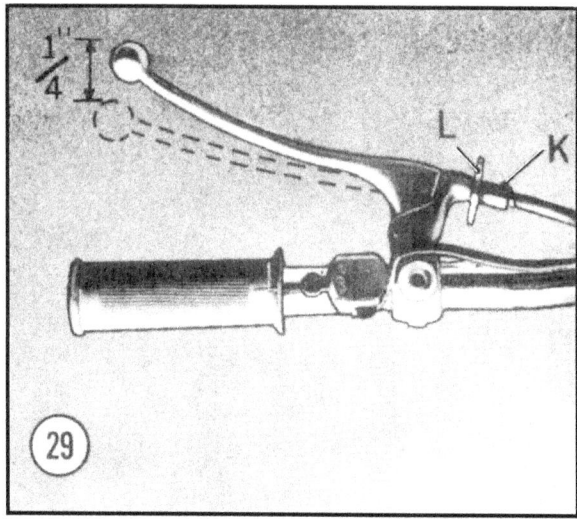

K. Adjuster screw   L. Locknut

checked at each oil change, or more often if the motorcycle is operated under dusty conditions.

1. Remove the filter element.

2. Replace the element if it is clogged with dirt or caked with oil or if the bonding material is cracked.

3. Light dust can be shaken off the element by tapping it while using a soft brush on the outside. If compressed air is available, force it through the filter from the inside.

4. Install the unit.

CARBURETORS AND EXHAUSTS

Unless the carburetor has been disassembled, it normally should not require adjustment. It should be worked on only as a last resort, when all other possible causes of such problems as rough idling or misfiring have been checked out. See Chapter Five for maintenance and repair.

WINTER STORAGE

Several months of inactivity can cause serious problems and a general deterioration of bike condition. This is especially important in areas of extreme cold weather. During the winter months it's advisable to specially prepare a bike for "hibernation."

Selecting A Storage Area

Most cyclists store their bikes in their home garage. If you don't have a home garage, facilities suitable for long-term motorcycle storage are readily available for rent or lease in most areas. In selecting a building, consider the following points.

1. The storage area must be dry, free from dampness and excessive humidity. Heating is not necessary but the building should be well insulated to minimize extreme temperature variations.
2. Buildings with large window area should be avoided, or such windows should be masked (a good security measure) if direct sunlight can fall on bike.
3. Buildings in industrial areas, where factories are liable to emit corrosive fumes, are not desirable for motorcycle storage, nor are facilities near bodies of salt water.
4. The area should be selected to minimize the possibility of loss by fire, theft, or vandalism. We strongly recommend that the areas be fully insured, perhaps with a package covering fire, theft, vandalism, weather, and liability. The advice of your insurance agent should be solicited on these matters. The building should be fireproof and items such as the security of doors and windows, alarm facilities, and proximity of police should be considered.

Preparing Bike for Storage

Careful pre-storage preparation will minimize deterioration and will ease restoring the bike to service in the spring. The following procedure is recommended.

1. Wash the bike completely, making certain to remove any accumulation of road salt that may have collected during the first weeks of winter. Wax all painted and polished surfaces.
2. Run the engine for 20-30 minutes to stabilize oil temperature. Drain oil regardless of mileage since oil change and replace with normal quantity of fresh oil.
3. Remove battery and coat cable terminals with petroleum jelly. If there is evidence of acid spillage in the battery box, neutralize with baking soda, wash clean, and repaint. Batteries should be kept in an area where they will not freeze, and where they can be recharged every 2 weeks.
4. Drain all gasoline from fuel tank, settling bowl, and carburetor float bowls. Leave petcock on the RESERVE position.
5. Remove spark plugs and add a small quantity of oil to each cylinder. Turn the engine a few revolutions by hand. Install spark plugs.
6. Run a business card, lightly saturated with silicone oil, between the points to clean them. Follow up with a dry card.
7. Check tire pressures. Move machine to storage area and store on center stand. If preparation is performed in an area remote from the storage facility, machines should be trucked, not ridden, into storage.

Inspection During Storage

Try to inspect bike weekly while in storage. Any deterioration should be corrected as soon as possible. For example, if corrosion of bright metal parts is observed, cover them with a light film of grease or silicone spray.

Restoring Bike to Service

A bike that has been properly prepared, and stored in a suitable area, requires only light maintenance to restore it to service. It is advisable, however, to perform a "spring tune-up."

1. Before removing the bike from the storage area, re-inflate tires to the correct pressures. Air loss during storage period may have nearly flattened the tires, and moving the bike can cause damage to tires, tubes, or rims.

2. When the bike is brought to the work area, immediately install the battery (fully charged) and fill the fuel tank. (The petcock should be on the RESERVE position; do not move yet.)

3. Check the fuel system for leaks. Remove carburetor float bowl or open the float bowl drain cock and allow several cups of fuel to pass through the system. Move the fuel cock slowly to the CLOSE position, remove the setting bowl and empty any accumulated water.

4. Perform normal tune-up, described earlier, apply oil to camshaft, and when checking spark plug add a few drops of oil to the cylinder. Be especially certain to degrease ignition points if an oily card was used to inhibit oxidation during storage; use a non-petroleum solvent such as trichloroethylene.

5. Check safety items, i.e., lights, horn, etc., as oxidation of switch contacts and/or sockets during storage may make one or more of these critical devices inoperative.

6. Test ride and clean the motorcycle.

CHAPTER THREE

TROUBLESHOOTING

Diagnosing mechanical problems is relatively simple if you use orderly procedures and keep a few basic principles in mind.

The troubleshooting procedures in this chapter analyze typical symptoms, and show logical methods of isolating causes. These are not the only methods. There may be several ways to solve a problem, but only a systematic, methodical approach can guarantee success.

Never assume anything. Don't overlook the obvious. If you are riding along and the bike suddenly quits, check the easiest, most accessible problem spots first. Is there gasoline in the tank? Is the gas petcock in the ON or RESERVE position? Has a spark plug wire fallen off? Check the ignition switch. Sometimes the weight of keys on a key ring may turn the ignition off suddenly.

If nothing obvious turns up in a cursory check, look a little further. Learning to recognize and describe symptoms will make repairs easier for you or a mechanic at the shop. Describe problems accurately and fully. Saying that "it won't run" isn't the same as saying "it quit on the highway at high speed and wouldn't start," or that "it sat in my garage for 3 months and then wouldn't start."

Gather as many symptoms together as possible to aid in diagnosis. Note whether the engine lost power gradually or all at once, what color smoke (if any) came from the exhaust, and so on. Remember that the more complicated a machine is, the easier it is to troubleshoot because symptoms point to specific problems.

After the symptoms are defined, areas which could cause the problems are tested and analyzed. Guessing at the cause of a problem may provide the solution, but it can easily lead to frustration, wasted time, and a series of expensive, unnecessary parts replacements.

You don't need fancy equipment or complicated test gear to determine whether repairs can be attempted at home. A few simple checks could save a large repair bill and time lost while the bike sits in a dealer's service department. On the other hand, be realistic and don't attempt repair beyond your capabilities. Service departments tend to charge heavily for putting together a disassembled engine that may have been abused. Some won't even take on such a job—so use common sense, don't get in over your head.

OPERATING REQUIREMENTS

An engine needs 3 basics to run properly: correct gas/air mixture, compression, and a spark at the right time. If one or more are missing, the engine won't run. The electrical system is the weakest link of the 3 basics. More problems result from electrical breakdowns than from any other source. Keep that in mind before you begin tampering with carburetor adjustments and the like.

If a bike has been sitting for any length of time and refuses to start, check the battery for a charged condition first, and then look to the gasoline delivery system. This includes the tank, fuel petcocks, lines, and the carburetors. Rust may have formed in the tank, obstructing fuel flow. Gasoline deposits may have gummed up carburetor jets and air passages. Gasoline tends to lose its potency after standing for long periods. Condensation may contaminate it with water. Drain old gas and try starting with a fresh tankful.

TROUBLESHOOTING INSTRUMENTS

Chapter One lists many of the instruments needed and detailed instruction on their use.

STARTING DIFFICULTIES

Check gas flow first. Remove the gas cap and look into the tank. If gas is present, pull off a fuel line at the carburetor and see if gas flows freely. If none comes out, the fuel tap may be shut off, blocked by rust or foreign matter, or the fuel line may be stopped up or kinked. If the carburetor is getting usable fuel, turn to the electrical system next.

Check that the battery is charged by turning on the lights or by beeping the horn. Refer to your owner's manual for starting procedures with a dead battery. Have the battery recharged if necessary.

Pull off a spark plug cap, remove the spark plug, and reconnect the cap. Lay the plug against the cylinder head so its base makes a good connection, and turn the engine over with the kickstarter. A fat, blue spark should jump across the electrodes. If there is no spark, or only a weak one, there is electrical system trouble. Check for a defective plug by replacing it with a known good one. Don't assume a plug is good just because it's new.

Once the plug has been cleared of guilt, but there's still no spark, start backtracking through the system. If the contact at the end of the spark plug wire can be exposed, it can be held about ⅛ in. from the head while the engine is turned over to check for a spark. Remember to hold the wire only by its insulation to avoid a nasty shock. If the plug wires are dirty, greasy, or wet, wrap a rag around them so you don't get shocked. If you do feel a shock or see sparks along the wire, clean or replace the wire and/or its connections.

If there's no spark at the plug wire, look for loose connections at the coil and battery. If all seems in order there, check next for oily or dirty contact points. Clean points with electrical contact cleaner, or a strip of paper. On battery ignition models, with the ignition switch turned on, open and close the points manually with a screwdriver.

No spark at the points with this test indicates a failure in the ignition system. Refer to Chapter Two (*Periodic Maintenance and Tune-up*) for checkout procedures for the entire system and individual components. Refer to the same chapter for checking and setting ignition timing.

Note that spark plugs of the incorrect heat range (too cold) may cause hard starting. Set gaps to specifications. If you have just ridden through a puddle or washed the bike and it won't start, dry off plugs and plug wires. Water may have entered the carburetor and fouled the fuel under these conditions, but wet plugs and wires are the more likely problem.

If a healthy spark occurs at the right time, and there is adequate gas flow to the carburetor, check the carburetor itself at this time. Make sure all jets and air passages are clean, check float level, and adjust if necessary. Shake the float to check for gasoline inside it, and replace or repair as indicated. Check that the carburetors are mounted snugly, and no air is leaking past the manifold. Check for a clogged air filter.

Compression, or the lack of it, usually enters the picture only in the case of older machines. Worn or broken pistons, rings, and cylinder bores could prevent starting. Generally a gradual power loss and harder starting will be readily apparent in this case.

Compression may be checked in the field by turning the kickstarter by hand and noting that an adequate resistance is felt.

An accurate cylinder compression check gives a good idea of the condition of the basic working parts of the engine. To perform this test, you need a compression gauge. The motor should be warm.

1. Remove the plug on the cylinder to be tested and clean out any dirt or grease.

2. Insert the tip of the gauge into the hole, making sure it is seated correctly.

3. Open the throttle all the way and make sure the choke on the carburetor is open.

4. Crank the engine several times and record the highest pressure reading on the gauge.

5. The normal compression is 155 to 170 psi.

6. Pour a tablespoon of motor oil into the suspect cylinder and record the compression.

If oil raises the compression significantly—10 psi in an old engine—the rings are worn and should be replaced.

Many owners of 2-stroke bikes are plagued by hard starting and generally poor running, for which there seems to be no cause. Carburetion and ignition may be good, and a compression test may show that all is well in the engine's upper end.

What a compression test does not show is lack of primary compression. The crankcase in a 2-stroke engine must be alternately under pressure and vacuum. After the piston closes the intake port, further downward movement of the piston causes the entrapped mixture to be pressurized so that it can rush quickly into the cylinder when the scavening ports are opened. Upward piston movement creates a slight vacuum in the crankcase, enabling fuel/air mixture to be drawn in from the carburetor.

If crankshaft seals or case gaskets leak, the crankcase cannot hold pressure or vacuum, and proper engine operation becomes impossible. Any other source of leak, such as defective cylinder base gaskets or porous or cracked crankcase castings will result in the same conditions.

It is possible, however, to test for and isolate engine pressure leaks. The test is simple and does not require elaborate equipment. Briefly, what is done is to seal off all natural engine openings, then apply air pressure. If the engine does not hold air, a leak or leaks is indicated. Then it is only necessary to locate and repair all leaks.

The following procedure describes a typical pressure test.

1. Remove the carburetor.

2. Install the pressure adapter and its gasket (**Figure 1**) in place of the carburetor.

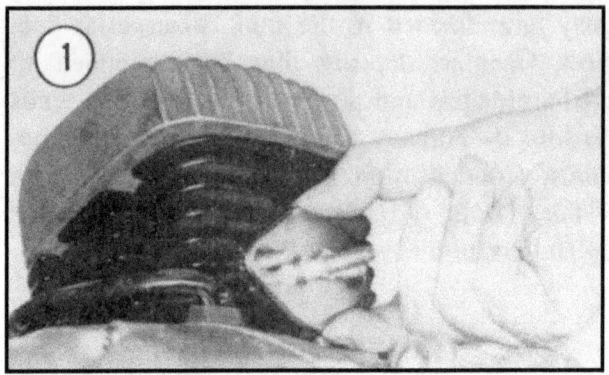

3. Block off the exhaust port, using suitable adapters and fittings (**Figure 2**).

4. Connect the pressurizing bulb and gauge to the pressure fitting installed where the carburetor was, then continue to squeeze the bulb until the gauge indicates approximately 6 pounds per square inch (**Figure 3**).

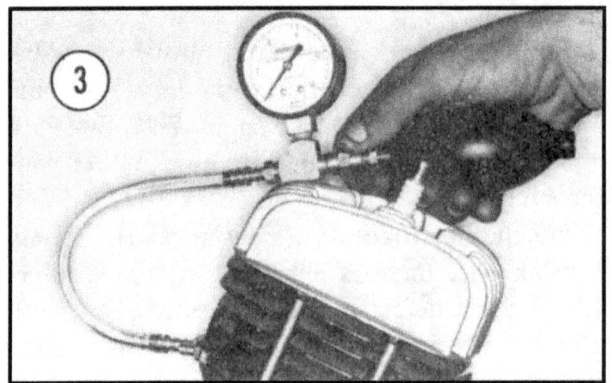

5. Observe the pressure gauge. If the engine is in good condition, pressure should not drop more than about one pound per square inch in several minutes. Any pressure loss of one pound per square inch in one minute indicates serious sealing problems.

Before condemning the engine, first be sure that there are no leaks in the test equipment itself. Then go over the entire engine carefully. Large leaks can be heard; smaller ones can be found by going over every possible leakage source with a small brush and soap suds solution. The following is a list of possible leakage points.

1. Crankshaft seals
2. Spark plug
3. Compression release
4. Cylinder head joint
5. Cylinder base joint
6. Carburetor mounting flange
7. Crankcase joint

POOR IDLING

This may be caused by incorrect carburetor adjustment, incorrect timing, or ignition system defects. Check gas cap vent for an obstruction.

MISFIRING

Misfiring can be caused by a weak spark or dirty plug. Check for fuel contamination. Run bike at night to check for spark leaks along plug wire and under spark plug cap.

> WARNING
> *Do not run engine in dark garage to check for spark leak. There is considerable danger of carbon monoxide poisoning.*

If misfiring occurs only at certain throttle settings, refer to the fuel system chapter for the specific carburetor circuits involved. Misfiring under heavy load, as when climbing hills or accelerating, is usually caused by a bad spark plug.

FLAT SPOTS

If the engine seems to die momentarily when the throttle is opened and then recovers, check for a dirty main jet in the carburetor, water in the fuel, or an excessively lean mixture.

POWER LOSS

Poor condition of rings, piston, or cylinder will cause a lack of power and speed. Ignition timing should be checked.

OVERHEATING

If the engine seems to run too hot all the time, be sure you are not idling it for long periods. Air-cooled engines are not designed to operate at a standstill for any length of time. Heavy stop and go traffic is hard on a motorcycle engine. A spark plug of the wrong heat range can burn a piston. An excessively lean gas mixture may cause overheating. Check ignition timing. Don't ride in too high a gear. Broken or worn rings may permit compression gases to leak past them, heating head and cylinder excessively. Check oil level and use the proper grade lubricants.

ENGINE NOISES

Experience is needed to diagnose accurately in this area. Noises are hard to differentiate and harder yet to describe. Deep knocking noises usually mean main bearing failure. A slapping noise generally comes from loose pistons. A light knocking noise during acceleration may be a bad connecting rod bearing. Pinging should be corrected immediately or damage to pistons will result. Compression leaks at the head-cylinder joint will sound like a rapid on-and-off squeal.

PISTON SEIZURE

Piston seizure is caused by incorrect piston clearances when fitted, fitting rings with improper end gap, too thin an oil being used, incorrect spark plug heat range, or incorrect ignition timing. Overheating from any cause may result in seizure.

EXCESSIVE VIBRATION

Excessive vibration may be caused by loose motor mounts, worn engine or transmission bearings, loose wheels, worn swinging arm bushings, a generally poor running engine, broken or cracked frame, or one that has been damaged in a collision. See also *Poor Handling*.

CLUTCH SLIP OR DRAG

Clutch slip may be due to worn or glazed plates, or improper adjustment. A dragging clutch could result from damaged or bent plates, improper adjustment, or even clutch spring pressure.

All clutch problems, except adjustments or cable replacement, require removal to identify the cause and make repairs.

1. *Slippage*—This condition is most noticeable when accelerating in high gear at relatively low speed. To check slippage, drive at a steady speed in fourth or fifth gear. Without letting up on the accelerator, push in the clutch long enough to let engine speed increase (one or two seconds). Then let the clutch out rapidly. If the clutch is good, engine speed will drop quickly or the bike will jump forward. If the clutch is slipping, engine speed will drop slowly and the bike will not jump forward.

Slippage results from insufficient clutch lever free-play, worn friction plates, or weak springs. Riding the clutch can cause the disc surfaces to become glazed, resulting in slippage.

2. *Drag or failure to release* — This trouble usually causes difficult shifting and gear clash especially when downshifting. The cause may be excessive clutch lever free-play, warped or bent plates, stretched clutch cable, or broken or loose disc linings.

3. *Chatter or grabbing*—Check for worn or misaligned steel plate and clutch friction plates.

TRANSMISSION

Transmission problems are usually indicated by one or more of the following symptoms:

   a. Difficult shifting gears
   b. Gear clash when downshifting
   c. Slipping out of gear
   d. Excessive noise in neutral
   e. Excessive noise in gear

Transmission symptoms are sometimes hard to distinguish from clutch symptoms. Be sure the clutch is not causing the trouble before working on the transmission.

POOR HANDLING

Poor handling may be caused by improper tire pressures, a damaged frame or swinging arm, worn shocks or front forks, weak fork springs, a bent or broken steering stem, misaligned wheels, loose or missing spokes, worn tires, bent handlebar, worn wheel bearing, or dragging brakes.

BRAKE PROBLEMS

Sticking brakes may be caused by broken or weak return springs, improper cable or rod adjustment, or dry pivot and cam bushings. Grabbing brakes may be caused by greasy linings which must be replaced. Brake grab may also be due to out-of-round drums or linings which have broken loose from the brake shoes. Glazed linings will cause loss of stopping power.

ELECTRICAL PROBLEMS

Bulbs which continuously burn out may be caused by excessive vibration, loose connections that permit sudden current surges, poor battery connections, installation of the wrong type bulb, or a faulty voltage regulator.

A dead battery or one which discharges quickly may be caused by a faulty alternator or rectifier. Check for loose or corroded terminals. Shorted battery cells or broken terminals will keep a battery from charging. Low water level will decrease a battery's capacity. A battery left uncharged after installation will sulphate, rendering it useless.

A majority of light and horn or other electrical accessory problems are caused by loose or corroded ground connections. Check those first, and then substitute known good units for easier troubleshooting.

TROUBLESHOOTING GUIDE

The following "quick reference" guide summarizes part of the troubleshooting process. Use it to outline possible problem areas, then refer to the specific chapter or section involved.

TROUBLESHOOTING GUIDE

Item	Problem or Cause	Things to Check
Loss of power	Poor compression	Piston rings and cylinders Head gaskets Crankcase leaks
	Overheated engine	Lubricating oil supply Clogged cooling fins Ignition timing Slipping clutch Carbon in combustion chamber
	Improper mixture	Dirty air cleaner Restricted fuel flow Gas cap vent hole
	Miscellaneous	Dragging brakes Tight wheel bearings Defective chain Clogged exhaust system
Brake troubles	Poor brakes	Brake adjustment Oil or water on brake linings Loose linkage or cables
	Noisy brakes	Worn or scratched lining Scratched brake drums Dirt in brakes
	Unadjustable brakes	Worn linings Worn drums Worn brake cams
Gearshifting difficulties	Clutch	Adjustment Springs Friction plates Steel plates Oil quantity
	Transmission	Oil Quantity Oil grade Return spring or pin Change lever or spring Drum piston plate Change drum Change forks

(continued)

TROUBLESHOOTING GUIDE (continued)

Item	Problem or Cause	Things to Check
Steering problems	Hard steering	Tire pressure Steering damper adjustment Steering stem head Steering head bearings
	Pulls to one side	Unbalanced shock absorbers Drive chain adjustment Front/rear wheel alignment Unbalanced tires Defective swinging arm Defective steering head
	Shimmy	Drive chain adjustment Loose or missing spokes Deformed rims Worn wheel bearings Wheel balance

CHAPTER FOUR

ENGINE, TRANSMISSION, AND CLUTCH

This chapter describes removal, disassembly, service, and reassembly of the engine, transmission, and clutch. It is suggested that the engine be serviced without removing it from the chassis except for overhaul of the crankshaft assembly, transmission, gearshift mechanism, or bearings. Operating principles of the 2-stroke engine is also discussed in this chapter, to help in understanding the work which needs to be done.

ENGINE PRINCIPLES

Figures 1 through 4 illustrate operation of the 2-stroke engine. During this discussion, assume that the crankshaft is rotating counter-clockwise. In **Figure 1**, as the piston travels downward, a scavenging port (A) between the crankcase and the cylinder is uncovered. The exhaust gases, which are under pressure, leave the cylinder through the exhaust port (B), which is also opened by the downward movement of the piston. A fresh fuel/air charge, which has previously been compressed slightly, travels from the crankcase (C) to the cylinder through the scavenging port (A) as the port opens. Since the incoming charge is under pressure, it rushes into the cylinder quickly and helps to expel the exhaust gases from the previous cycle.

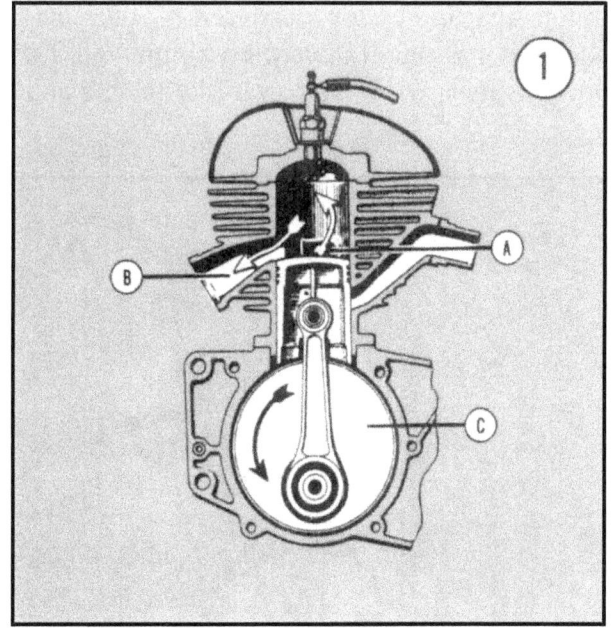

Figure 2 illustrates the next phase of the cycle. As the crankshaft continues to rotate, the piston moves upward, closing the exhaust and scavenging ports. As the piston continues upward, the air/fuel mixture in the cylinder is compressed. Notice also that a low pressure area is created in the crankcase at the same time. Further upward movement of the piston uncovers the intake port (D). A fresh fuel/air charge is then drawn into the crankcase through the intake port

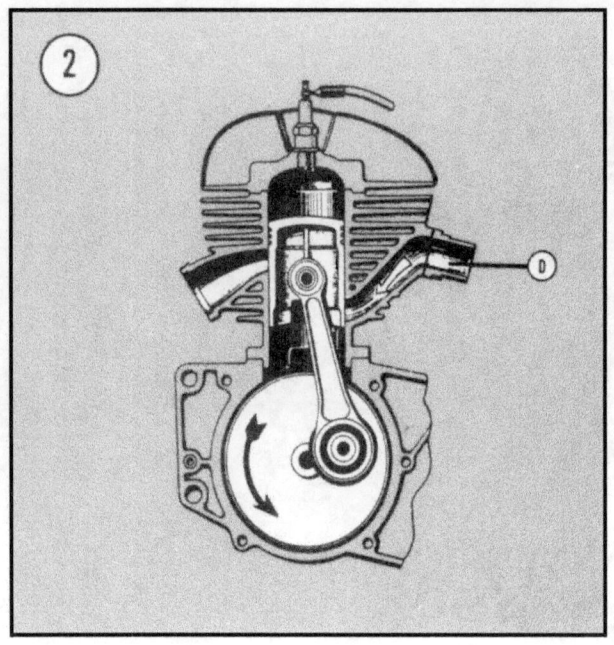

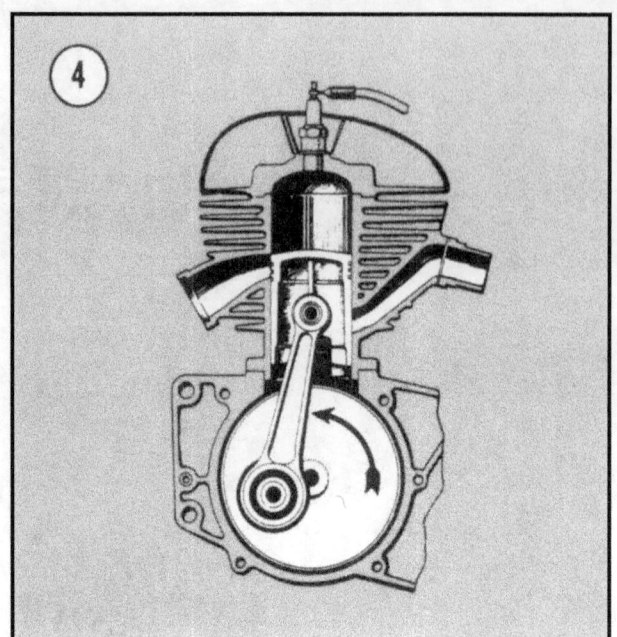

because of the low pressure created by the upward piston movement.

The third phase is shown in **Figure 3**. As the piston approaches top dead center, the spark plug fires, igniting the compressed mixture. The piston is then driven downward by the expanding gases.

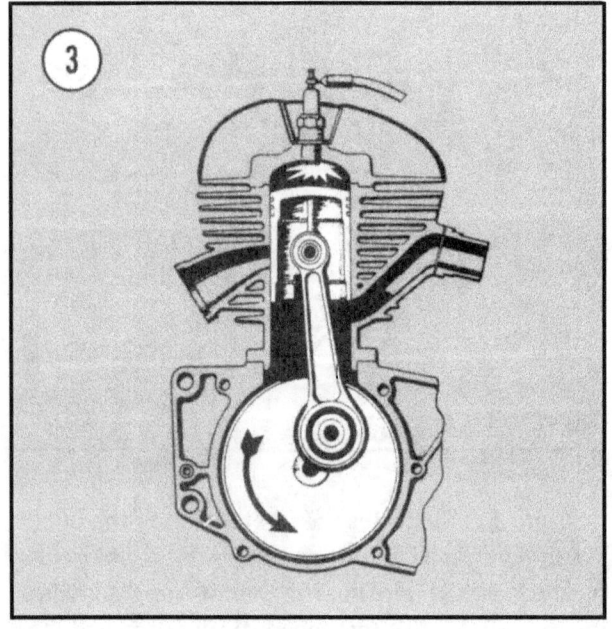

When the top of the piston uncovers the exhaust port, the fourth phase begins, as shown in **Figure 4**. The exhaust gases leave the cylinder through the exhaust port. As the piston continues downward, the intake port is closed and the mixture in the crankcase is compressed in preparation for the next cycle.

It can be seen from the foregoing discussion that every downward stroke of the piston is a power stroke.

CYLINDER HEAD AND CYLINDER

Figure 5 shows an exploded view of the cylinder and head.

Removal

1. Remove the spark plug. Remove the exhaust pipe nut. Remove the air cleaner rubber hose.
2. Remove intake stud nuts and the carburetor from the manifold.
3. Remove the cylinder head nuts, head, and aluminum gasket.
4. Push the kickstarter until the piston reaches top dead center.
5. Raise the cylinder and stuff a clean rag in the crankcase (see **Figure 6**) to keep out debris.
6. Remove the cylinder and place on bench with head end down.

Piston Removal

1. Remove the wrist pin circlips with a long nosed pliers (see **Figure 7**).

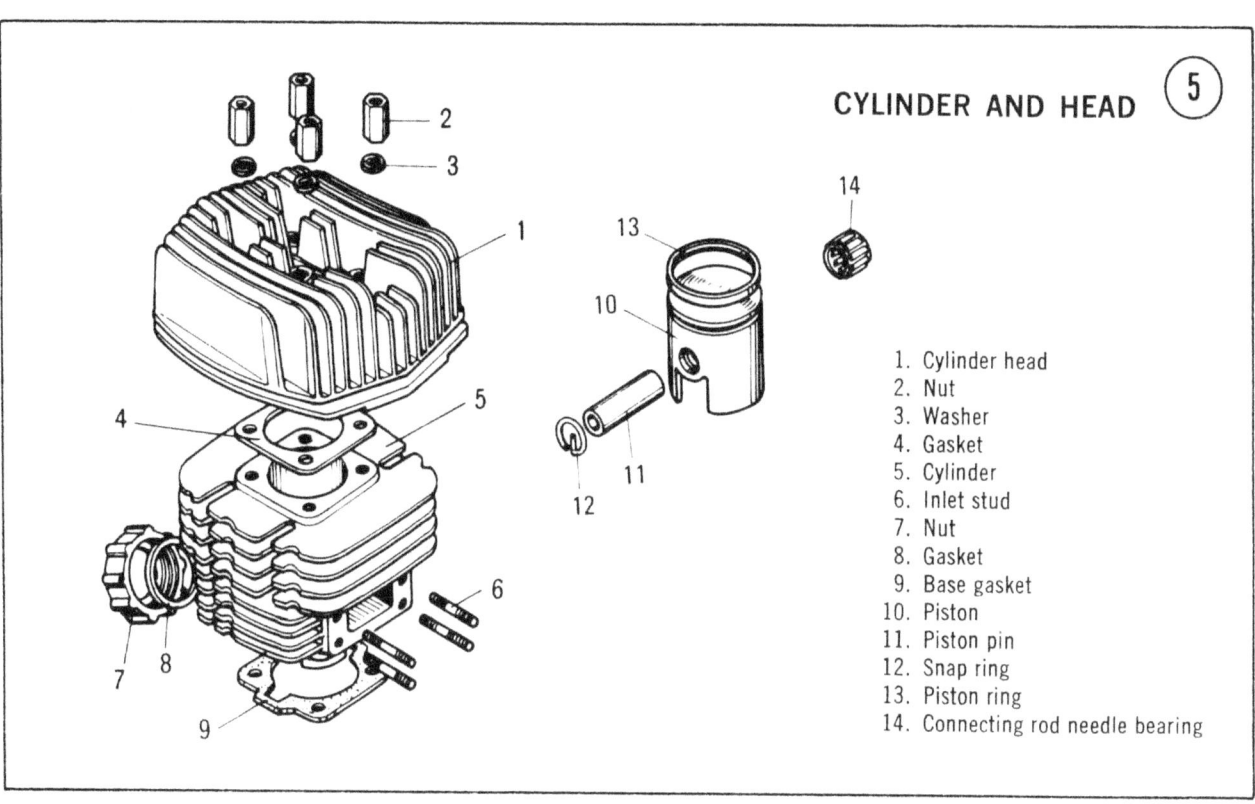

CYLINDER AND HEAD

1. Cylinder head
2. Nut
3. Washer
4. Gasket
5. Cylinder
6. Inlet stud
7. Nut
8. Gasket
9. Base gasket
10. Piston
11. Piston pin
12. Snap ring
13. Piston ring
14. Connecting rod needle bearing

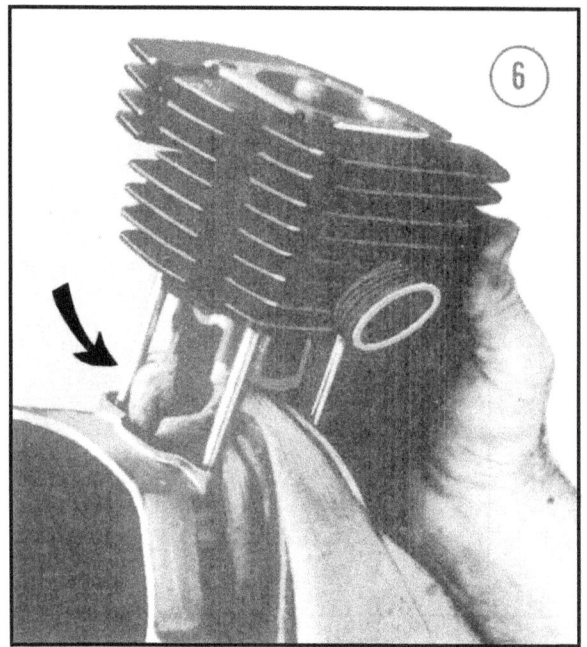

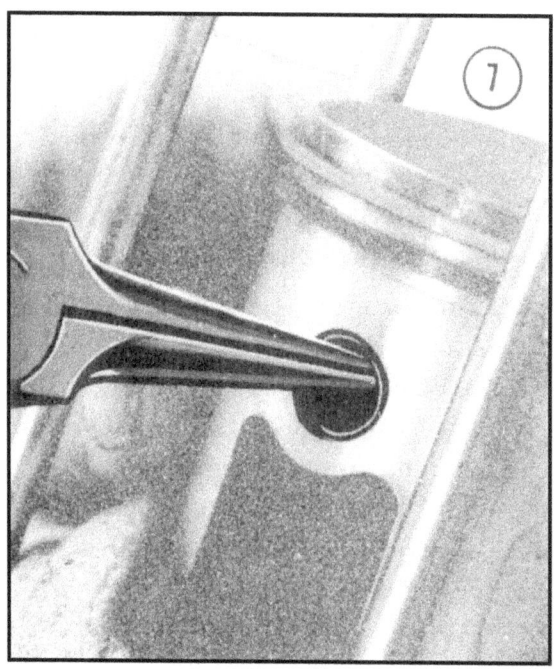

2. Hold the piston and push the wrist pin part way out with a round dowel.

3. Remove wrist pin with long nosed pliers (see Figure 7). It may be necessary to heat the piston lightly with a torch before removing pin.

4. Remove the piston from the rod and remove the cloth from the crankcase.

5. Remove the cylinder base gasket and cover the crankcase with the cloth again.

DECARBONIZING

1. Scrape carbon deposits from the exhaust passage with a knife. Finish the job with No. 200 grit sandpaper.

2. Remove the carbon from the piston ring grooves with a groove scraper or a piece of broken piston ring. Be sure not to remove any metal.

3. Clean the carbon from the cylinder head, being careful not to gouge the surfaces.

4. Run a 14mm tap through the spark plug threads to remove carbon.

5. Clean the exhaust pipe and muffler of carbon as detailed in Chapter Eleven.

6. Clean the parts in solvent and dry with air or a clean cloth.

7. Clean the piston sidewalls with soap-filled steel wool pads and rinse with running water.

8. Lightly hone the cylinder wall to remove the glaze.

9. Remove any aluminum deposit on cylinder wall from piston seizure with muriatic acid. Rinse the acid carefully with running water.

10. Clean the cylinder with solvent after honing and cover the wall with oil.

CYLINDER AND PISTON SCORES

1. Rebore the cylinder to the next oversize if scores of more than 0.002 in. remain after honing.

2. Replace the piston if scores are deeper than 0.003 in. or more than ½ in. wide.

CYLINDER AND PISTON MEASURING

1. Measure the piston at the bottom of the skirt at right angles to the sides.

2. Replace the piston if wear is more than 0.002 in. of diameter given in the specification tables.

3. Measure the piston ring clearance with new rings and a feeler gauge (see **Figure 8**). The clearance should be 0.0008 to 0.0024 in. Replace the piston if ring groove wear is greater.

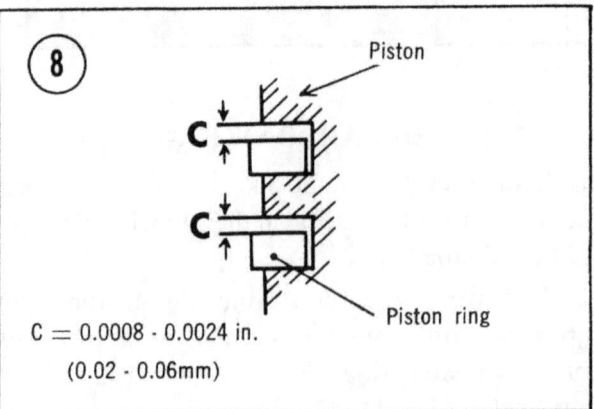

4. Measure the cylinder bore at the top and bottom. If the difference is more than 0.004 in., rebore to the next oversize.

5. Compare the diameter of the piston skirt (see **Figure 9**) and the bottom of the cylinder (see **Figure 10**). If the clearance is more than 0.006 in., rebore to next oversize.

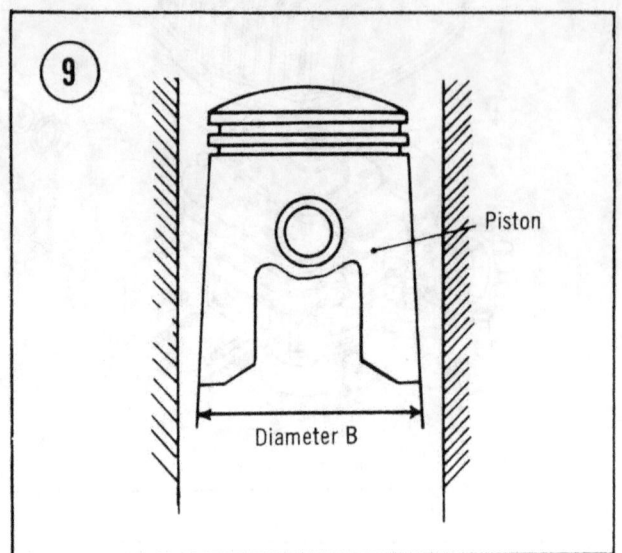

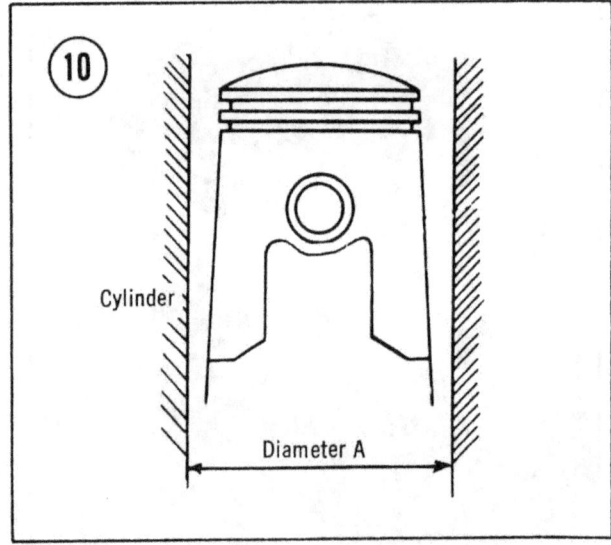

CYLINDER BORING

1. After reboring, fit the new piston to 0.003 to 0.004 in. total clearance. Finish fitting with a hone, moving the hone rapidly in and out of the cylinder to get a cross-hatched surface in the bore.

2. Bevel the port edges 1/64 in. with a fine file to prevent the rings from hooking the edge of the ports. Clean cylinder and piston thoroughly

with solvent after fitting to remove all abrasives. Coat parts with oil.

3. Push the wrist pin through the pin bosses. If it won't go, ream the bosses lightly with a bar reamer until it will.

NEW CYLINDER RINGS

1. Put the new ring into the cylinder and push down ½ in. with the piston skirt (see **Figure 11**).

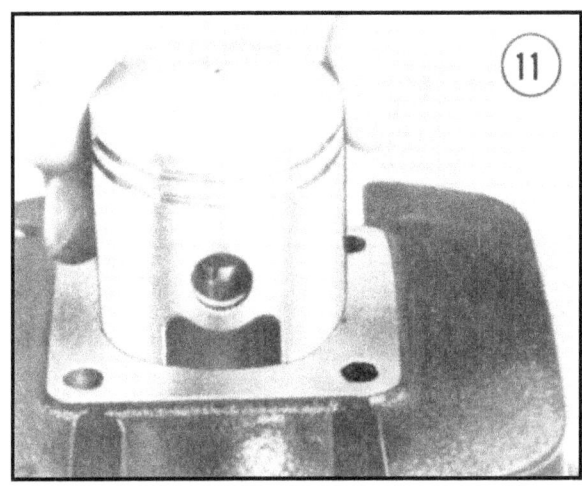

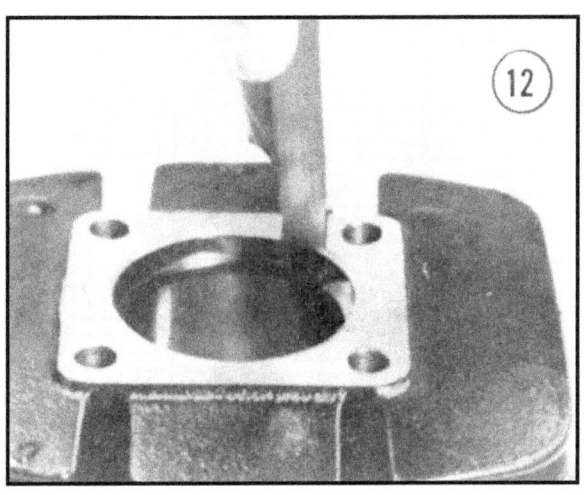

2. Measure the end gap with a feeler gauge (see **Figure 12**). Top ring gap is 0.006 to 0.014 in. Bottom ring gap is 0.004 to 0.012 in. (see **Figure 13**).

3. Do not use the ring if the gap is wrong. Recheck ring and cylinder size.

REASSEMBLY

Piston

1. Install the rings on the piston with the cutaway at the ring gap facing toward the anti-rotation pegs. The top ring is chrome faced and a steel expanded ring must be installed in the lower ring groove before the ring is installed.

2. Coat the piston with a film of oil.

3. Push the wrist pin into the piston until it clears the pin boss.

4. Install the piston over the rod with the top groove anti-rotation peg toward the rear of the engine. Push the pin through the rod bushing on Ace 90 models (see **Figure 14**).

5. On 100cc and 125cc models, a needle bearing is used instead of a bushing. Replace the

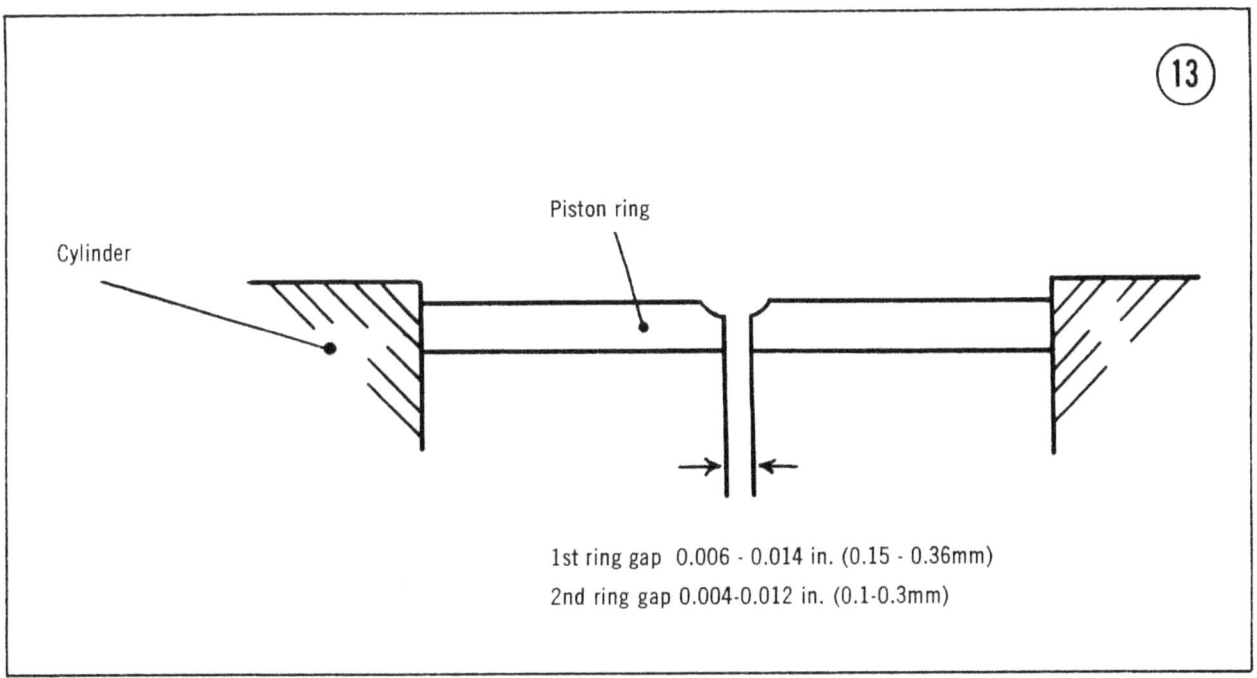

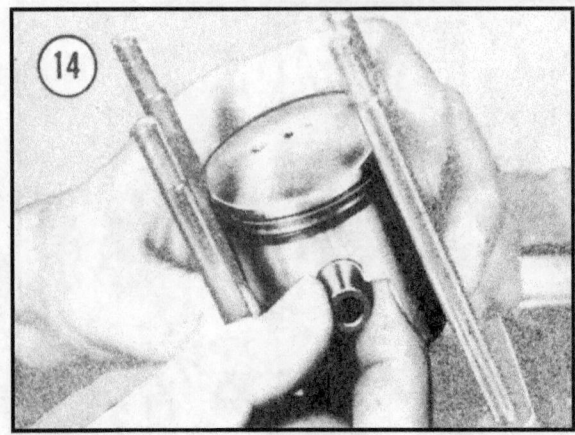

bearing and wrist pin each time the piston is replaced.

6. Install new circlips with long nosed pliers.

7. Lubricate the rod eye with an oil can, rocking the piston back and forth.

Cylinder and Head

1. Install a new cylinder base gasket (see **Figure 15**).

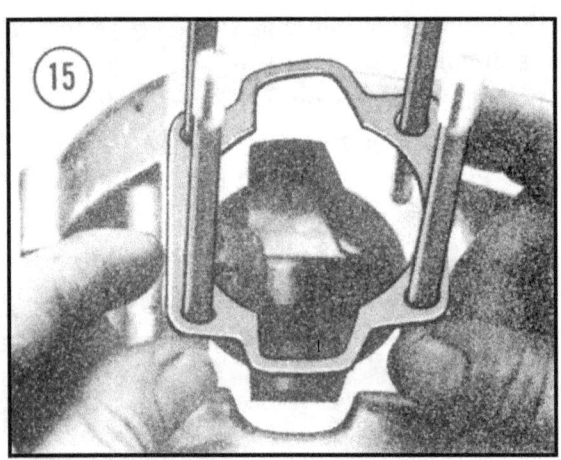

2. Pull the piston to the top of its stroke, with ring gaps properly positioned.

3. Install the cylinder over the studs and over the piston. Compress the rings with your fingers to fit inside cylinder (see **Figure 16**).

4. Seat the cylinder firmly on the base gasket.

5. Install a new head gasket and install the head.

6. Install the washers and nuts on studs and torque to 105 in.-lb. (see **Figure 17**). Torque slowly and evenly to prevent warping.

7. Install the carburetor on the manifold, torqueing nuts evenly.

8. Install the rubber air cleaner hose.

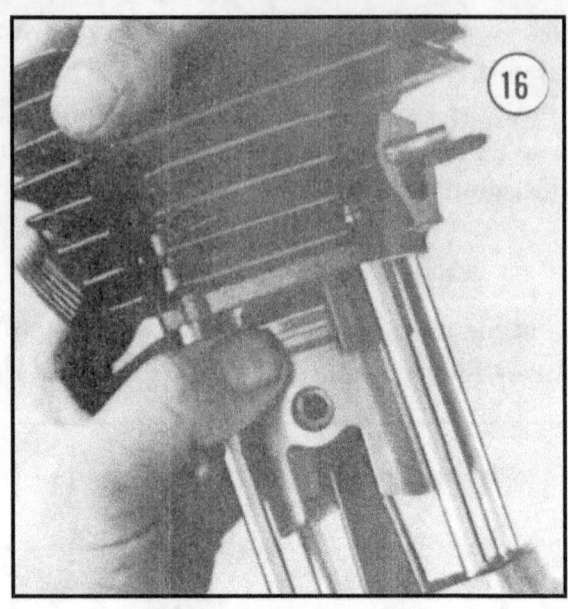

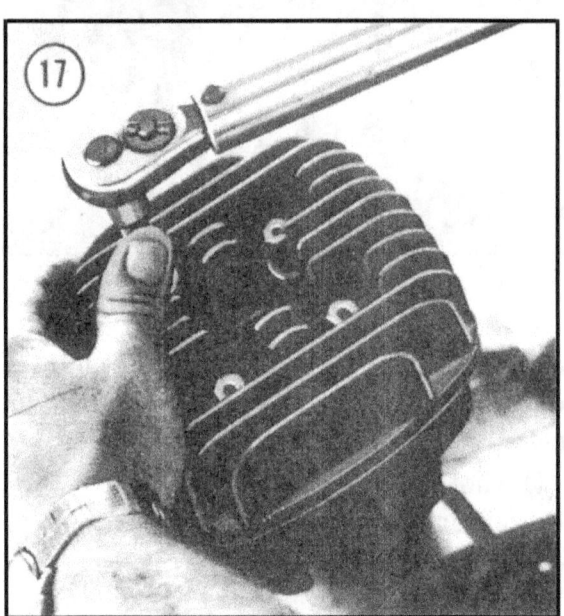

9. Install the spark plug and spark plug wire.

10. Use a new exhaust gasket and install the exhaust pipe.

CLUTCH

Hodaka uses a crankshaft-mounted multidisc clutch. It is designed to operate in the transmission case oil supply. **Figure 18** shows an exploded view of the clutch assembly. **Figure 19** is a cross-section view showing the clutch in the disengaged position. The engaged position is indicated by the dotted lines.

Adjustment

Refer to Chapter Two for clutch adjustment.

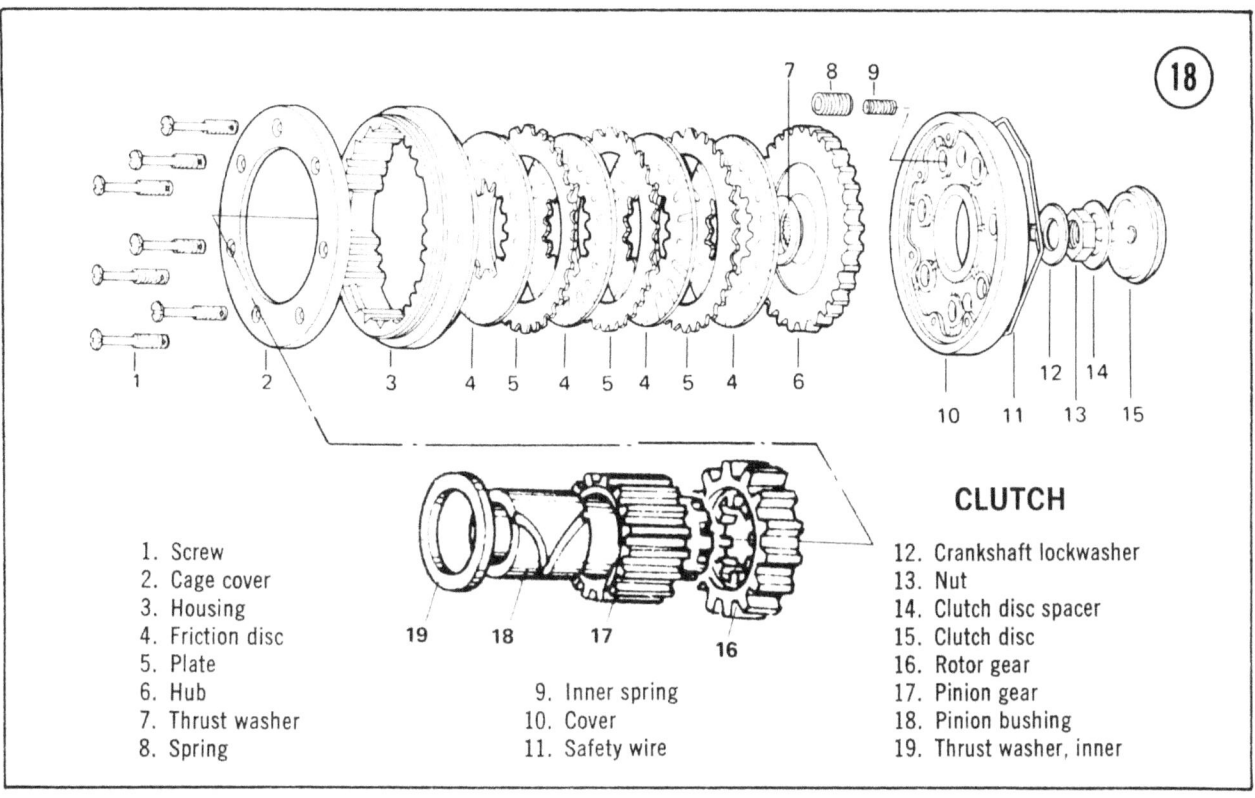

CLUTCH

1. Screw
2. Cage cover
3. Housing
4. Friction disc
5. Plate
6. Hub
7. Thrust washer
8. Spring
9. Inner spring
10. Cover
11. Safety wire
12. Crankshaft lockwasher
13. Nut
14. Clutch disc spacer
15. Clutch disc
16. Rotor gear
17. Pinion gear
18. Pinion bushing
19. Thrust washer, inner

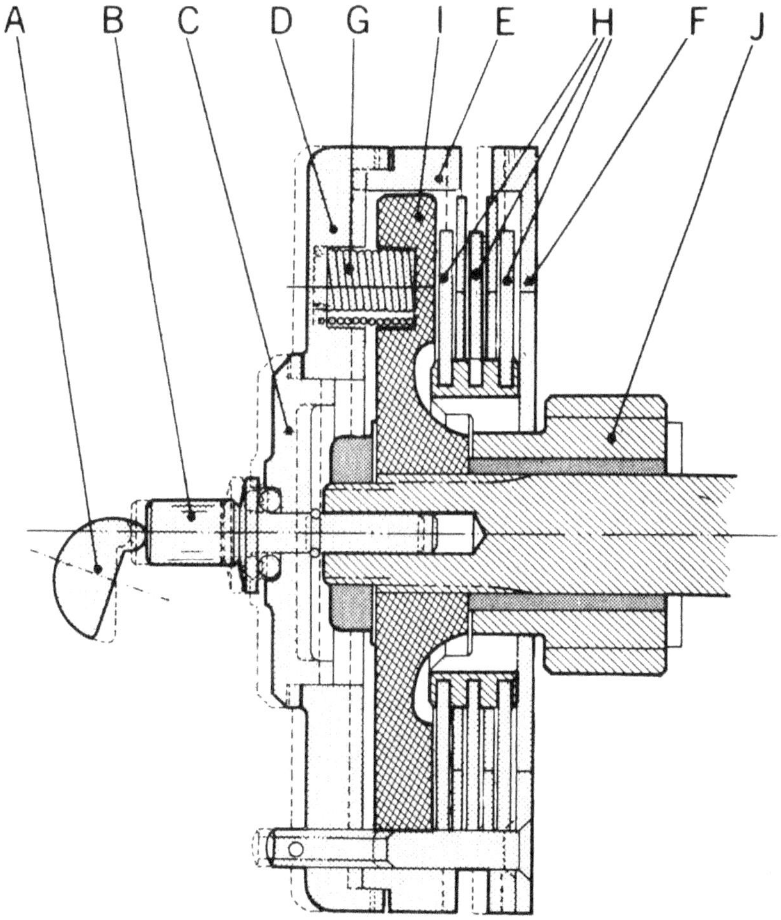

CLUTCH

A. Cam-ended clutch lever
B. Clutch pressure shaft
C. Clutch disc
D. Cover
E. Housing
F. Cover
G. Clutch springs
H. Friction discs
I. Hub
J. Pinion gear

Clutch Lever

1. Push down the kickstarter lever and insert a screwdriver in the frame to prevent it from returning (see **Figure 20**).

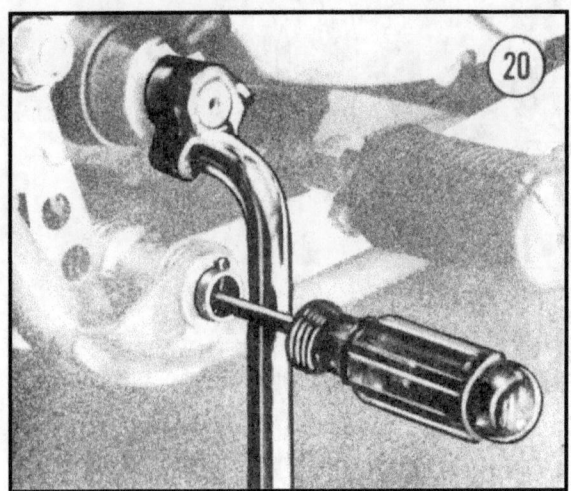

2. Loosen the cable adjuster and remove the cable end from the crankcase clutch lever, and remove the adjuster from the case cover.

3. Remove the drain plug and drain the transmission oil (see **Figure 21**).

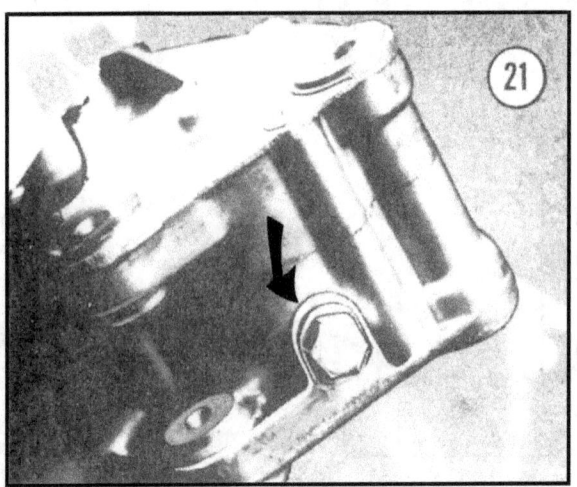

4. Remove the 4 screws and the clutch case cover (see **Figure 22**). Be sure to put the clutch pressure shaft aside so it doesn't get lost before reassembly.

5. Remove clutch disc and spacers from the clutch cover (see **Figure 23**).

6. The lever free-play is controlled by the disc spacers, which come in 3 thicknesses for this purpose. Thicker spacers decrease lever play, and thinner spacers increase it. Adjust for 3/32 in. play at the end of the lever.

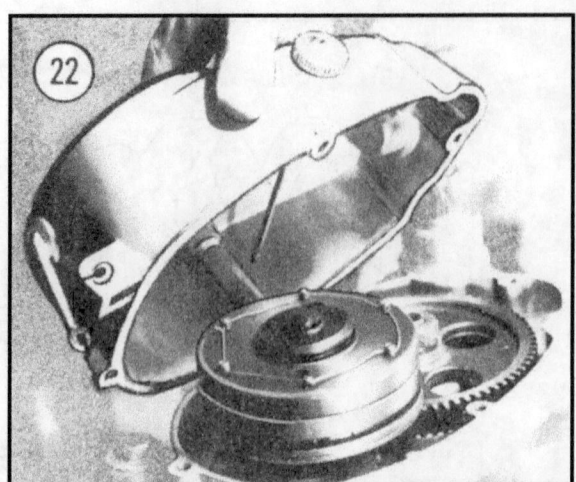

7. Reassemble in reverse sequence. Be sure the lever play is correct before installing clutch cable again.

8. Clean the clutch side cover with solvent and a stiff brush.

9. Lubricate the clutch pressure piece with grease to hold it in place while reassembling.

10. Remove the old side cover gasket and clean the mating faces with lacquer thinner. Put gasket sealer on mating faces and use a new gasket for reassembly.

11. Don't forget to refill the transmission with oil before starting the engine for testing.

Removal

1. Remove the clutch side cover and disc as described before.

2. Bend the locking tab away from the crankshaft nut.

3. Insert a holding tool into the clutch cover (see **Figure 24**) and remove the crankshaft nut.

This nut has a left-hand thread, remove by turning clockwise.

4. Remove the clutch assembly, pinion gear, and bushing from the crankshaft.

5. Remove the thrust washer from the crankshaft. It is not necessary to remove the shift lever because the complete shift mechanism comes off with the cover. Removal of this cover plate will allow the mechanic to inspect the shifter parts for possible wear or damage, and to replace any parts if necessary.

6. The clutch lever is fastened to the side cover with a brass rivet.

7. Center punch the rivet exactly in the center.

8. Drill straight through the rivet with a No. 40 drill bit (0.098 in.) and remove the fragments with a pick.

9. Remove the lever from the side cover and the O-ring from the lever.

Disassembly

1. Remove the pinion gear and bushing.
2. Remove the rotor gear and thin thrust washer.
3. Remove the safety wire from the ends of the clutch screws.
4. Remove the screws by turning each one gradually and evenly. Be sure to follow this procedure exactly or the cover could warp.
5. Remove the cover, housing, friction discs, steel plates, hub, and springs.

Inspection

1. Clean all parts with solvent and a stiff brush and dry with a clean cloth or compressed air.

2. Remove all gasket material and sealer from the cases with lacquer thinner.

3. Spread a clean cloth on the work bench and lay out the clutch components in sequence (see Figure 18).

4. Check the clutch screws for wear or damage. If any is present, replace the entire set.

5. Lay the cover on a sheet of plate glass and hold it lightly. Try to insert a 0.002 in. feeler gauge under it at any point. If it can be done, replace the cover.

6. Check the clutch housing internal gear teeth for wear. If teeth are indented more than 0.010 in., replace.

7. Measure the friction disc thicknesses with a micrometer. If they are 0.067 in. or less, replace the disc. If the friction material is blackened or charred from heat, replace the discs.

8. Check the steel plates for scoring or cracking. Lay each one on a sheet of plate glass to check for flatness. Replace if warped.

9. Check the clutch hub and center for scored friction surfaces or worn splines. Replace if worn or damaged.

10. Measure the length of the clutch springs. The standard free length of the outer spring is 0.79 in.; the inner spring is 0.67 in. Replace the springs as a set if they are below standard.

11. Check the clutch cover for wear or damage. Replace if necessary.

12. Check the crankshaft nut and lockwasher for wear or damage. If in doubt, always replace the part.

13. Rotate the center piece of the clutch disc. If the bearings run rough or appear damaged, replace the part.

14. Put the pinion bushing on the crankshaft and the pinion gear over the bushing. Rock the gear with your fingers. If the movement in any direction exceeds 0.003 in., replace the bushing.

15. Check the pinion gear and rotor drive teeth for wear or damage. If the teeth are indented, replace the part. If the pinion gear is replaced, be sure to replace the primary gear on the transmission main shaft also, or noisy gear operation will result.

16. Check the rotor gear for wear or damage. Replace if necessary.

17. Check the clutch side cover for wear or damage. If the clutch lever can move up and down more than 0.010 in., replace the side cover and lever.

18. If the lever has been removed from the side cover, replace the O-ring.

19. On most models the clutch is similar to that of Ace 90 except for larger diameter (see **Figure 25**), one more friction disc and steel plate, and 7 dual clutch springs and 7 flathead retaining screws. Service procedures for the later clutch are the same.

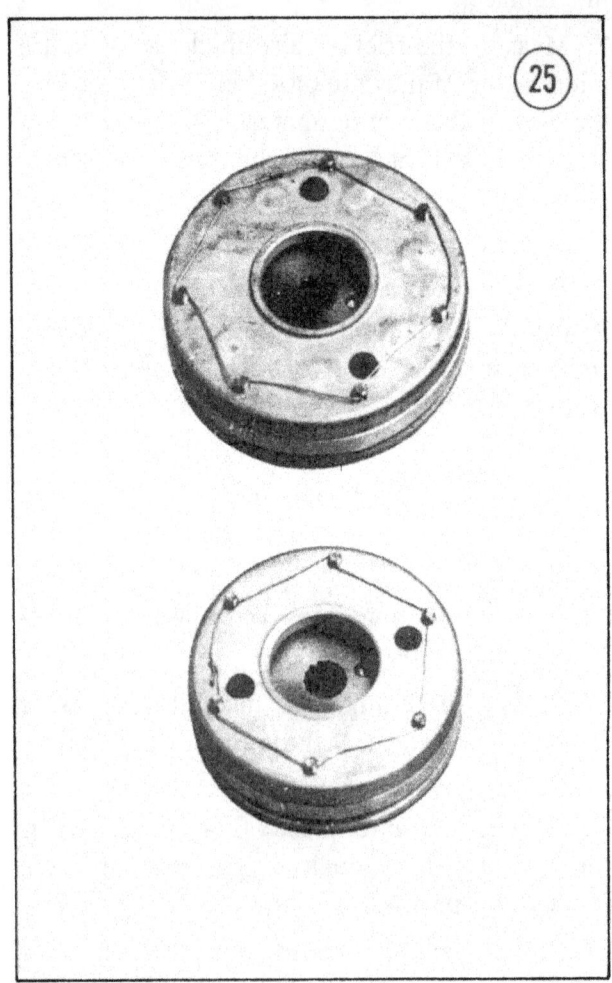

Reassembly

1. Put the clutch cover outer surface down on the work bench.

2. Install the outer and inner springs in the cover pockets.

3. Install the hub on the springs. Be sure the springs fit in the hub pockets.

4. Install the housing over the hub with the ventilating groove up and blank tooth spaces aligned over the screw holes in the cover.

5. Install 3 of the flat head clutch screws between the cage and the cover to prevent the cage from dropping onto the cover.

6. Install the friction discs and clutch plates in sequence (see Figure 18).

7. Install the thin thrust washer into the backside of the rotor gear.

8. Slip the rotor gear through the friction gear teeth. If the friction discs are new, soak them in oil and then touch up the teeth with a 3-cornered file so they will slip on the rotor gear.

9. Install the cage cover in position, aligning the screw holes with those in the clutch cover.

10. Remove the 3 screws from between the cage and the cover. Hold the cage to keep it from dropping until all flat head screws have been installed and tightened several turns.

11. Install the pinion gear into the rotor gear. Install the bushing inside the pinion gear and install the loosely assembled clutch onto the crankshaft. This will center the components of the clutch assembly.

12. Remove the assembly from the crankshaft and place face down on the bench.

13. Gradually and evenly tighten the screws to prevent warping.

14. Safety wire the screw ends. Be sure the wire tends to tighten the screws. Fold the twisted end of the wire away from the center of the clutch hub, so that centrifugal force will not tend to untwist it.

15. Install a new O-ring in the groove nearest the claw end of clutch lever.

16. Lubricate the lever with grease and insert into the side cover chamber.

17. Flatten the brass rivet with a flat-ended punch while holding the lever firmly in place in the side cover.

18. Lubricate the pressure shaft with grease and install.

Installation

1. Install the thick thrust washer with its rounded edge toward the engine.

2. Be sure the open ends of the oil groove of the pinion gear bushing face the engine side of the pinion gear (see **Figure 26**).

3. Install the clutch assembly on the crankshaft.
4. Install the lockwasher with square tab on the crankshaft, with the tab in the blind hole of the clutch hub.
5. Install the crankshaft nut, tightening the left-hand thread counterclockwise. Torque to 250 in.-lb. Do not overtighten, or the pinion bushing will swell and seize.
6. Fold the lockwasher over one flat of the crankshaft nut with a screwdriver. Be careful not to damage the clutch disc seat on the cover.
7. Install the clutch disc, spacers, and side cover. Adjust the lever play as described in Chapter Two.

ENGINE

Removal

Figure 27 is an exploded view of the engine and transmission. Refer to it in the following procedures.

1. Drain the transmission oil as described in Chapter Two.
2. Disconnect the fuel line at the carburetor and disconnect the air cleaner rubber hose.
3. Remove the carburetor top cap and remove the throttle slide from the carburetor.
4. Remove the exhaust pipe and muffler from the machine.
5. Disconnect the magneto harness at the battery junction and remove the harness from the frame clips.
6. Engage 1st gear, lock the rear wheel with the brake to prevent it from turning, and unscrew the countershaft sprocket nut (**Figure 28**). Remove the sprocket from the countershaft.

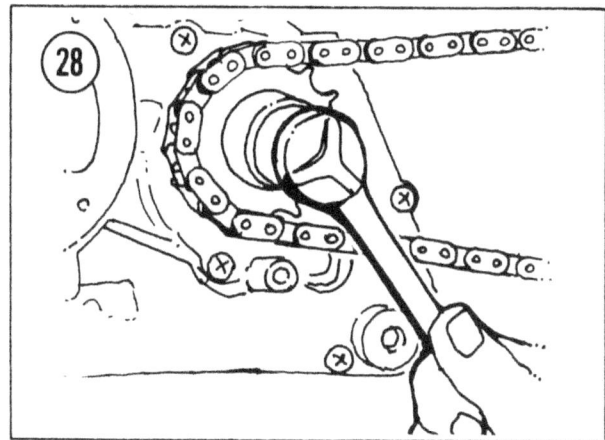

7. Remove the 3 engine mounting bolts and the clutch cable from the clutch cover. Remove the engine from the frame.

Engine Case Disassembly

Refer to Figure 27 for an exploded view of the crankcase.

1. Remove magneto cover (**Figure 29**, page 46), flywheel, and magneto frame assembly.
2. Remove the clutch side cover (**Figure 30**, page 47), clutch assembly, and pinion gear.
3. Remove cylinder head, cylinder, and piston.
4. Release the kickstarter lever and rotate it until the return spring is free from tension.
5. Remove the kickstarter lever (**Figure 31**, page 48) from its shaft.
6. Remove the kickstarter spring and cover from the case.
7. Hold the primary gear still while removing the main shaft nut (see **Figure 32**).
8. Remove the primary gear.
9. Remove the countershaft sprocket and collar from the shaft (see **Figure 33**).
10. Use an impact-type Phillips wrench to remove the 11 crankcase screws from the left side.
11. Gently tap the crankcase halves apart with a soft mallet (see **Figure 34**).

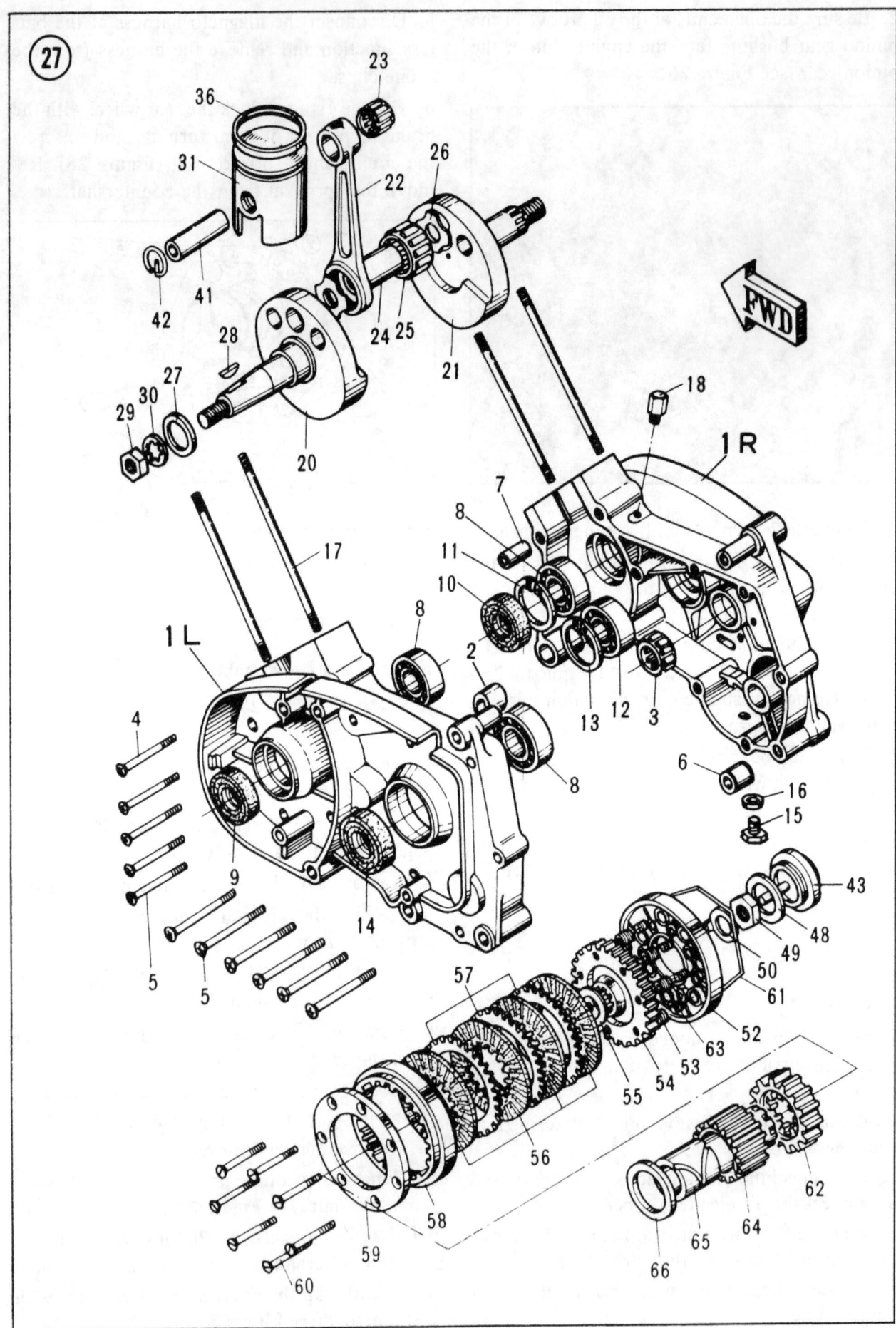

ENGINE AND TRANSMISSION

1. Crankcase assembly
2. Main shaft bushing
3. Countershaft bearing
4. Crankcase screw
5. Crankcase screw
6. Crankcase alignment dowel (large)
7. Crankcase alignment dowel (small)
8. Ball bearing
9. Crankshaft oil seal (L)
10. Crankshaft oil seal (R)
11. Crankshaft thrust snap ring
12. Ball bearing
13. Main shaft snap ring
14. Countershaft oil seal
15. Drain plug
16. Drain plug gasket
17. Cylinder stud bolt
18. Breather
20. Crankshaft (magneto side)
21. Crankshaft (clutch side)
22. Connecting rod
23. Connecting rod needle bearing (small end)
24. Crank pin
25. Needle roller bearing (large end)
26. Crank pin thrust washer
27. Crankshaft washer (L)
28. Crankshaft key
29. Flywheel nut
30. Flywheel lockwasher
31. Piston
36. Piston ring
41. Piston pin
42. Piston pin snap ring
43. Clutch disc
48. Clutch disc spacer
49. Crankshaft nut (left-hand thread)
50. Crankshaft lockwasher
52. Clutch cover
53. Spring
54. Clutch hub
55. Thrust washer
56. Friction disc
57. Clutch plate
58. Clutch housing
59. Cover
60. Screw
61. Safety wire
62. Rotor gear
63. Inner spring
64. Pinion gear
65. Bushing
66. Thrust washer

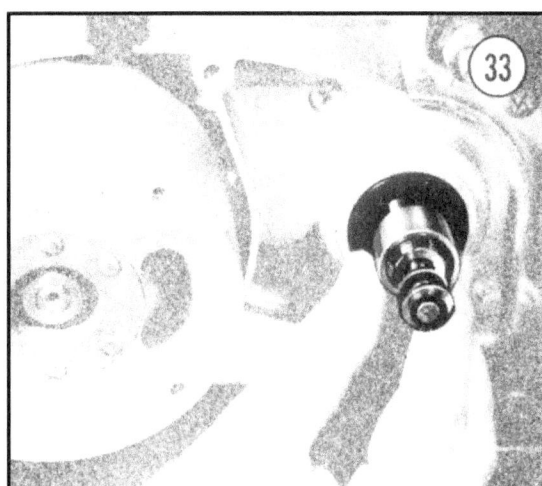

H. Crankcase alignment dowel

MAGNETO COVER

1. Magneto cover
2. Grease nipple
3. Grease nipple
4. Spring seat
5. Shifter cover
6. Screw
7. Shifter guide
8. Shifter arm
9. Shifter pin
10. Guide spacer
11. Sliding pin
12. Pin snap ring
13. Adjusting bolt
14. Spring washer
15. Nut
16. Shift shaft
17. Shaft key
18. Pin
19. Snap ring
20. Ratchet
21. Ratchet spring
22. Center screw
23. Washer
24. Snap ring
25. Plunger
26. Plunger spring
27. Inside cover
28. Cover gasket
29. Screw
30. Spring washer
31. Shift lever
32. Lever rubber
33. Bolt
34. Spring washer
35. Magneto cover screw
36. Magneto cover screw
37. Cover seal

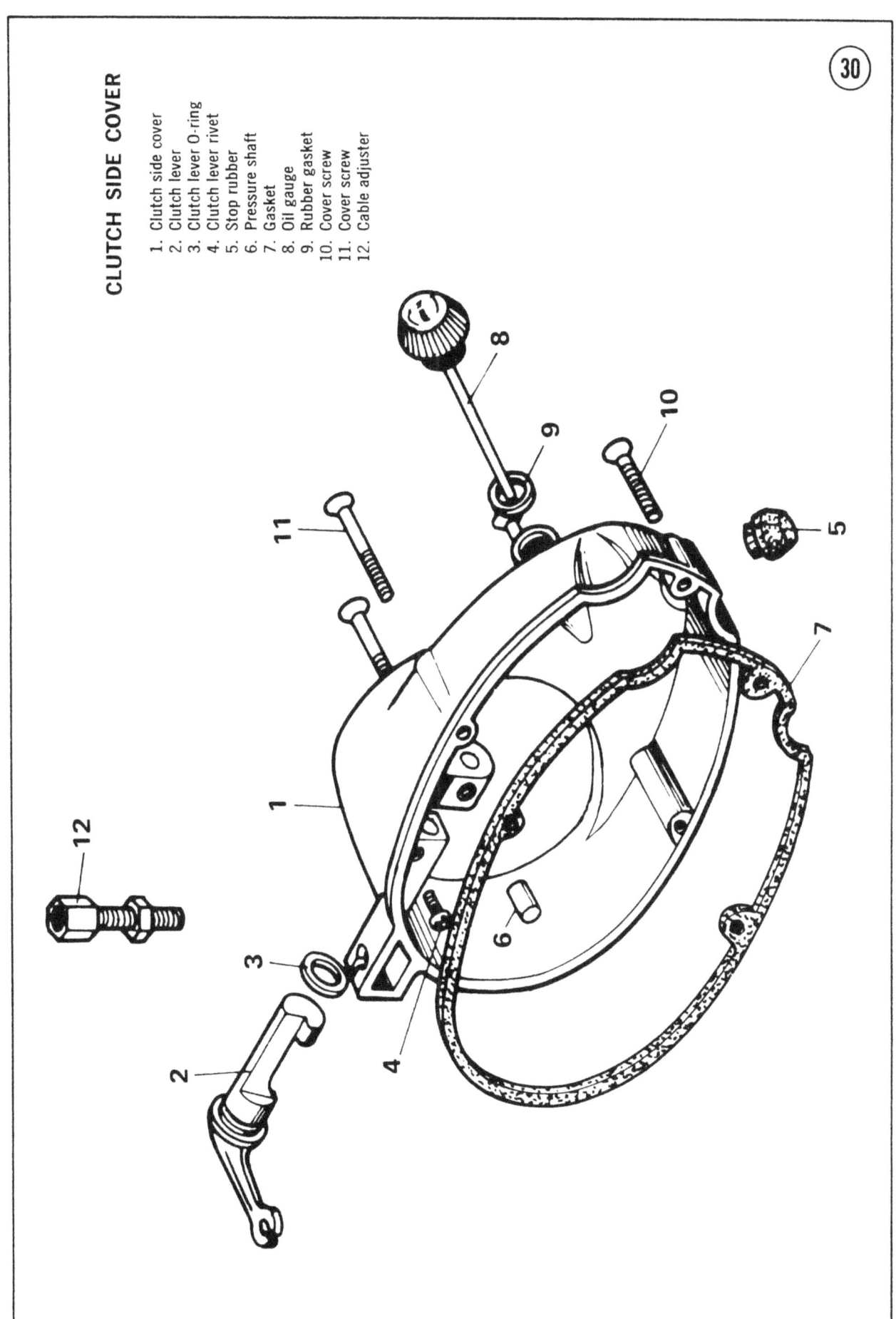

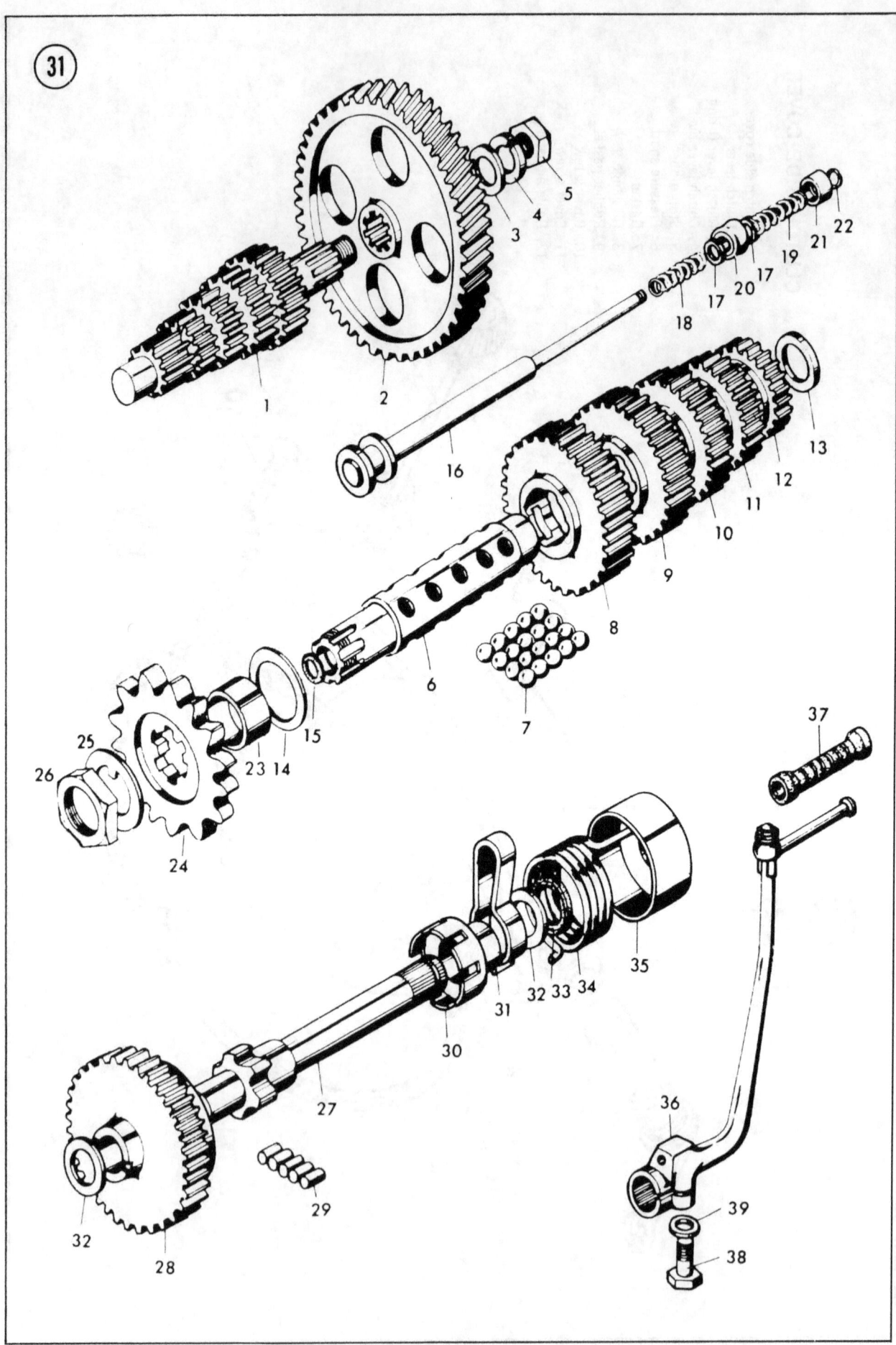

TRANSMISSION 5-SPEED MODEL (4-SPEED SIMILAR)

1. Main shaft
2. Primary gear
3. Lockwasher
4. Spring washer
5. Nut
6. Countershaft
7. Ball
8. Low gear
9. 2nd gear
10. 3rd gear
11. 4th gear
12. Top gear
13. Countershaft spacer (R)
14. Countershaft spacer (L)
15. Control shaft O-ring
16. Control shaft
17. Washer
18. Spring (L)
19. Spring (R)
20. Ball receiver
21. Spring stopper
22. Snap ring
23. Secondary sprocket collar
24. Secondary sprocket
25. Lockwasher
26. Sprocket nut
27. Kickstarter shaft
28. Kickstarter gear
29. Roller
30. Retainer
31. Washer
32. Thrust washer
33. O-ring
34. Spring
35. Spring cover
36. Kickstarter crank
37. Kick pedal rubber
38. Crank bolt
39. Spring washer

12. Lay the crankcase on its right side and remove the left half by pushing on the countershaft and crankshaft with the thumbs.

13. Remove the crankshaft, transmission, and kickstarter assembly from the right crankcase half. The steel balls on the countershaft are likely to fall out, so disassemble over a flat pan to catch them.

14. The crankshaft, transmission, and kickstarter assembly can be removed separately for services without removing the others.

15. Depress the control shaft spring stopper with a screwdriver (see **Figure 35**) and remove the circlip from the shaft.

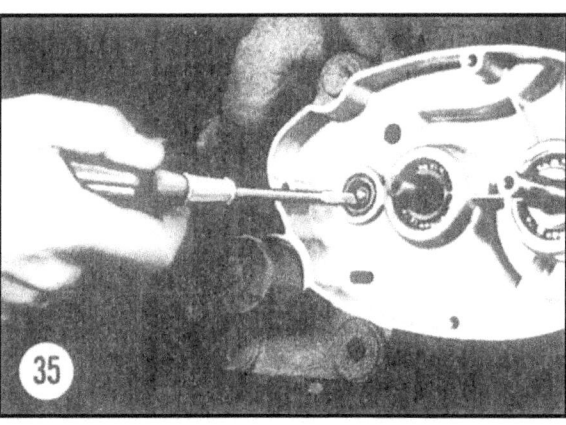

16. Remove control shaft from the opposite end.

17. Remove the stopper, 2 springs, and 2 washers from the control shaft.

18. The control shaft can be removed for service without splitting the cases. Remove the magneto cover and clutch side cover to gain access to control shaft.

19. Remove crankshaft oil seals and countershaft oil seal with a screwdriver and discard.

20. Remove the O-ring from the right case kickstarter passage and discard it.

21. Remove the ball bearing circlips in the right case.

22. If the bearings need replacement, heat the cases around the bearing bosses with a torch (see **Figure 36**) and remove the bearings with a brass drift and hammer. Be sure not to heat the bearings during this operation.

23. If the bushings show wear, tap the countershaft bushing from the right case with a bushing driver.

24. Thread the main shaft bushing with a 14mm bottom tap (see **Figure 37**). Put the countershaft collar and flat washer over the bushing and thread a 14mm bolt into the bushing (see Figure 37) and remove.

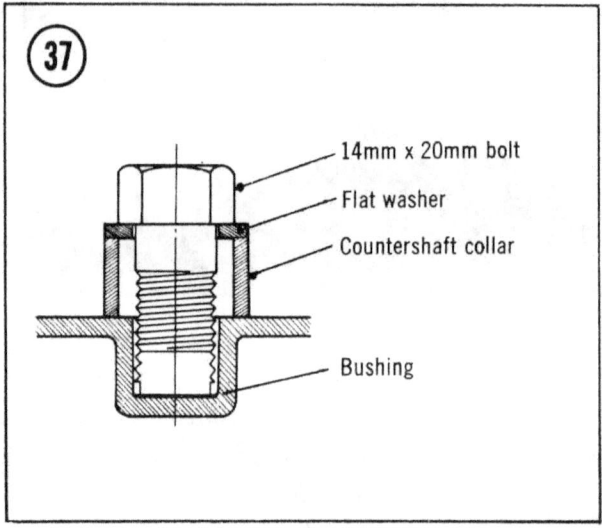

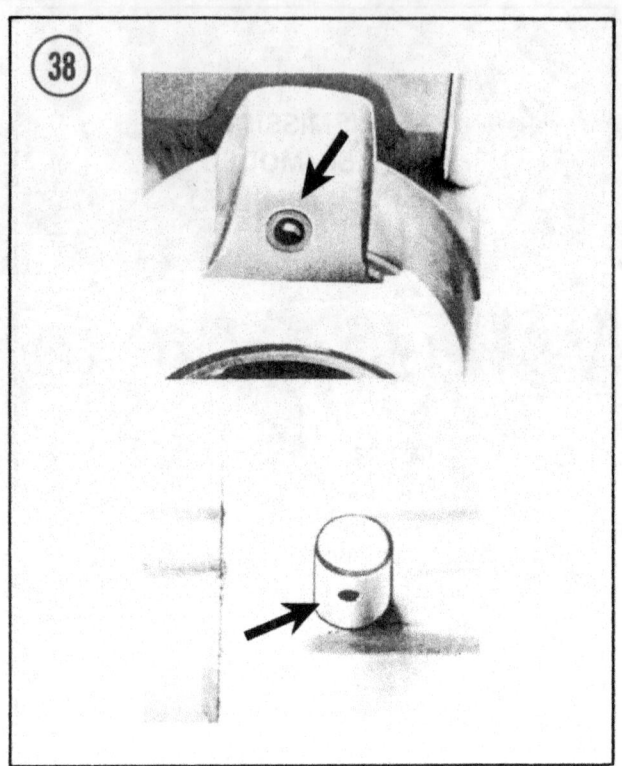

Inspection

1. Clean all components in solvent and dry with air or a clean lint-free cloth.

2. Carefully clean the crankshaft bearing oil passage in the left case and the transmission breather in the right case (see **Figure 38**).

3. Check the ball bearings for wear or damage. Replace if in doubt.

4. Check the cases for wear or damage. Replace if necessary. Replacement crankcase sections must be bought in **pairs only**.

5. Check the countershaft and gears for wear or damage. Replace if necessary.

6. Check the countershaft sprocket for wear or damage. Replace if necessary.

7. Check the control shaft for wear or damage. The shaft must be straight.

8. Replace the control shaft springs and circlip with new parts.

9. Check the steel balls, spacers, nut, and lockwasher carefully.

10. Check the main shaft gear cluster for wear or damage. Replace if necessary.

11. Check the kickstarter assembly for wear or damage. Replace any doubtful parts, especially the spring.

12. Carefully check the crankshaft and connecting rod assembly for wear or damage. Disassemble to replace any defective parts.

13. Check the crankshaft assembly for the following: wrist pin bushing clearance, 0.0005 in.; crank pin thrust washer clearance, 0.002 to 0.004 in.; crankshaft bearing surface runout, 0.0008 in. maximum (see **Figure 39**), excessive rod big end bushing wear. Replace any parts necessary.

14. On 100-125cc models, the connecting rod has needle bearings at both ends. Replace the small end bearing each time the engine is to be disassembled.

15. Heat the area around the crankpin and use a 2 leg puller to remove the flywheel. Heat the

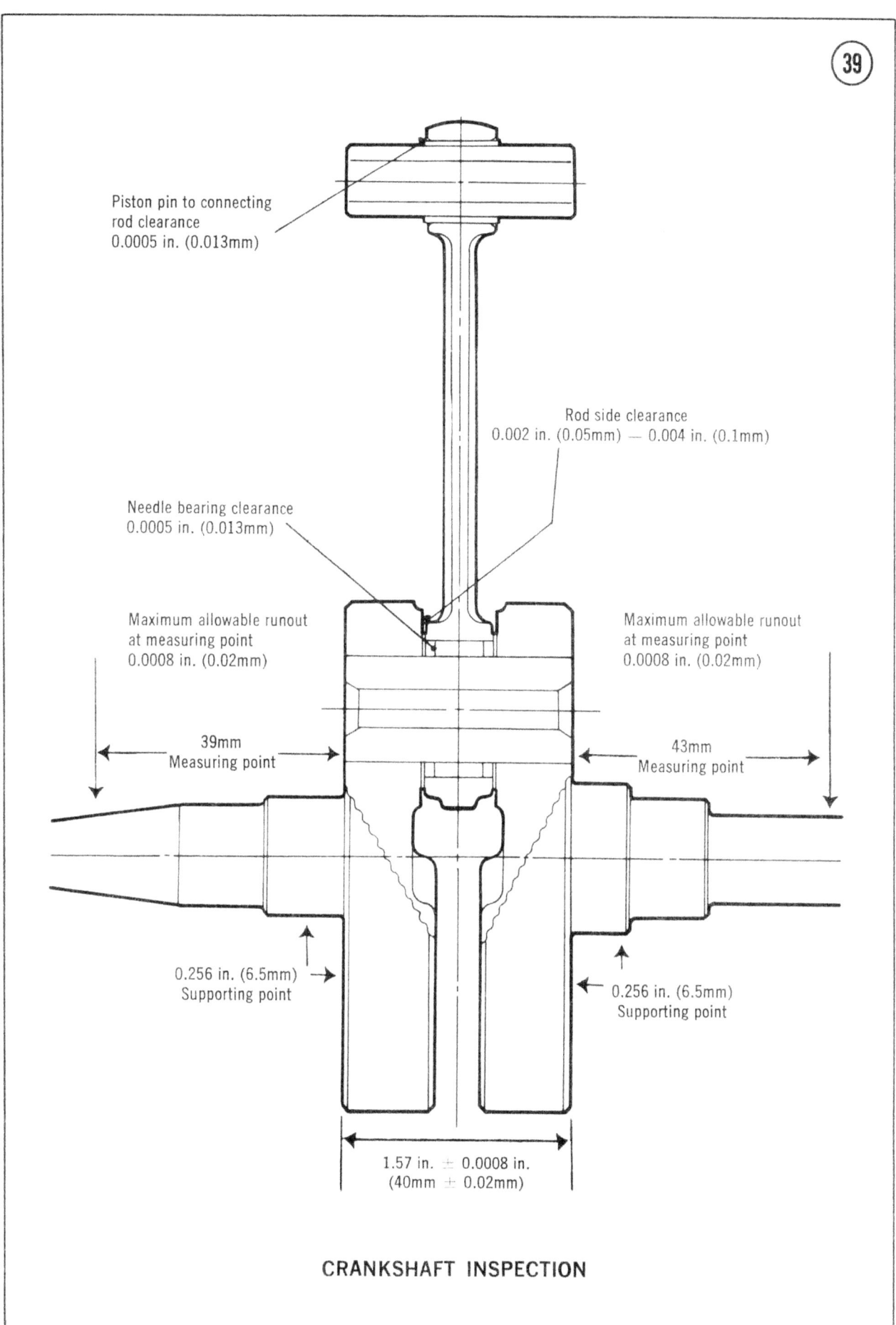

CRANKSHAFT INSPECTION

other flywheel and remove the crankpin from the mounting bore with the puller.

16. Replace the crankpin, thrust washers, rod, and bearing as a unit if any parts are defective.

Crankshaft Reassembly

See **Figure 40** for an exploded view of the crankshaft assembly.

1. Press a new crankpin into half the crankshaft. Install the thrust washer, needle bearing, connecting rod, and second thrust washer (see **Figure 41**). Press the other half of the shaft on

1. Crankshaft thrust washer

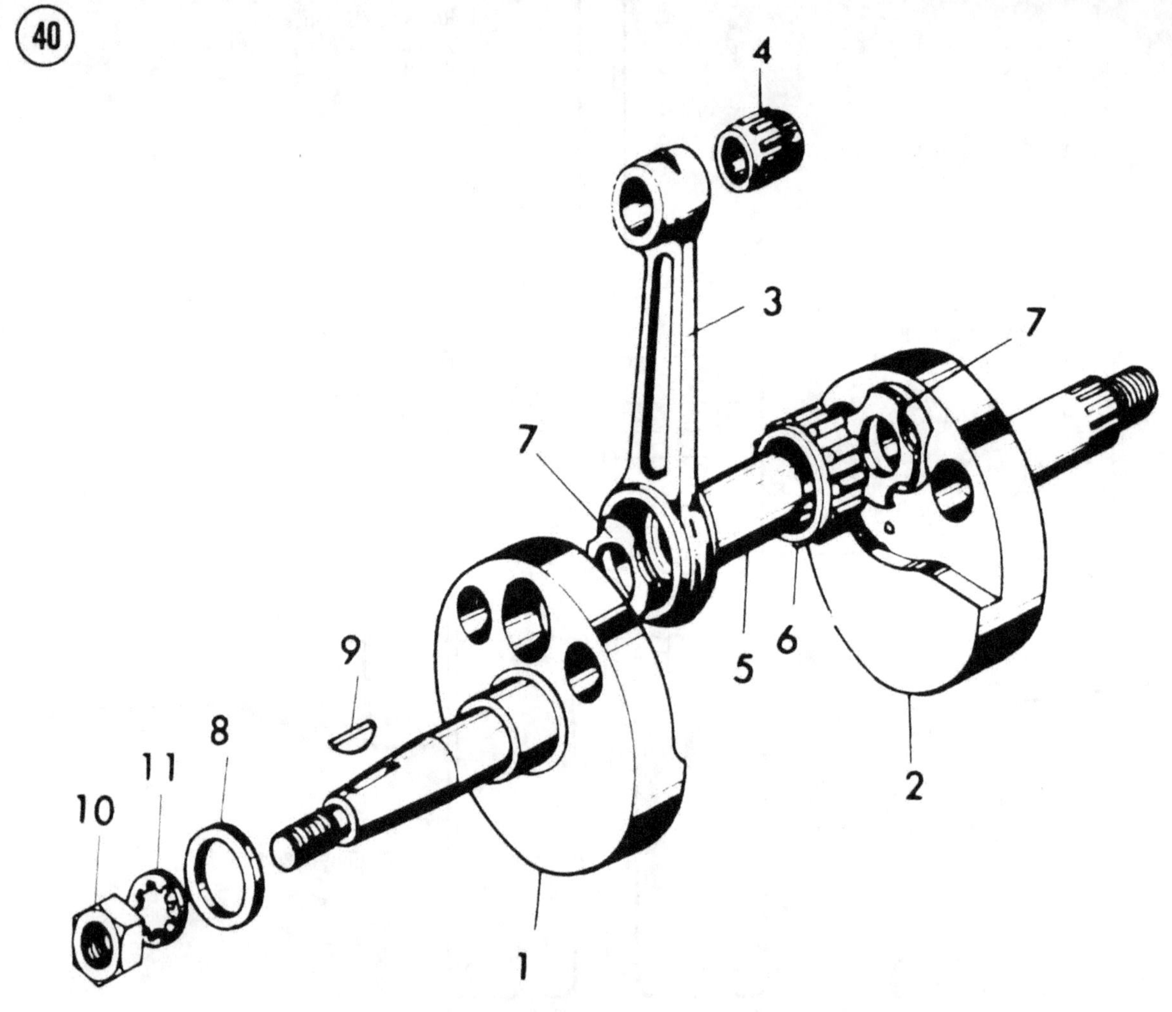

CRANKSHAFT ASSEMBLY

1. Crankshaft (magneto side)
2. Crankshaft (output side)
3. Connecting rod
4. Needle bearing
5. Crank pin
6. Needle roller bearing (large end)
7. Thrust washer
8. Washer (L)
9. Key (L)
10. Setting nut
11. Spring washer

the pin with a 0.004 in. feeler gauge between the thrust washer and crank half to insure correct side clearance for the rod.

2. Check the bearing runout with an alignment jib. Runout must be less than 0.001 in. Check the rod side clearance and oil the needle bearings.

3. The connecting rod side clearance should be 0.010 inch in the 100-MX models.

Engine Case Reassembly

1. Heat the bearing bosses in the cases and install the ball bearings.

2. Install the circlip in the right case.

3. Tap the countershaft bushing in the right case with a bushing driver. Be sure to drive it in far enough to clear oil supply grooves in the case.

4. Install the main shaft bushing flush with the left case surface.

5. Install the inner right case crankshaft oil seal with the cupped side toward the bearing and flush with the case surface.

6. Install a new O-ring in the kickstarter passage in the right case.

7. Install the outer left case crankshaft and countershaft oil seals with their cupped sides toward the bearings and flush with the case surface.

8. Oil the seals and bearings and install the crankshaft in the right case. Be sure the splined end of the shaft extends from the primary side of the right case and the connecting rod does not damage the sealing face of the case.

9. Install a new O-ring at the threaded end of the countershaft bore.

10. Oil the O-ring at the threaded end of the countershaft bore.

11. Install the left-hand wound spring, washer, ball receiver, washer, right wound spring, and spring stopper with its collar side toward the circlip groove over the tip end of the control shaft (**Figure 42**).

12. Install the circlip on the control shaft. A simple tool can be made for this task by screwing a ¼ in. nut two to three turns onto a bolt (**Figure 42**). The recess in the nut must face out.

13. Grease the countershaft ball pockets and install the steel balls.

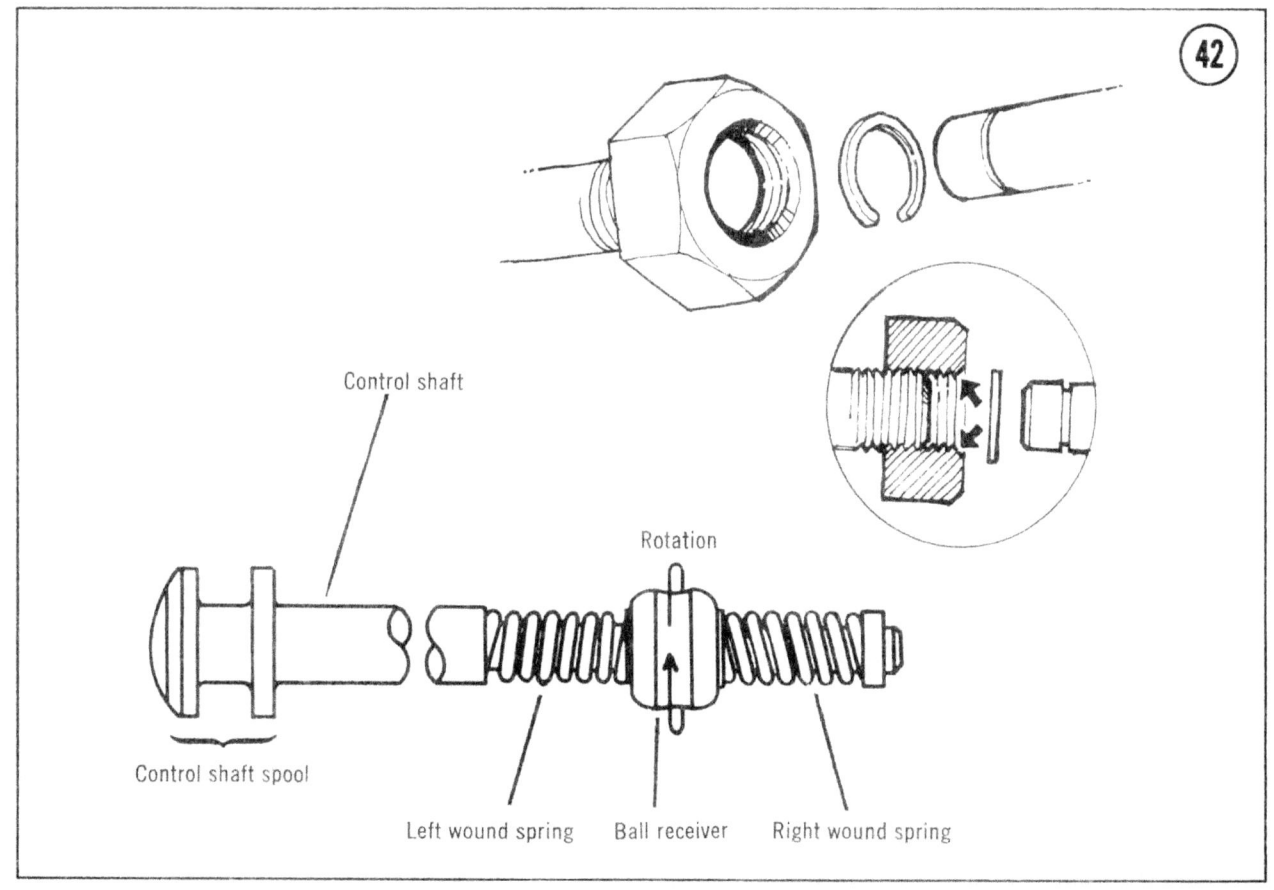

14. Grease the right case countershaft bushing. Install the spacer on the countershaft bushing end and install the shaft in the right case.

15. Install the main shaft in the right case ball bearing.

16. Put the gears on the countershaft with the gear shoulder toward the threaded end of shaft.

17. Mesh the kickstarter gear with the small countershaft gear and then install the large countershaft gear on the shaft, shoulder side out.

18. Install the notched side of the kick shaft roller retainer on kick shaft from the splined end.

19. Install the roller retainer hold snap on the back of the retainer.

20. Hold the kick shaft vertical, with the retainer against the kick shaft shoulder and install the 5 steel rollers with grease to hold them.

21. Install the kick gear over the blind end of the shaft so the gear shoulder covers the rollers.

22. Install the kick gear thrust washers on both ends of the kick shaft. Install the shaft in the right case with the splined end first.

23. Install the hold snap tang between the casing webs in the right case.

24. Install the kick shaft assembly. Mesh the kick gear with the countershaft gear. Install the countershaft gear with shoulder side out.

25. Install the spacer on the threaded end of the shaft.

26. Install the spacer over the tapered end of the crankshaft.

27. Be sure the crankcase alignment dowels are in place. Put sealer on both case halves (see **Figure 43**) and install the left case on the right. Tighten the case screws (see **Figure 44**). Note that the three 40mm screws fit into the holes marked J and the eight 45mm screws fit into the K-holes.

28. Install the countershaft collar and sprocket, lockwasher, and nut. Hold the sprocket with the special tool and tighten the nut. Bend the lockwasher over.

29. Lay the engine on its left side and install the kick spring (see **Figure 45**).

30. Install the spring cover over spring. Align the kick lever over the shaft splines and spring prong, and install the lever and bolt.

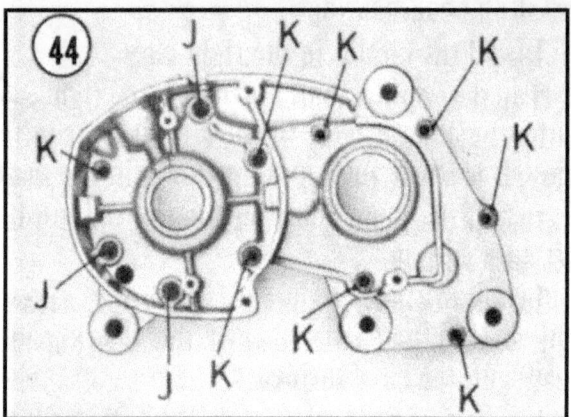

31. Install the primary gear on the main shaft, with the washer and lockwasher and nut. Tighten to 180 in.-lb.

SHIFTER ASSEMBLY

Shift mechanism details are given in **Figures 46 and 47**.

Removal

1. Remove the magneto cover and the screws of the foot change cover.

FOUR-SPEED SHIFT MECHANISM

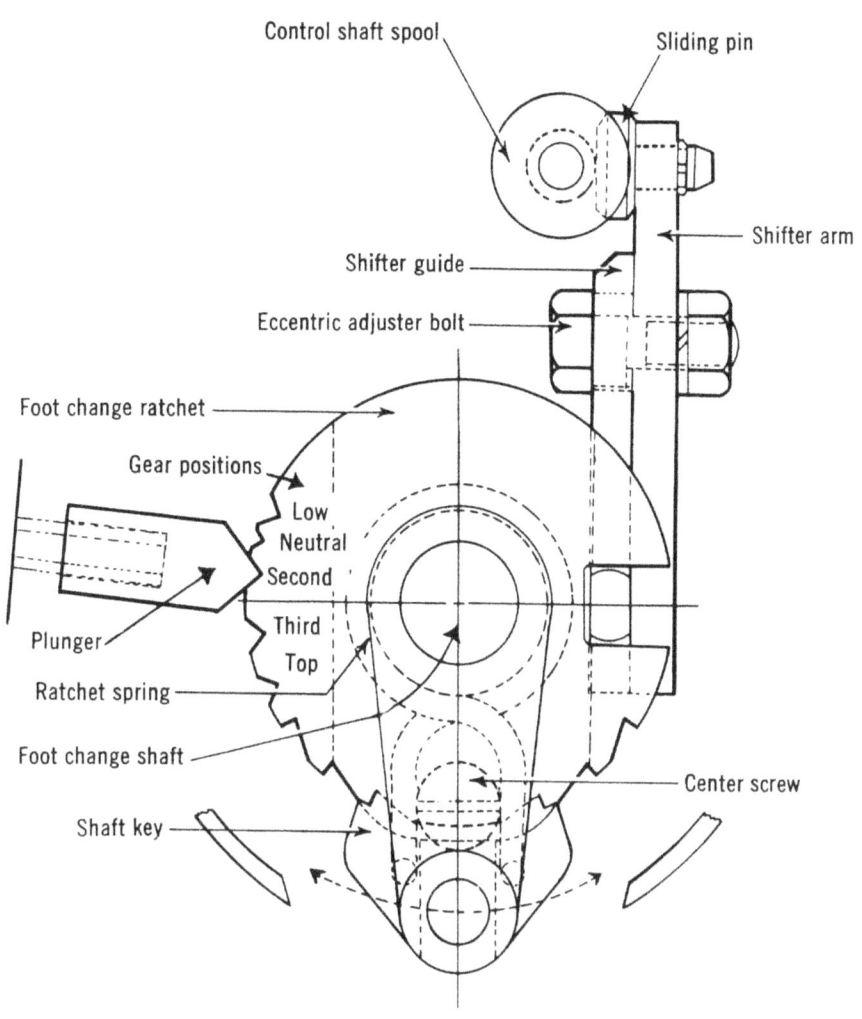
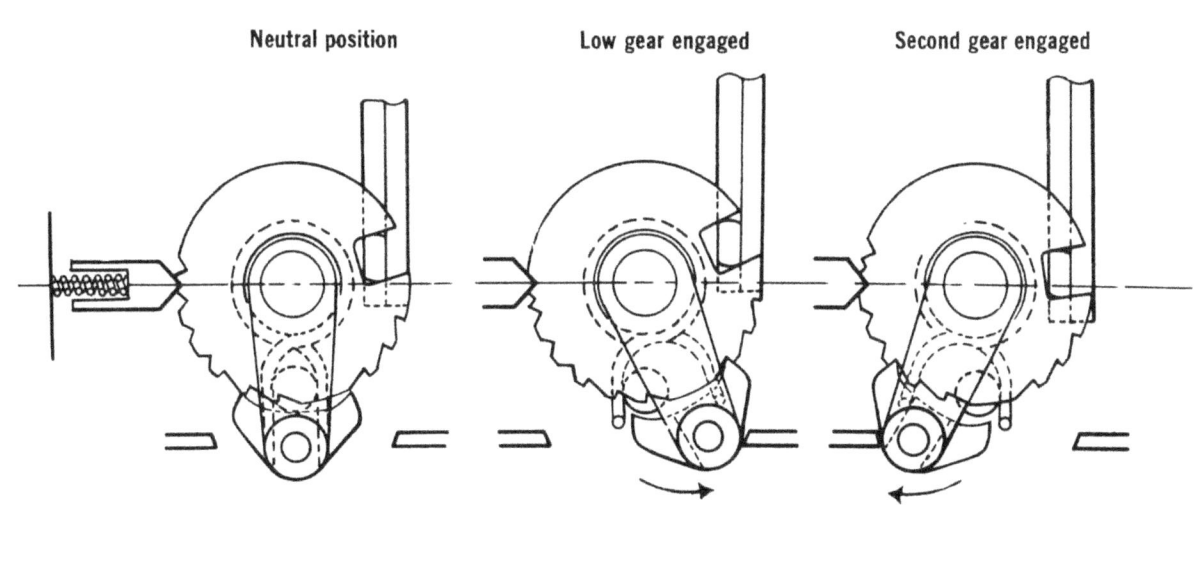

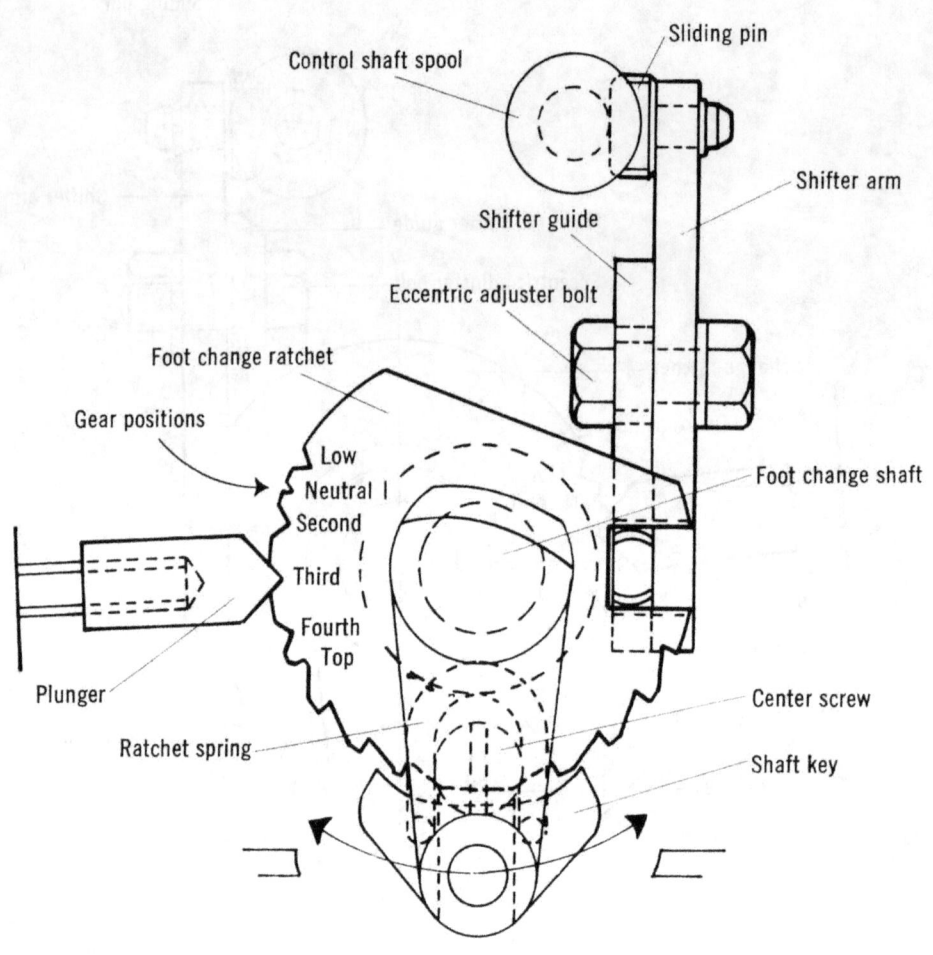

**ACE 100-B SHIFT MECHANISM — 5-SPEED
(OTHER 5-SPEED MODELS ARE SIMILAR)**

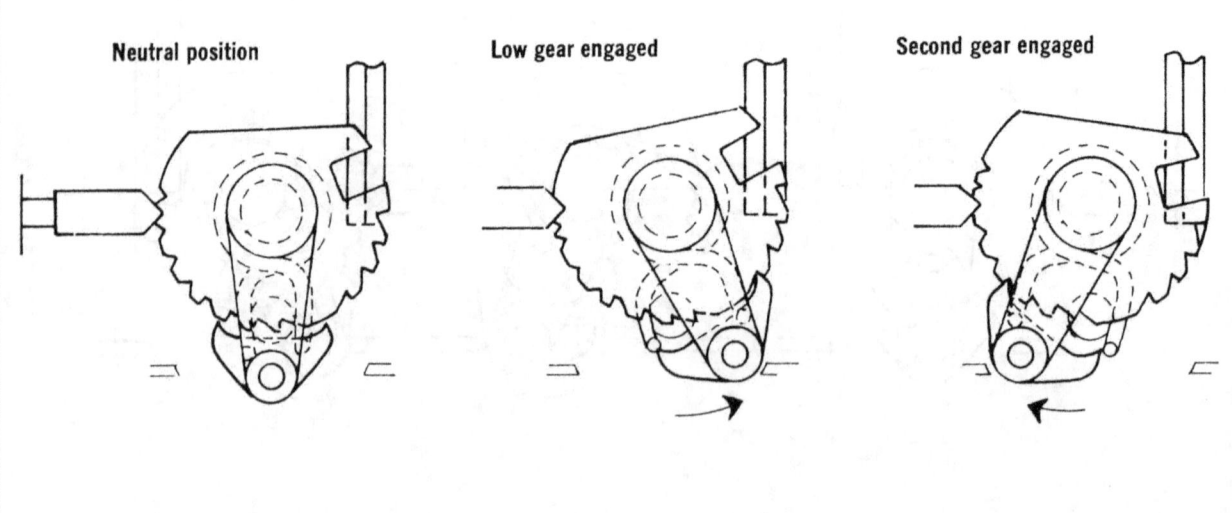

2. Remove the foot change bolt and the foot change lever.

3. Remove circlip from foot change shaft.

4. Remove the shaft from the magneto cover and remove the ratchet and spring.

5. Remove the shaft key circlip and the key.

6. Remove the ratchet plunger and spring and grease nipple.

7. Remove the shifter pin from the cover with a dowel. Don't lose the spacers.

8. Remove the circlip from sliding pin and locknut from adjusting bolt.

9. Remove the shifter arm assembly.

Inspection

1. Clean all parts in solvent and dry with air or a clean lint-free cloth.

2. Check the magneto cover for wear or damage. Replace if necessary.

3. Check the shaft for wear or damage. Replace, with lever, if necessary.

4. Check the shaft key for wear or damage. Replace if in doubt.

5. Replace the sliding pin and shaft circlips with new parts.

6. Check the ratchet and spring for wear or damage. Replace if necessary.

7. Check the shifter arm and guide for wear or damage. Replace if necessary.

8. Check the plunger and spring for wear or damage. Replace if necessary.

Reassembly

1. Lubricate all parts as detailed before.

2. Install the sliding pin in shifter arm and install circlip.

3. Install the adjusting bolt through shifter guide and arm. Install the lockwasher and nut and tighten.

4. Install the shifter pin through the guide and arm to align.

5. Install the shifter assembly in the case. Be sure there is 0.02mm clearance.

6. Tap the shifter pin through the cover until visible in the shifter arm slot. Install the shifter arm assembly in the slot and tap the pin through the arm and guide. Install the spacers and use a center punch to make a depression in the magneto cover to prevent the pin from working into the flywheel cavity.

7. Install the ratchet spring prongs facing outward (see Figure 46).

8. Install the ratchet plunger and spring in the cover.

9. Engage the plunger in the neutral notch and put the shifter guide pawl in the large notch on the ratchet (see Figure 46).

10. Install the shaft key with the shoulder side out and install the circlip.

11. Install the shaft through the ratchet and cover and center the shaft key shoulders between the spring prongs.

12. Install the washer and circlip on outside of the shaft.

13. Check the shaft end-play. It should be between 0.008 and 0.012 in.

14. Install the foot change lever and check the ratchet action.

15. Lubricate as detailed in Chapter Two.

16. Install the inside cover on the magneto cover and install the assembly. Rough timing can be accomplished with the marks provided on the case. When the line on the flywheel coincides with the right-hand marks on the case, the points should just open. For a more accurate setting, a dial indicator is recommended. See Chapter Two for timing.

17. See the sections on cylinder head and clutch for assembly.

CHAPTER FIVE

FUEL AND EXHAUST SYSTEMS

The fuel system consists of the fuel tank, fuel shutoff valve, and carburetor. **Figures 1** (page 60) **and 2** (page 62) illustrate these.

For proper operation, a gasoline engine must be supplied with fuel and air, mixed in the proper proportions by weight. A mixture in which there is an excess of fuel is said to be rich. A lean mixture is one which contains insufficient fuel. It is the function of the carburetor to supply the proper mixture to the engine under all operating conditions.

An essential functional part of the carburetor is a float and float valve mechanism for maintaining a constant fuel level in the float bowl, a pilot system for supplying fuel at low speeds, a main fuel system which supplies the engine at medium and high speeds, and a starter system, which supplies the very rich mixture needed to start a cold engine.

The carburetor was designed to provide the proper mixture under all operating conditions. Little or no benefit will result from experimenting. However, unusual operating conditions such as sustained operation at high altitudes, or unusually high or low temperatures, may make modifications to the standard specifications desirable.

There is no set rule regarding frequency of carburetor overhaul. A carburetor used on a machine used primarily for street riding may go 5,000 miles without attention. If the machine is used in dirt, the carburetor might need an overhaul in less than 1,000 miles. Poor engine performance, hesitation, and little or no response to idle mixture adjustment are all symptoms of possible carburetor malfunctions. As a general rule, it is good practice to overhaul the carburetor each time you perform a routine decarbonization of the engine.

CARBURETOR

The carburetors are accurately adjusted at the factory and rarely require adjustment. Before suspecting the fuel system, always make certain that the valve clearance is proper and that the ignition system is accurately timed and in good condition.

Adjustment

1. Road test at full throttle on a straight, level road.

2. Back off the throttle slightly. If rpm increases, the main jet is too small. If it decreases, the jet is correct or slightly large.

3. If the engine misses, smokes, or 4-strokes with open throttle, the main jet is too large.

Main Jet Replacement

1. Turn off the fuel. Remove the air cleaner rubber hose.

2. Remove the carburetor from the manifold. Remove the float bowl.

3. Remove the main jet (see **Figure 3**). Replace the jet and reassemble in reverse order. Road test again.

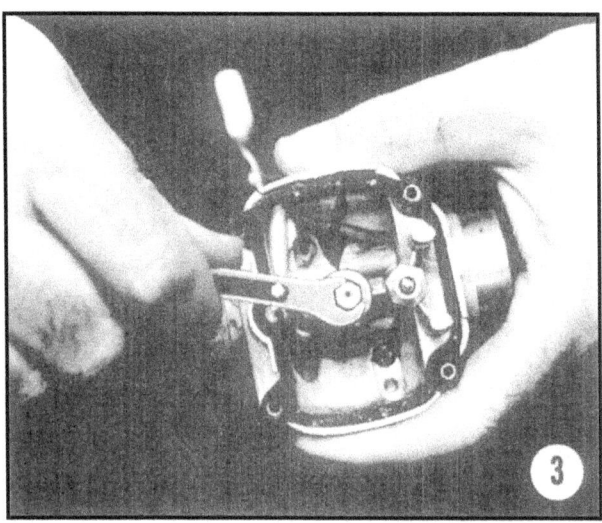

Pilot Jet Adjustment

1. Turn pilot screw all the way in (**Figure 4**) then back out 1¼ turns.

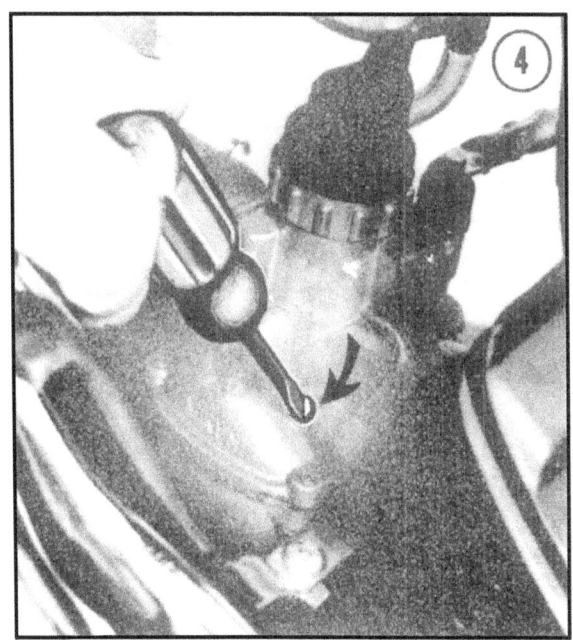

2. Warm up engine to operating temperature.
3. Turn the throttle adjuster (see **Figure 5**) so the engine idles at 1,800 rpm.

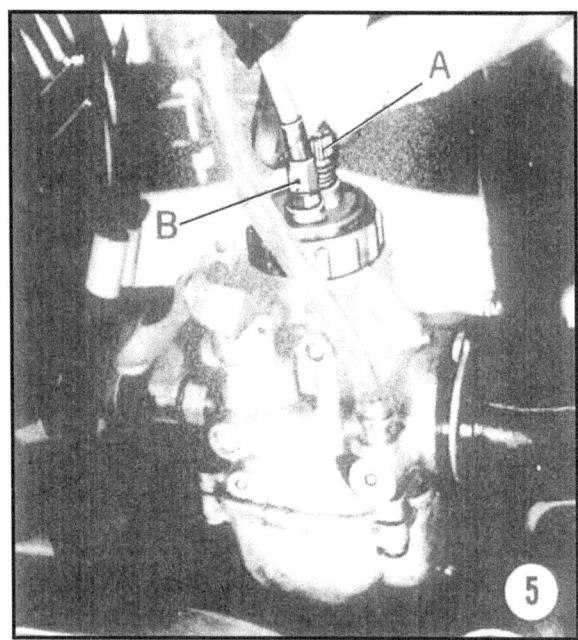

A. Knurled throttle adjuster
B. Cable adjuster

4. Turn the pilot screw in until engine reaches slowest speed. Then back off ¼ turn.

5. Turn the throttle adjuster until the engine almost stops.

6. Turn the pilot screw in and out until the engine runs well.

Throttle Valve

1. Throttle valves are numbered. A higher number means more cutaway (see **Figure 6**).

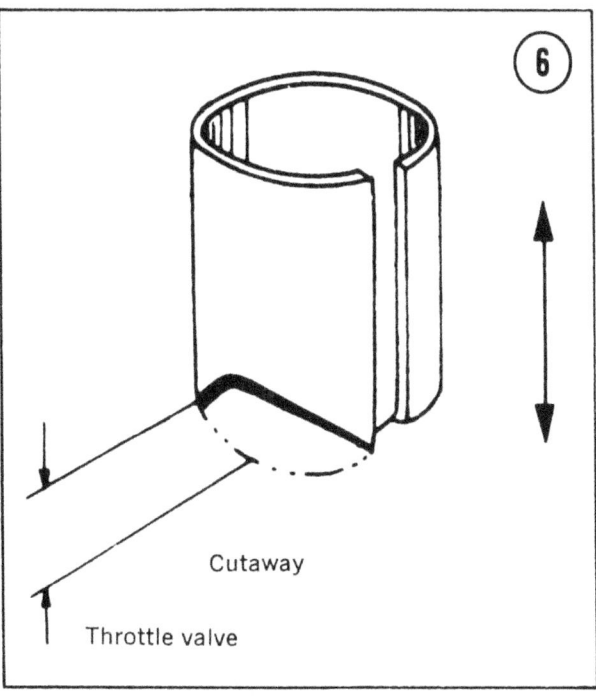

59

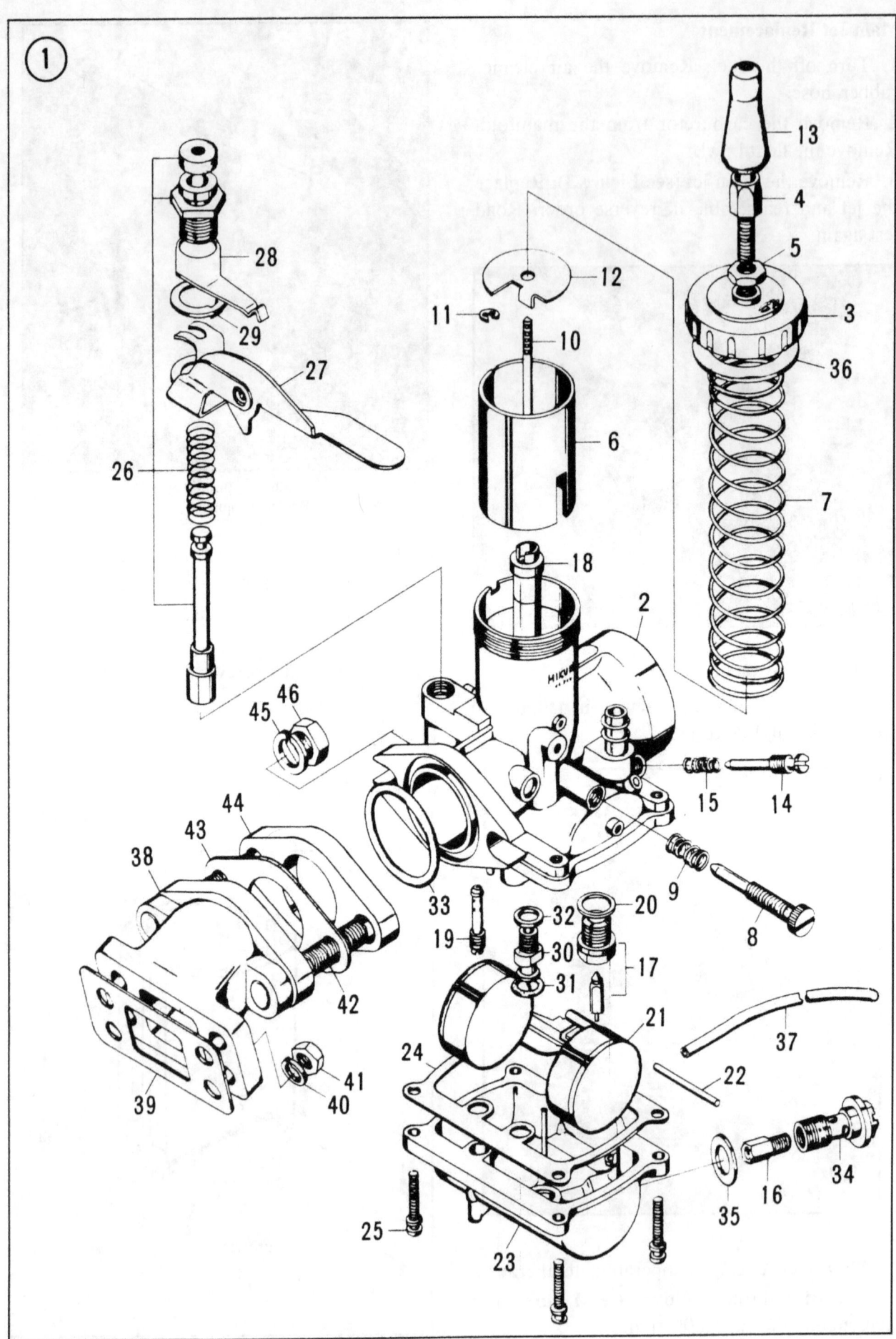

MIKUNI CARBURETOR (TYPICAL TO ALL MODELS)

1. Nut
2. Mixing chamber body
3. Mixing chamber top
4. Throttle cable adjuster
5. Adjuster locknut
6. Throttle valve (slide)
7. Valve spring
8. Throttle adjuster
9. Throttle adjuster spring
10. Jet needle
11. Needle clip
12. Cable seat
13. Mixing chamber top rubber cap
14. Air screw
15. Air adjusting spring
16. Main jet
17. Float valve and seat
18. Needle jet
19. Pilot jet
20. Float valve gasket
21. Float
22. Float pin
23. Float chamber body
24. Gasket
25. Screw
26. Choke plunger unit
27. Choke lever
28. Spring
29. Washer
30. Needle jet bolt
31. O-ring
32. Washer
33. Carburetor O-ring
34. Banjo bolt
35. Banjo bolt washer
36. Top gasket
37. Vent tube
38. Intake manifold
39. Manifold gasket
40. Spring washer
41. Nut
42. Stud
43. Gasket
44. Heat shield block
45. Spring washer
46. Nut

2. A higher numbered valve leans the carburetor mixture. A smaller numbered one enriches it.

3. Except for racing applications, do not replace the standard throttle valve.

Jet Needle Adjustment

1. The needle has 5 grooves (see **Figure 7**). The standard setting is the center groove, No. 3.

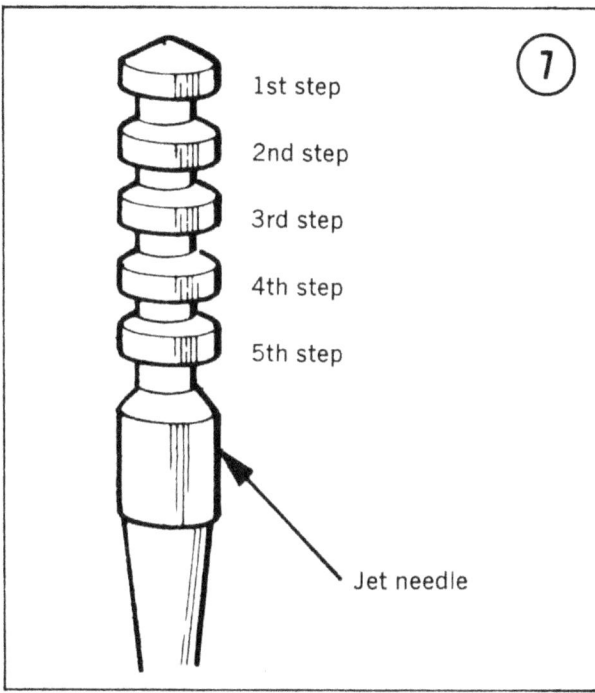

2. Road test the machine with the throttle ½ to ¾ open.

3. White exhaust smoke, sluggish running, or 4-stroking means the mixture is too rich.

4. Fluctuating engine speed or lack of power means the mixture is too lean.

5. Remove the top carburetor cap and the throttle valve assembly.

6. Remove the jet needle and move the needle clip higher to lean or lower to enrich the mixture. Reassemble in reverse order and road test again.

7. Always check main jet with road test after changing the needle position.

Idle Adjustment

1. Set throttle cable for 1/32 to 1/16 in. slack.

2. Set idle with throttle adjuster for 1,500 rpm with the light on.

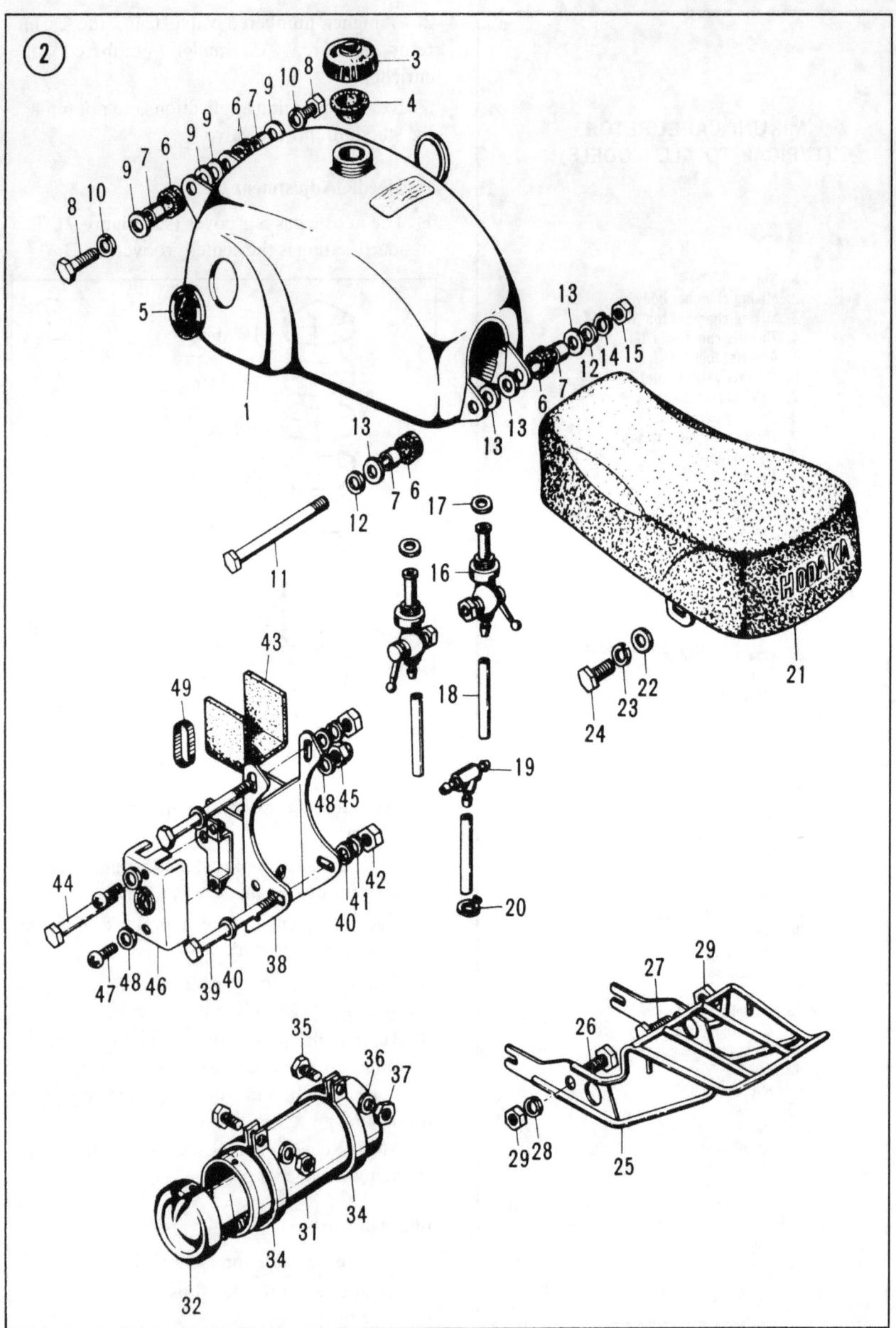

FUEL TANK

1. Fuel tank
2. Fuel tank emblem
3. Filler cap
4. Gasket
5. Fuel tank emblem
6. Rubber mount
7. Collar
8. Bolt (front)
9. Washer (front)
10. Spring washer
11. Bolt (rear)
12. Washer
13. Washer (rear)
14. Spring washer
15. Nut
16. Fuel petcock
17. Gasket
18. Fuel line
19. Connector
20. Clip
21. Seat
22. Washer
23. Spring washer
24. Bolt
25. Rear carrier rack
26. Bolt
27. Bolt
28. Spring washer
29. Nut
31. Tool box body
32. Tool box cover
33. Spring
34. Band
35. Band bolt
36. Spring washer
37. Nut
38. Battery bracket
39. Bolt
40. Washer
41. Spring washer
42. Nut
43. Rubber seat
44. Battery bolt
45. Self-locking nut
46. Cover
47. Screw
48. Washer
49. Rubber band

Float Level Adjustment

1. Remove the float bowl from the carburetor.

2. Hold the carburetor upside down and check the float height for 7/8 in. (see **Figure 8**).

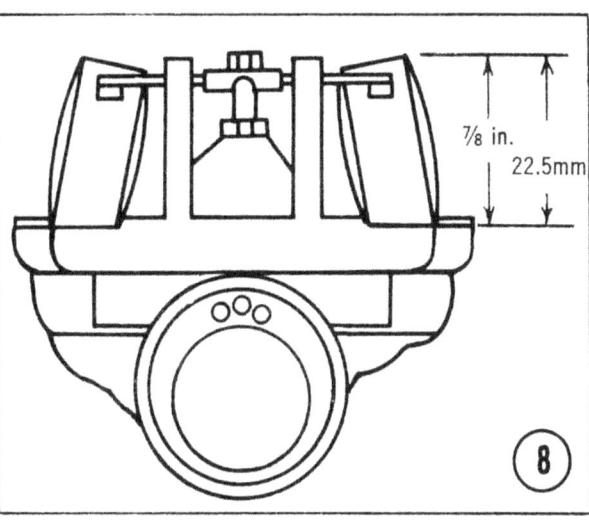

3. Bend the needle actuating tab (see **Figure 9**) to adjust.

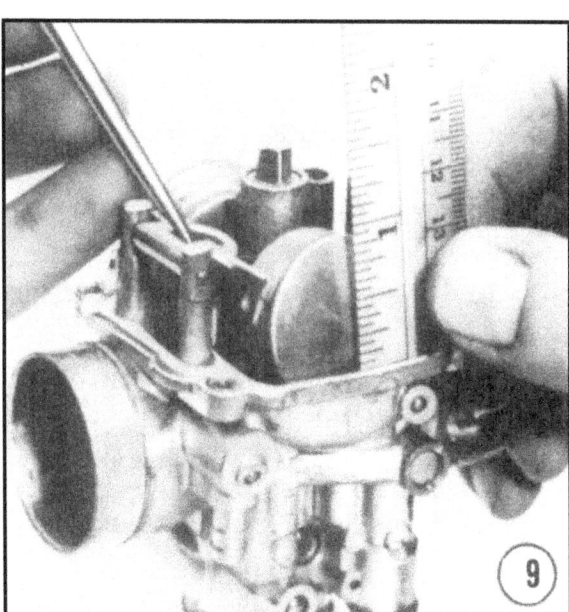

4. Measure both sides for the same height. Reassemble in reverse order.

CARBURETOR OVERHAUL

Disassembly

1. Remove the top cap and the throttle valve assembly.

2. Compress the throttle spring and remove the cable from the throttle valve.

3. Remove the float bowl and discard the gasket.
4. Remove the float arm pin, float, needle, and main jet.
5. Remove the float valve seat and discard the gasket.
6. Use a hardwood dowel to remove the needle jet through the carburetor body.
7. Remove the pilot jet, starter plunger unit, and lever assembly.
8. Remove the rubber cap from the plunger and disassemble the plunger assembly.
9. Remove the O-ring from the mixing chamber and discard.
10. Remove the cotter pin from the throttle adjusting screw.
11. Remove the cable adjuster and throttle adjusting screw from the top cap.
12. Remove the jet needle and spring from the throttle valve. Remove the needle clip.

Inspection

1. Clean all parts in solvent and dry with compressed air.
2. Clean all air passages so they're free of obstructions.
3. Be sure not to damage the nylon valve guide or neoprene plunger tip.
4. Check all parts for wear or damage. Replace if there's any doubt.
5. Replace the gaskets, O-ring, jet needle clip, and cotter pin with new parts.

Reassembly

1. Assemble the starter plunger parts and install in the body.
2. Install the pilot jet, needle jet, and main jet.
3. Install the float valve seat with a new gasket.
4. Install the float arm, needle, and pin. Check the float height.
5. Install the float bowl with new gasket.
6. Install the pilot air screw and spring. Turn all the way in and back out 1¼ turns.
7. Install the new O-ring in the mounting flange groove.
8. Install the carburetor on the intake manifold.
9. Install the air cleaner hose and fuel line.
10. Install a new clip in the third notch of the needle and install the needle in the throttle valve.
11. Install the cable adjuster, adjusting screw, and spring on the top cap.
12. Install the throttle valve assembly on the top cap.
13. Install throttle cable into throttle valve.
14. Install assembly in carburetor body with the throttle valve cutaway facing the air cleaner.
15. Adjust carburetor as detailed before.

MANIFOLD

1. Replace the gaskets if the carburetor has been removed from the cylinder.
2. Replace the manifold if it is warped more than 0.001 in.
3. Tighten the manifold nuts slowly and evenly to prevent warping.
4. Be sure the phenolic heat shield is installed between the cylinder and the manifold.

FUEL TANK

1. Remove the tank and drain every 5,000 miles or 6 months.
2. Plug fuel outlet and fill with soapy detergent water and a handful of nuts, bolts, or B-B's.
3. Shake the tank vigorously and drain. Flush with gasoline and drain again.
4. Check all parts for wear or damage. Replace parts if necessary.
5. The fuel cocks can be repaired with valve lapping compound to stop leaks, but it is advisable to replace damaged ones if possible.
6. Replace the fuel lines every 6 months to prevent age cracking.

THROTTLE CABLE

1. Remove the throttle cable and oil the inner cable while working the housing up and down.
2. Install the throttle cable and adjust.
3. Disassemble the twist grip assembly and clean with solvent.
4. Lubricate with grease and reassemble.

5. To install a new twist grip rubber, pour gasoline inside the rubber and then install quickly. The gas will evaporate quickly leaving the grip firm.

AIR CLEANER

An exploded view of the air cleaner is shown in **Figure 10**. See Chapter Two for maintenance intervals.

Removal and Installation

1. To remove the air cleaner, detach the spring as shown in **Figure 11**.

2. Release the spring clips which hold the body to the mouthpiece (**Figure 12**).

3. Remove the mouthpiece and rubber joint from the carburetor and lift out the element as shown in **Figure 13**.

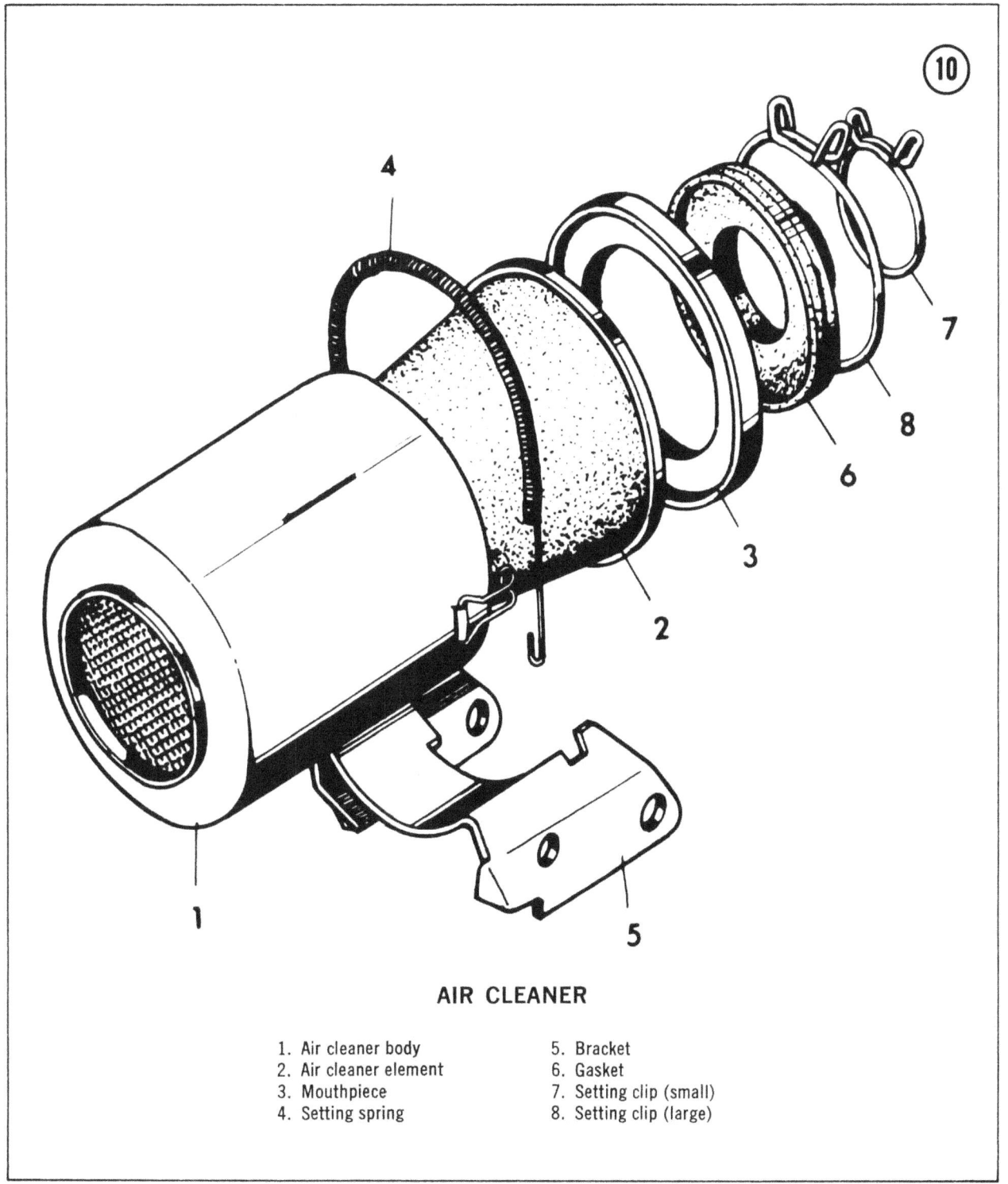

AIR CLEANER

1. Air cleaner body
2. Air cleaner element
3. Mouthpiece
4. Setting spring
5. Bracket
6. Gasket
7. Setting clip (small)
8. Setting clip (large)

4. Tilt the air cleaner body (see **Figure 14**) and lift out.

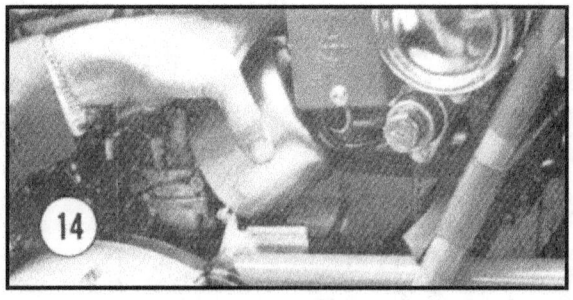

5. Clean all parts in solvent and dry with compressed air.

6. Lubricate the element with SAE 10W oil and squeeze out the excess.

7. Installation procedures are the reverse of removal.

EXHAUST SYSTEM

The exhaust system consists of a steel exhaust pipe connected to an expansion chamber muffler. A baffle pipe contained within is removable for cleaning. The exhaust pipe is fixed to the cylinder exhaust port by means of a bezel nut. The exhaust pipe-to-muffler coupling is sealed by a rubber sleeve. A ventilated heat shield is fastened to the muffler body. See **Figure 15**.

The exhaust systems for the Ace 100, Ace 100-B (Figure 15 and **Figure 16**), and 100-MX (**Figure 17**) are similar in construction, except that the 100-MX does not have a removable inner pipe. All other models will be similar to either of these models.

EXHAUST PIPE AND MUFFLER

Disassembly

1. Remove the exhaust flange nut.
2. Remove the exhaust pipe from the frame.
3. Remove the Phillips screw holding the inner baffle pipe and remove the pipe with a pliers.
4. Remove the heat shield from the pipe.

Inspection

1. Slide a length of old chain through the pipe. By twisting and pulling on the chain, clean excess carbon from inside the pipe.
2. Clean loose carbon out with compressed air. A more thorough job can be done by your local radiator shop, using their immersion solution.
3. Check all parts for any signs of wear or damage. Replace if necessary.
4. Use a new gasket and rubber seats when installing.

Reassembly

1. Install the nut over the pipe with the open end toward the flange.
2. Install rubber sleeve in heat shield clamp.
3. Install the rubber seats under the heat shield mounting holes.
4. Install the side cover screws and tighten.
5. Install muffler assembly on mounting studs.
6. Install the pipe on the cylinder with a new gasket.
7. Install the baffles in the muffler.
8. Tighten the heat shield saddle clamp screws. Do not overtighten.

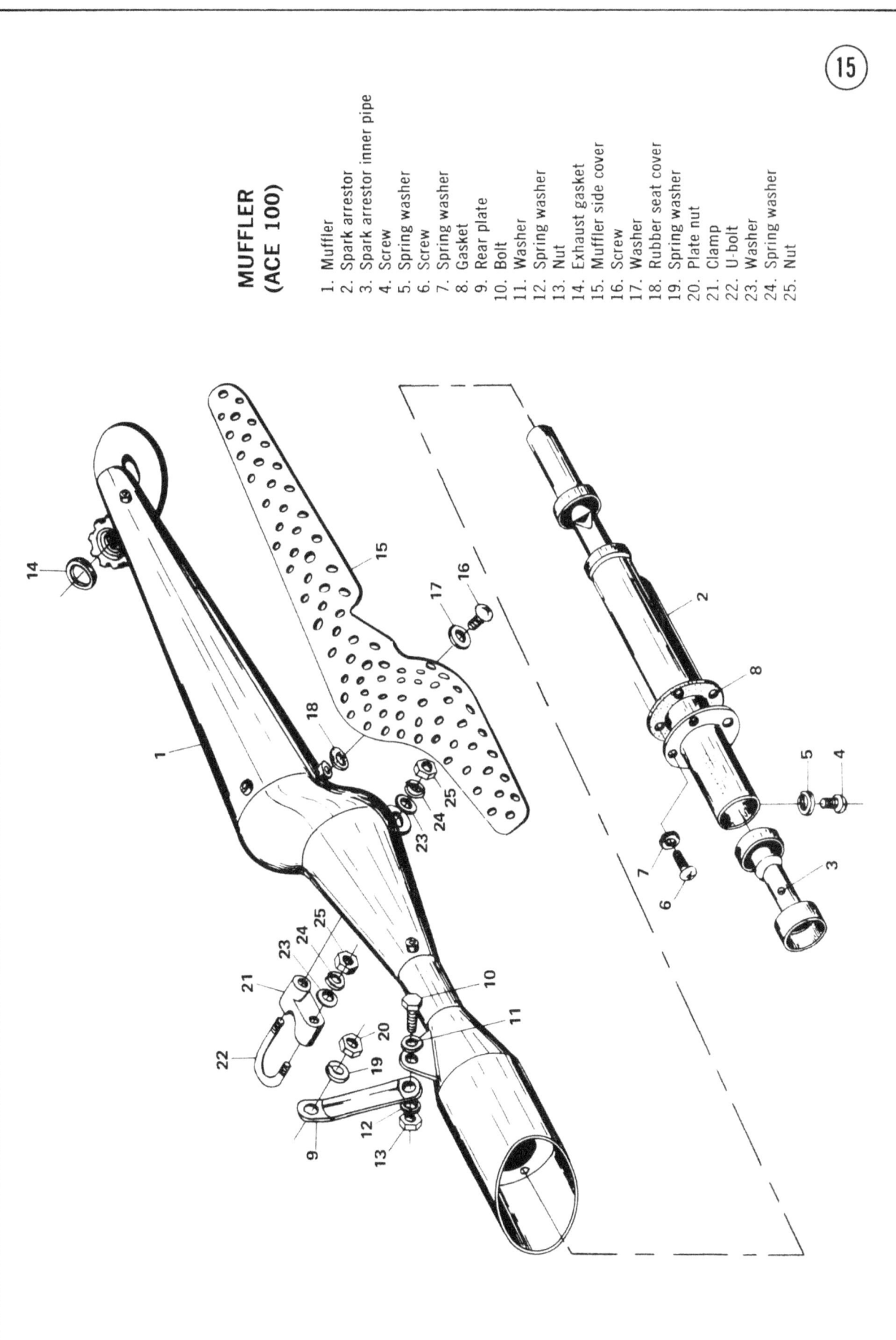

MUFFLER (ACE 100)

1. Muffler
2. Spark arrestor
3. Spark arrestor inner pipe
4. Screw
5. Spring washer
6. Screw
7. Spring washer
8. Gasket
9. Rear plate
10. Bolt
11. Washer
12. Spring washer
13. Nut
14. Exhaust gasket
15. Muffler side cover
16. Screw
17. Washer
18. Rubber seat cover
19. Spring washer
20. Plate nut
21. Clamp
22. U-bolt
23. Washer
24. Spring washer
25. Nut

MUFFLER (ACE 100-B)

1. Muffler
2. Inner pipe
3. Setscrew
4. Lockwasher
5. Tailpipe
6. Setscrew
7. Lockwasher
8. Gasket
9. Rear mounting bracket
10. Bolt
11. Washer
12. Lockwasher
13. Nut
14. Exhaust pipe gasket
15. Side cover
16. Mounting screw
17. Washer
18. Mounting seat
19. Washer
20. Lockwasher
21. Nut
22. Mounting clamp
23. U-bolt
24. Flat washer
25. Hex nut

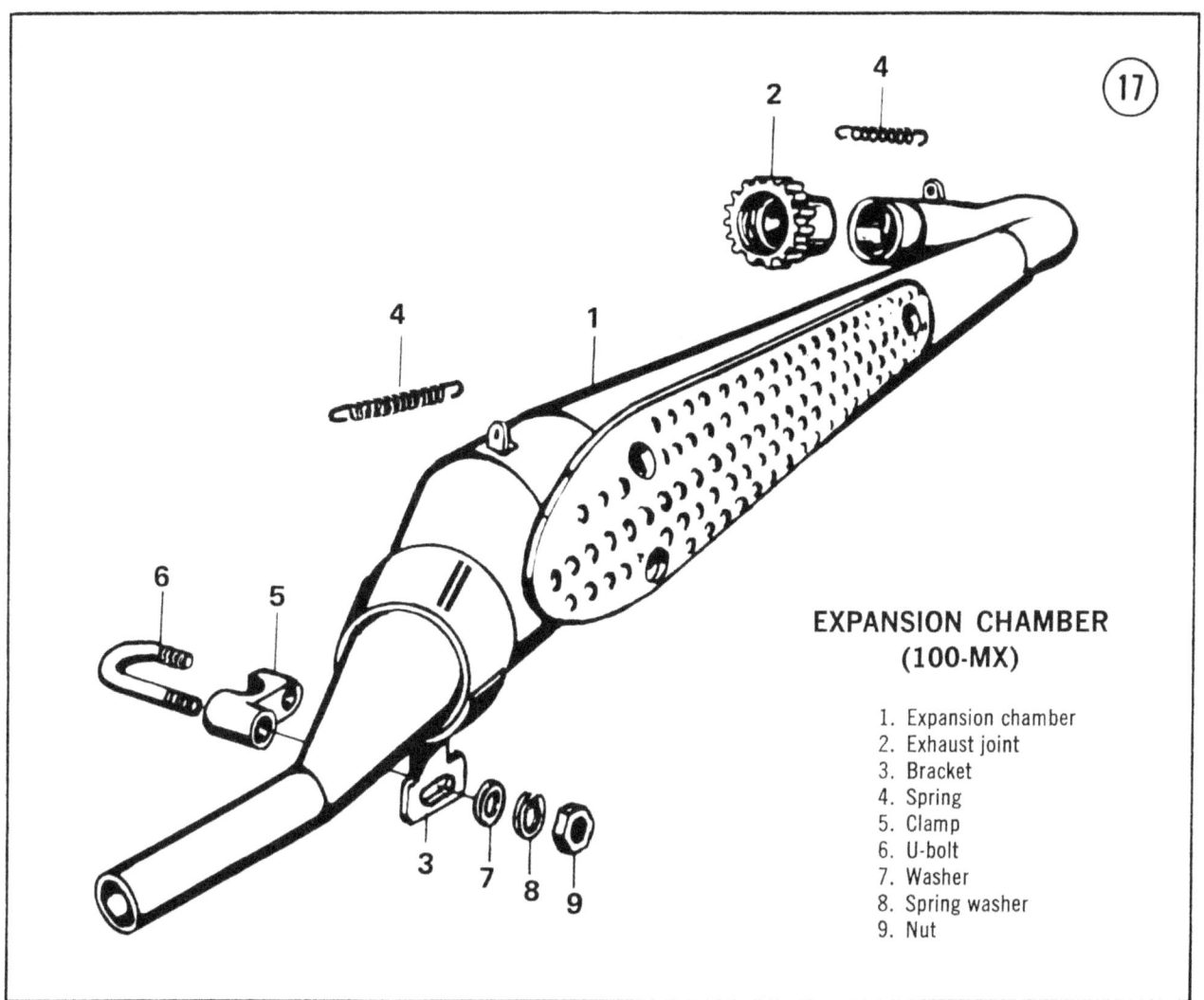

EXPANSION CHAMBER (100-MX)

1. Expansion chamber
2. Exhaust joint
3. Bracket
4. Spring
5. Clamp
6. U-bolt
7. Washer
8. Spring washer
9. Nut

CHAPTER SIX

ELECTRICAL SYSTEM

This chapter covers maintenance and repair of the following.

a. Starting system   d. Lighting
b. Ignition system   e. Horn
c. Charging system

The magneto/alternator assembly (**Figure 1**) has been modified to incorporate an energy transfer ignition system. The MX models have the same system, except that they are racing models and do not have an alternator, wiring harness, battery, or rectifier. Service procedures for all models are very similar, except where detailed otherwise.

FLYWHEEL REMOVAL

1. Remove the magneto cover.
2. Use holding tool No. P/N 909523 or equivalent to prevent flywheel rotation and remove the flywheel nut (see **Figure 2**).
3. Screw the flywheel puller body into the flywheel hub in a counterclockwise direction. Back off the puller stud so it can't contact the crankshaft until the puller body is tight.
4. Hold the puller body with a wrench (see **Figure 3**) and tighten the stud clockwise against the crankshaft until flywheel comes off the tapered seat.

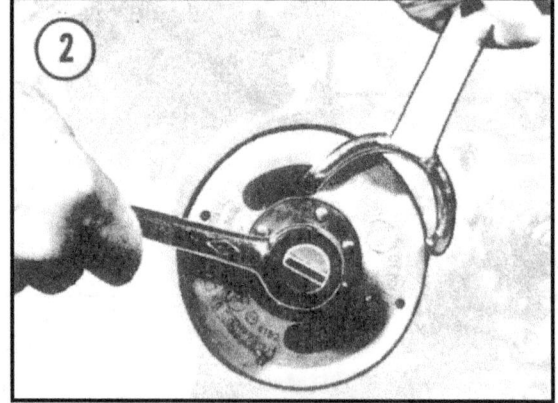

5. Do not strike or heat the flywheel in any way. Handle carefully.
6. Remove the crankshaft key and store for reassembly.

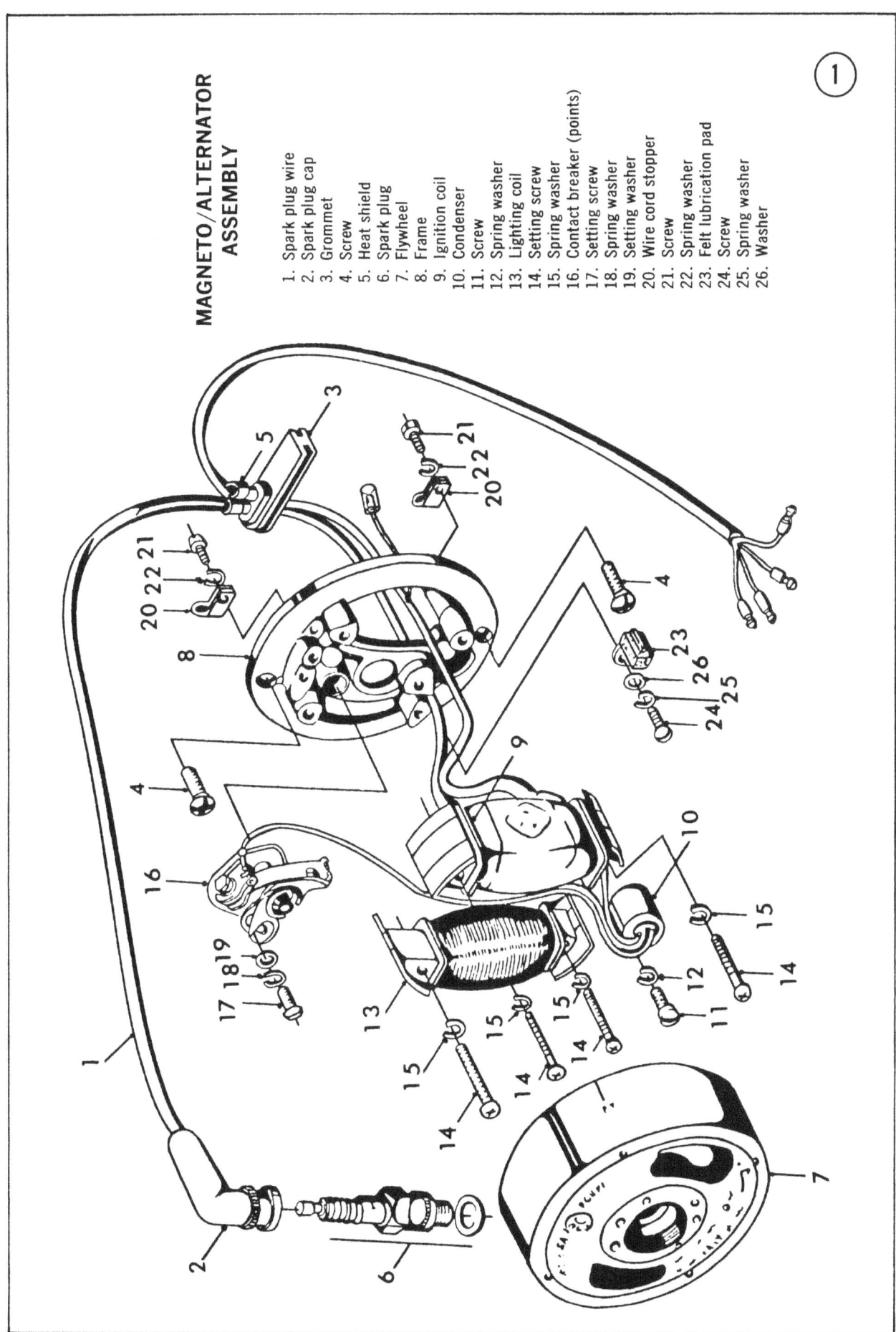

MAGNETO/ALTERNATOR ASSEMBLY

1. Spark plug wire
2. Spark plug cap
3. Grommet
4. Screw
5. Heat shield
6. Spark plug
7. Flywheel
8. Frame
9. Ignition coil
10. Condenser
11. Screw
12. Spring washer
13. Lighting coil
14. Setting screw
15. Spring washer
16. Contact breaker (points)
17. Setting screw
18. Spring washer
19. Setting washer
20. Wire cord stopper
21. Screw
22. Spring washer
23. Felt lubrication pad
24. Screw
25. Spring washer
26. Washer

MAGNETO

Frame Assembly Removal

1. Use a Phillips head impact tool to remove the 2 screws in the magneto frame (**Figure 4**).

C. Felt lubricating pad   D. Frame mounting screws

2. Disconnect the magneto harness from the frame clip and remove the spark plug wire.
3. Remove the magneto frame and wiring from the engine case.

Disassembly

1. Remove the 2 screws holding the wire cord stoppers to the back of the frame face.
2. Unsolder the red primary wire from the condenser and remove the 2 screws holding the coil core to the frame.
3. Unscrew the high tension wire terminal. Remove the high tension wire from the grommet and remove the coil.
4. Unsolder the wire connection on top of the condenser and remove the screw. Remove the condenser.
5. Remove the lighting coil core screws and wires from the harness. Remove the lighting coil.
6. Loosen the nut holding the blue wire to the insulated terminal of the breaker points. Remove the wire and unscrew the contact breaker screw. Remove breaker assembly from frame.

Inspection

1. Wash all parts with solvent and dry with compressed air.
2. Check the breaker points for pitting or burning. If light sanding with a points stone will not restore them, replace points. See Chapter Two for more detail.
3. Check the breaker point spring for wear or damage.
4. Check the rubbing block on the movable breaker point for wear or damage.
5. Check the insulated terminal for carbonized surfaces. Remove with a knife or sandpaper.
6. Test the continuity of all magneto wiring with a continuity light or ohmmeter. Replace all damaged wiring. Wiring diagrams are shown in **Figures 5 and 6**.
7. Sandpaper the magneto frame surfaces lightly to insure positive ground connection with engine when reassembled. Do the same for all mountings. Spray with WD-40 or equivalent to prevent rust.
8. Check the flywheel magneto surface for signs of touching the coil core ends. This indicates worn crankshaft bearings, faulty flywheel mounting, worn taper fit flywheel mounting, or faulty spacing of coil cores. Replace any parts as necessary.

Reassembly

1. Install the ignition coil on the magneto frame and tighten the screws.
2. Install the condenser to the frame with the setting screw.
3. Run the blue wire from the points to condenser between the contact breaker mounting lugs on the frame.
4. Install the breaker points on the mounting lugs. Center the pivot shaft in the locating hole and set the screw loosely.
5. Install the lighting coil on the frame and the magneto harness over the lighting coil leads.
6. Solder the red wire from the ignition coil, the blue wire from the breaker point terminal, and the black wire from the magneto harness to the condenser.
7. Install the wire cord stoppers on the back of the magneto frame. Be sure the grommet and high tension terminal are in place and oil the felt pad.

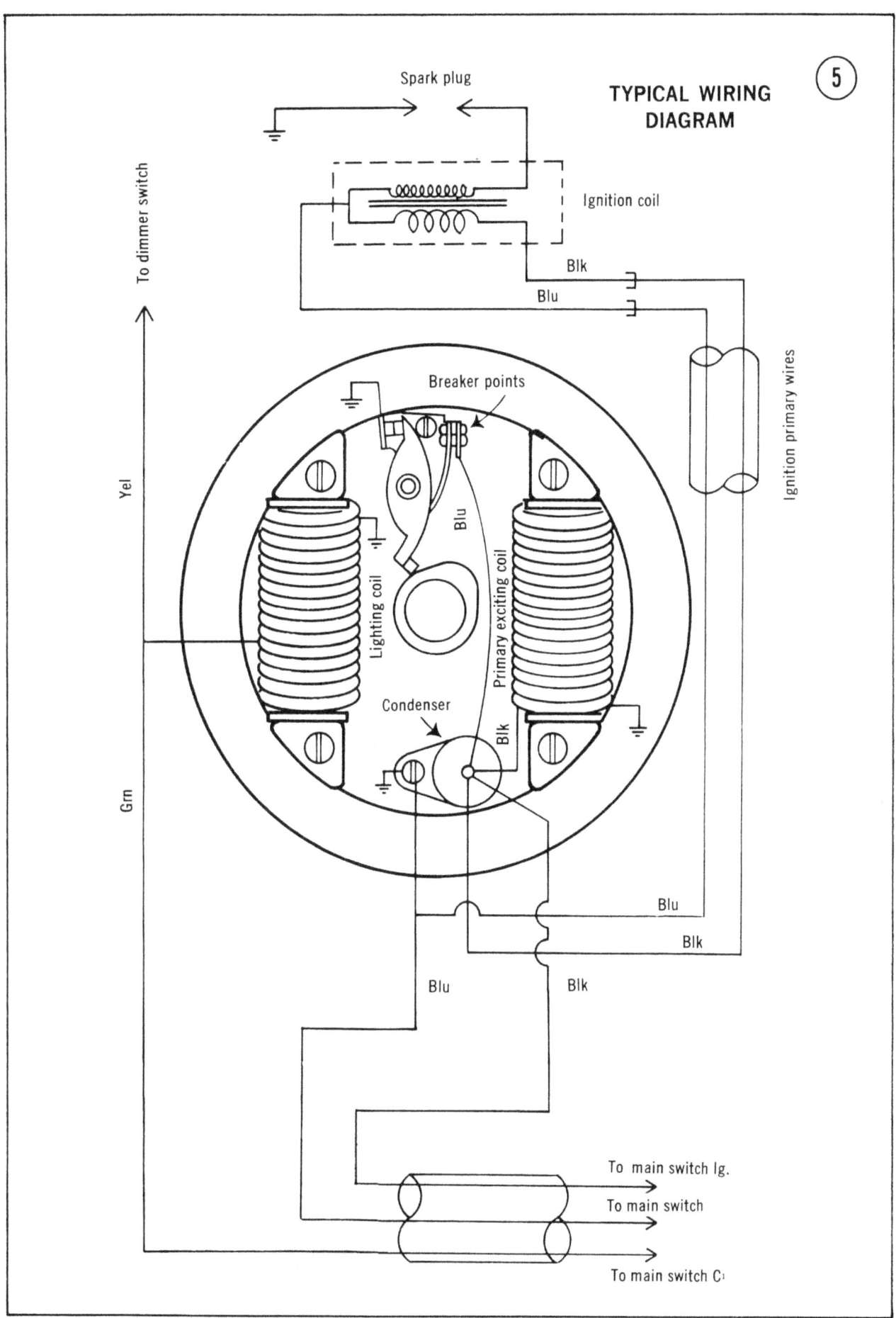

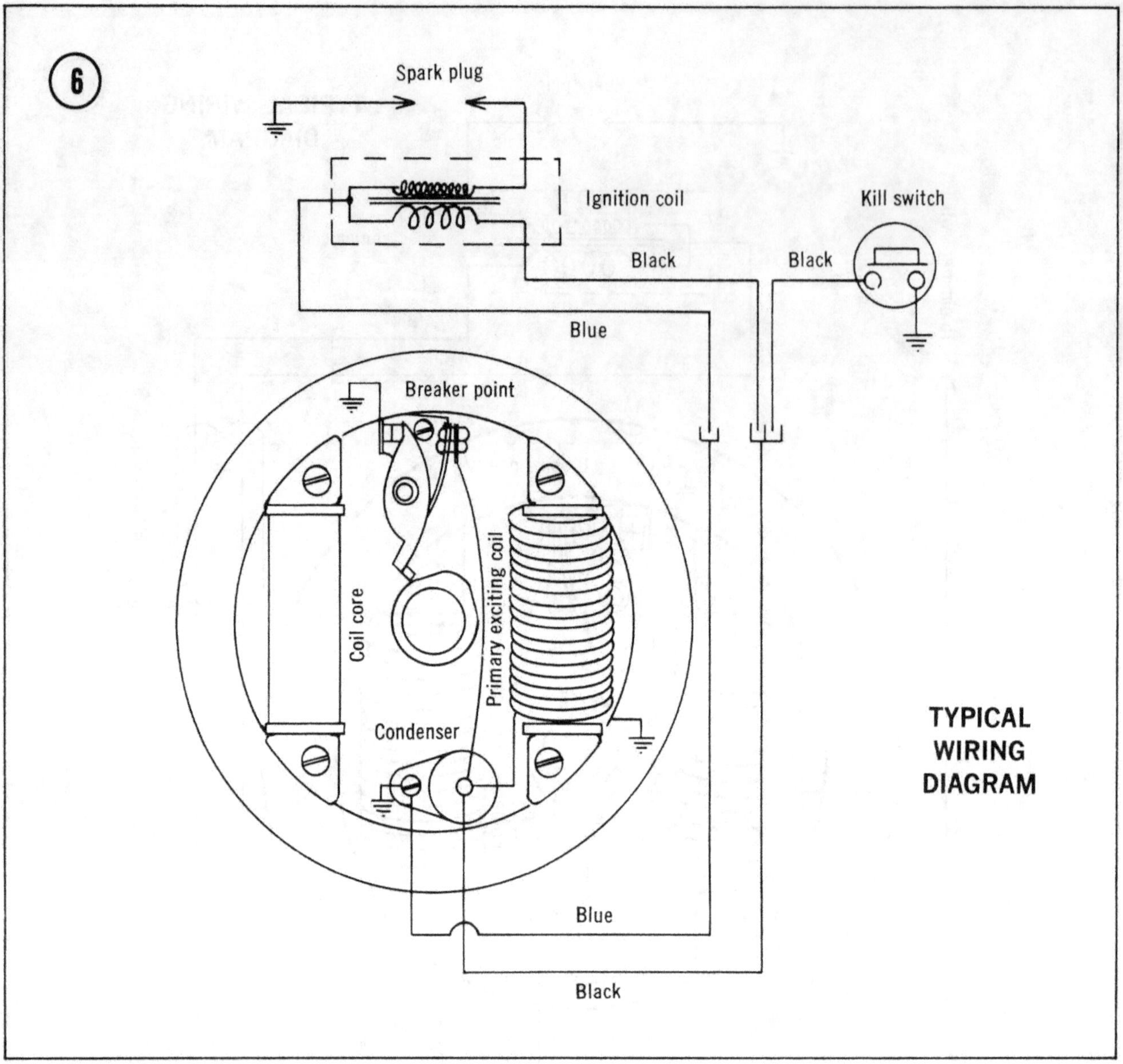

(6) TYPICAL WIRING DIAGRAM

MAGNETO AND FLYWHEEL INSTALLATION

Magneto Frame

1. Install the frame into the engine case and the grommet into the slot.
2. Tighten the frame mounting screws and check for any pinched wires.
3. Connect the wiring according to matching color code at battery junction.
4. Connect the spark plug wire last, and clean points with a paper strip or business card.

Flywheel

1. Install the key in the crankshaft and tap down with a brass drift pin.
2. Lubricate the cam with a thin film of 10W oil and install the flywheel (**Figure 7**) on the crankshaft.

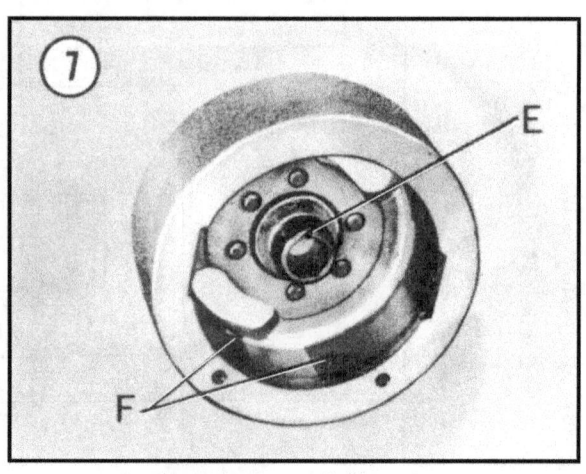

E. Flywheel cam   F. Magnets

3. Install the lockwasher and crankshaft nut. Hold the flywheel with the holding tool and tighten the nut to 170 in.-lb. (14 ft.-lb.).

4. Measure the coil core ends for 0.010 in. gap from flywheel magneto, using a feeler gauge through the flywheel inspection openings.

5. Remove the paper strips and check the gap again. Repeat for both the ignition coil and lighting coil, on both ends of the coil at the same time.

6. Set ignition timing (Chapter Two).

7. Install the magneto cover on the engine case. Be sure to engage the shifter sliding pin in the control shaft groove.

8. Tighten the setting screws and install the shifter cover on the magneto cover and tighten the screws.

9. Check condition of the spark of the spark plug wire with a 5mm gap test plug.

HEADLIGHT

Adjustment

See Chapter Two.

Disassembly

1. Remove the rim setting screw. See **Figures 8 and 9**. Pull the rim up and out to remove.

2. Disconnect the cannon plug and remove the light assembly.

3. Remove the rim from the light assembly.

4. Remove the speedometer lights from below.

5. Remove the speedometer bracket and speedometer.

6. Remove the headlight case.

Inspection

1. Clean the hardware with solvent and dry with compressed air.

2. Clean the case and rim with soap and water and dry with air.

3. Check all parts for wear or damage. Replace if necessary. Be especially careful when checking the insulation of the wiring.

4. Connect wiring according to color code.

5. Install the headlight in rim with TOP mark opposite the set screw.

6. Connect the speedometer lights and the headlight cannon plug.

7. Install the rim and headlight into case.

8. Adjust beam position as detailed in Chapter Two. Tighten all hardware.

TAILLIGHT

Replacement

1. Remove the lens screws and taillight lens. See **Figure 10**.

2. Push bulb in and twist to remove.

3. Check all parts for wear or damage. Replace if necessary.

4. Replace rubber grommets or socket boot if deteriorated.

HORN

Adjustment

1. Remove the gas tank and seat.

2. Disconnect the black wire from the horn at the nearest connector.

3. Loosen the locknut on the armature adjusting screw (see **Figure 11**, page 80).

4. Ground the black horn wire to the frame and turn the adjusting screw until the desired horn tone is achieved.

5. Tighten the locknut after adjusting.

SPARK PLUG SERVICE

See Chapter Two for *Maintenance and Service*.

BATTERY

The battery electrolyte level should be checked regularly, especially in hot weather.

Removal

1. Remove the retaining strap. Disconnect the ground, or negative (−) cable first, then the positive (+) cable.

2. Lift the battery from the mounting, noting the location of the terminal covers, mounting pads, and vent tube for reinstallation later.

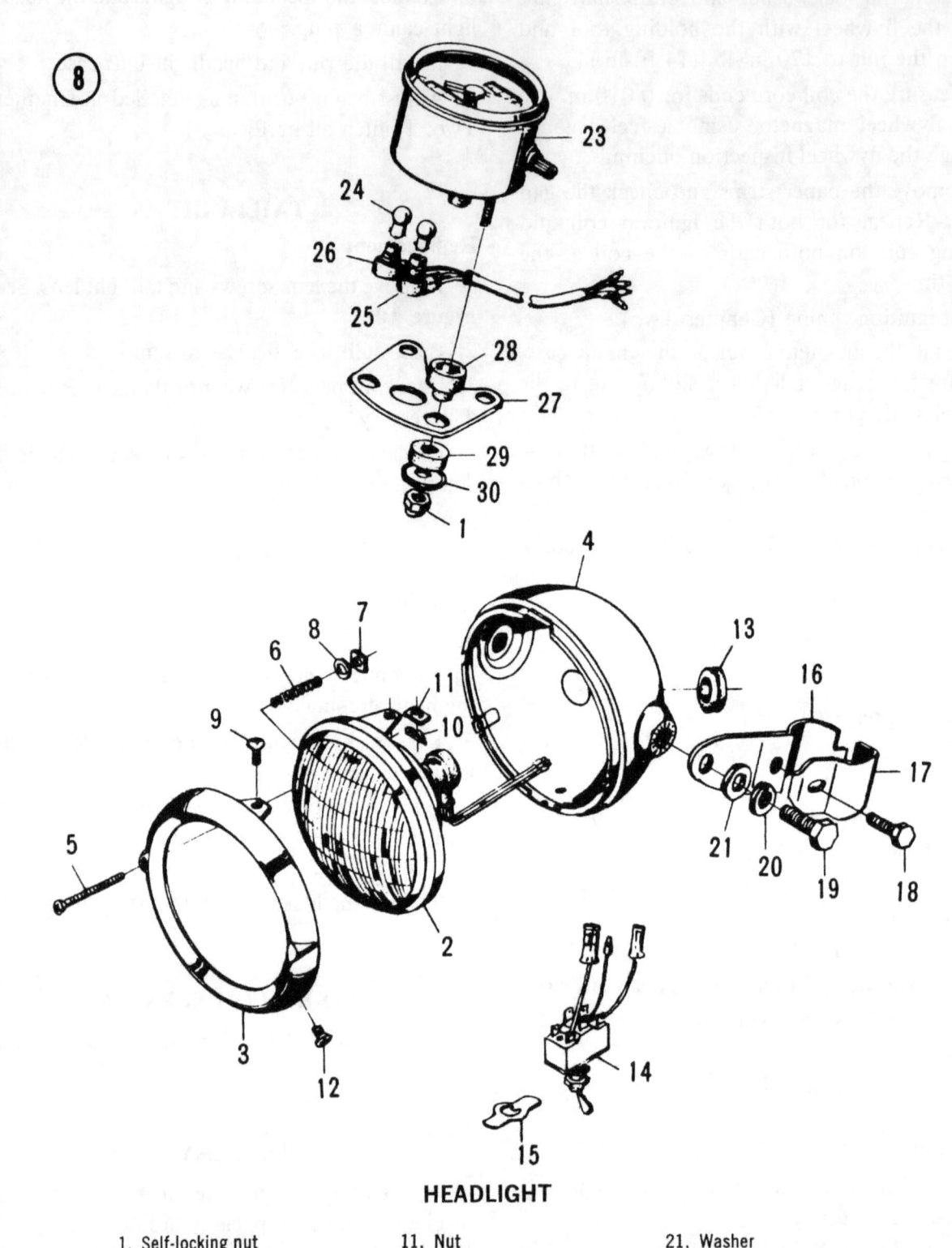

HEADLIGHT

1. Self-locking nut
2. Sealed beam unit
3. Headlight rim
4. Headlight body
5. Adjusting screw
6. Adjusting spring
7. Nut
8. Washer
9. Screw
10. Clip
11. Nut
12. Rim screw
13. Rubber bushing
14. Emergency switch
15. Name plate
16. Headlight bracket
17. Clamp
18. Bolt
19. Bolt
20. Spring washer
21. Washer
23. Speedometer (with trip meter)
24. Speedometer light bulb
25. Light socket
26. High beam indicator light socket
27. Speedometer bracket
28. Rubber mount A (upper)
29. Rubber mount B (lower)
30. Washer

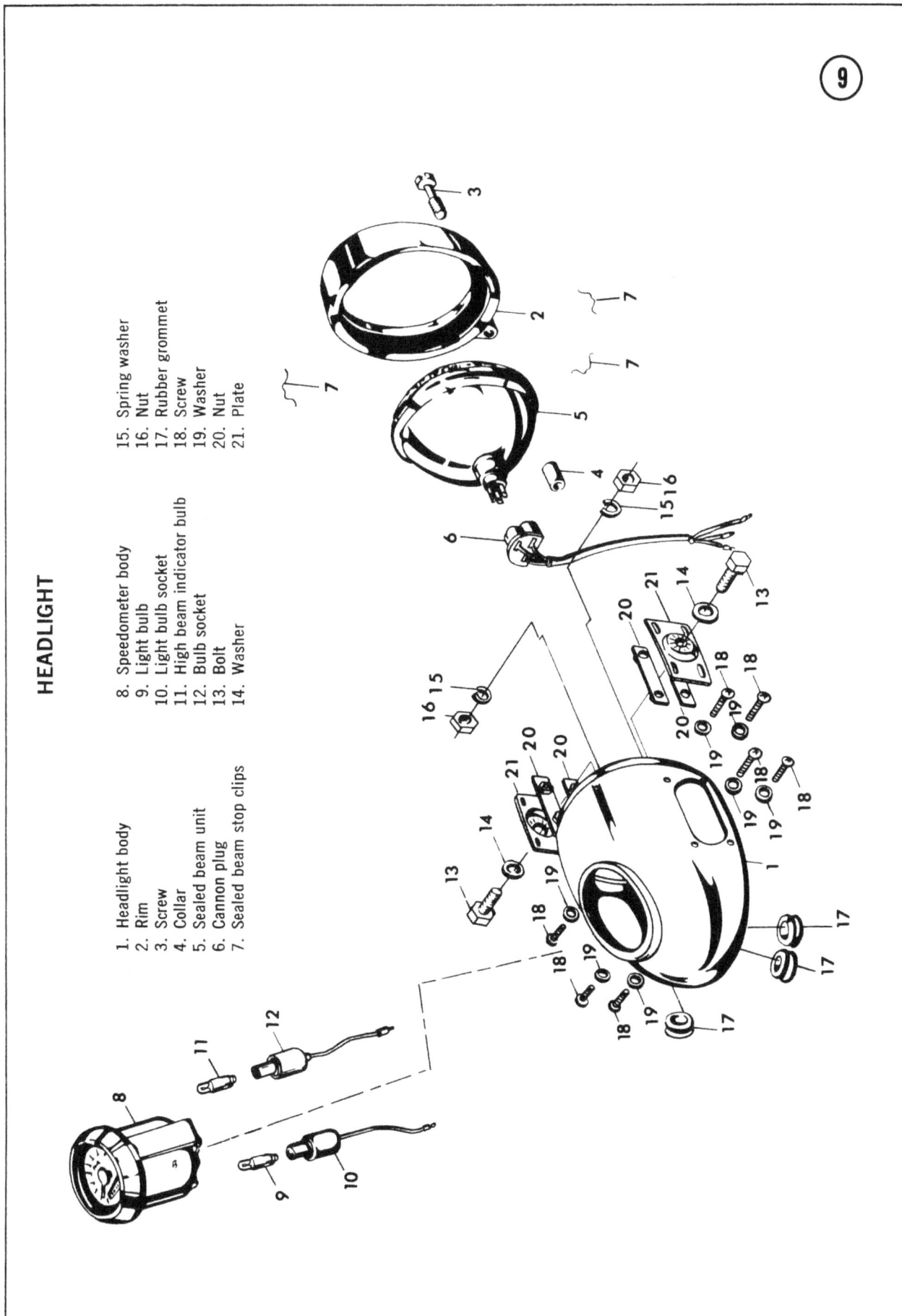

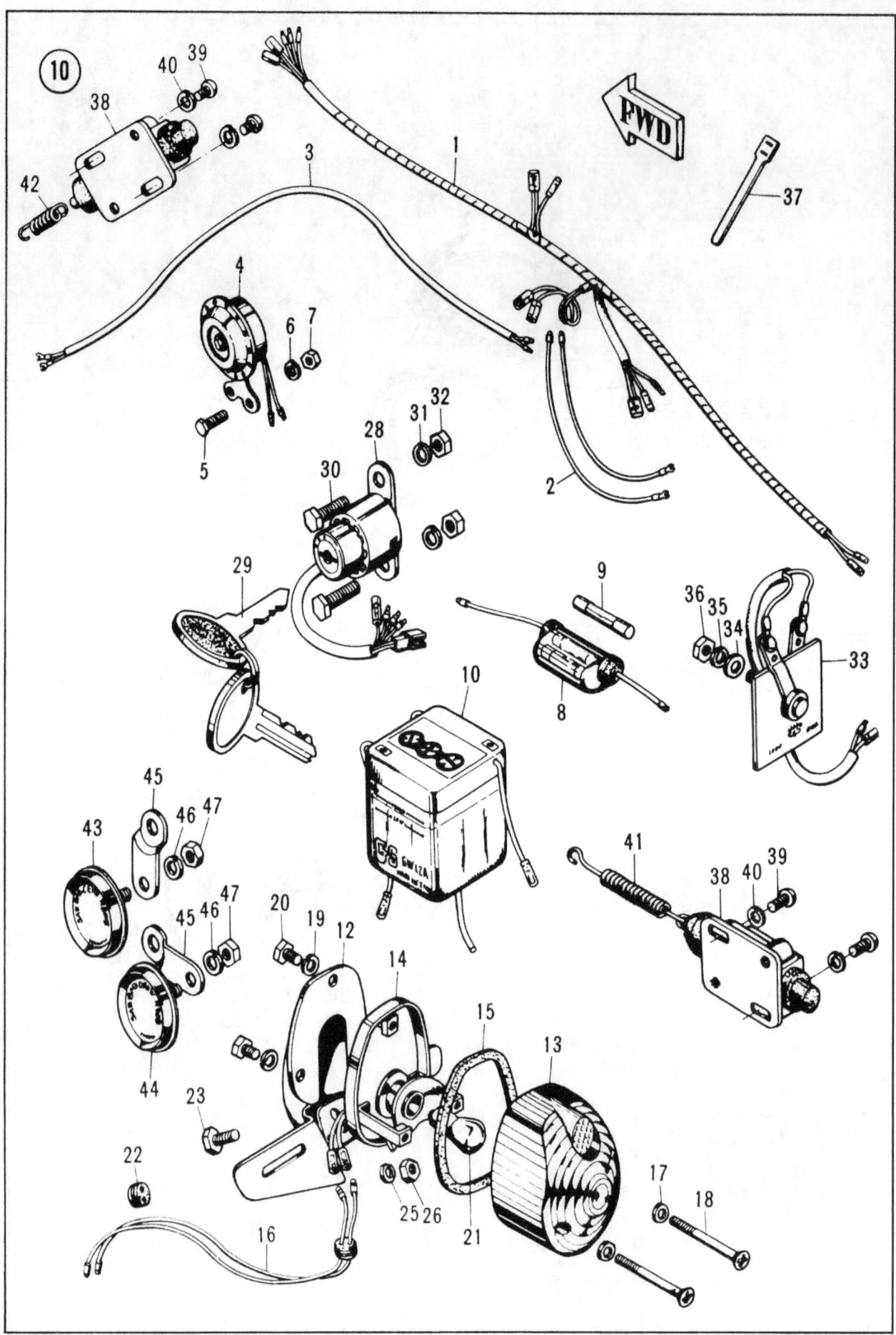

ELECTRICAL EQUIPMENT

1. Main wire harness
2. Stoplight switch wire
3. Front stoplight switch wire harness
4. Horn
5. Bolt
6. Spring washer
7. Nut
8. Fuse box
9. Fuse
10. Battery
12. License plate bracket
13. Tail- and stoplight lens
14. Tail- and stoplight socket
15. Lens gasket
16. Tail- and stoplight wiring
17. Washer
18. Screw
19. Spring washer
20. Screw
21. Tail- and stoplight bulb
22. Wiring harness grommet
23. Bolt
25. Spring washer
26. Nut
28. Main switch body unit
29. Main switch key
30. Bolt
31. Spring washer
32. Nut
33. Selenium rectifier
34. Washer
35. Spring washer
36. Nut
37. Wiring harness clip
38. Stoplight switch (rear, front)
39. Screw
40. Spring washer
41. Spring
42. Spring
43. Front reflector (amber)
44. Rear reflector (red)
45. Reflector bracket
46. Spring washer
47. Nut

Inspection and Testing

1. Corrosion on the battery terminals causes leakage of current. Clean them with a wire brush or a solution of baking soda and water.

2. The electrolyte level should be between the upper and lower fill marks. Top up low cells with distilled water only.

3. Measure the specific gravity of the electrolyte with a bulb hydrometer, reading is as shown in **Figure 12**. Generally, the reading should be between 1.26 and 1.28. If the value is less than 1.189 at 68°F (20°C), the battery is in poor condition and should be charged. Figure 12 shows the relationship between specific gravity and residual battery capacity.

Charging

A "trickle" charger is recommended for restoring a low voltage battery to normal. Most such inexpensive chargers have outputs ranging from 1 to 6 amps.

The so-called "quick" chargers found at gas stations drastically shorten battery life by overheating which causes plate warpage.

1. **Figure 13** shows the connection of a charger. Note that the positive lead must be clipped to the positive terminal and the negative lead to the corresponding terminals or damage will result.

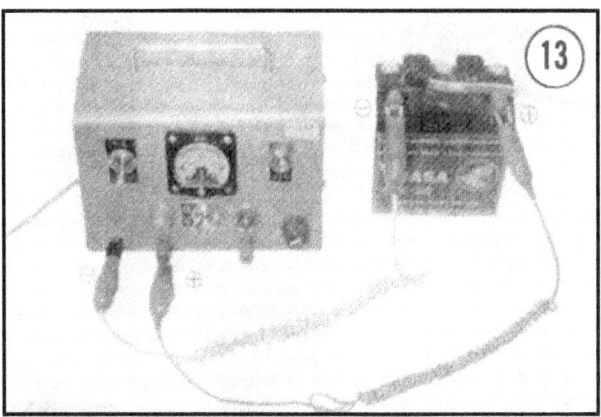

2. The electrolyte will begin bubbling, signifying that explosive hydrogen gas is being released. Make sure the area is adequately ventilated and there are no open flames.

3. It will take at least 8 hours to bring the battery to full charge. Test the electrolyte periodically with a hydrometer to see if the specific

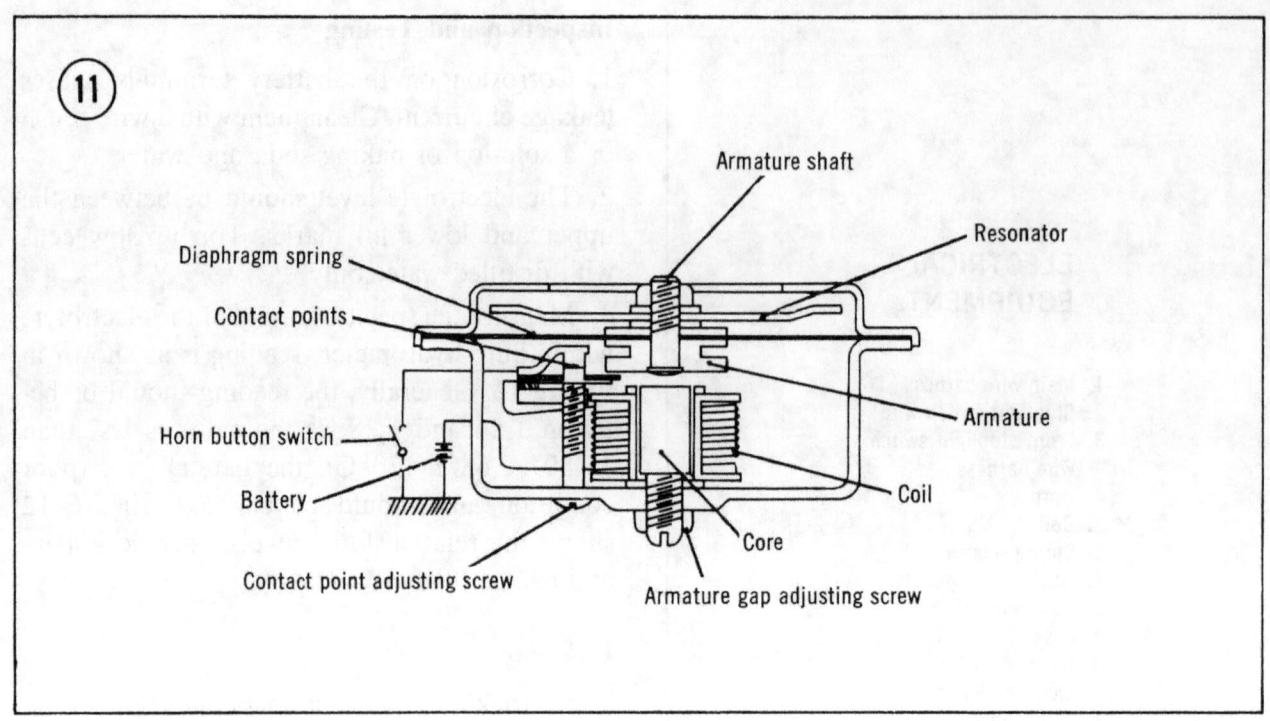

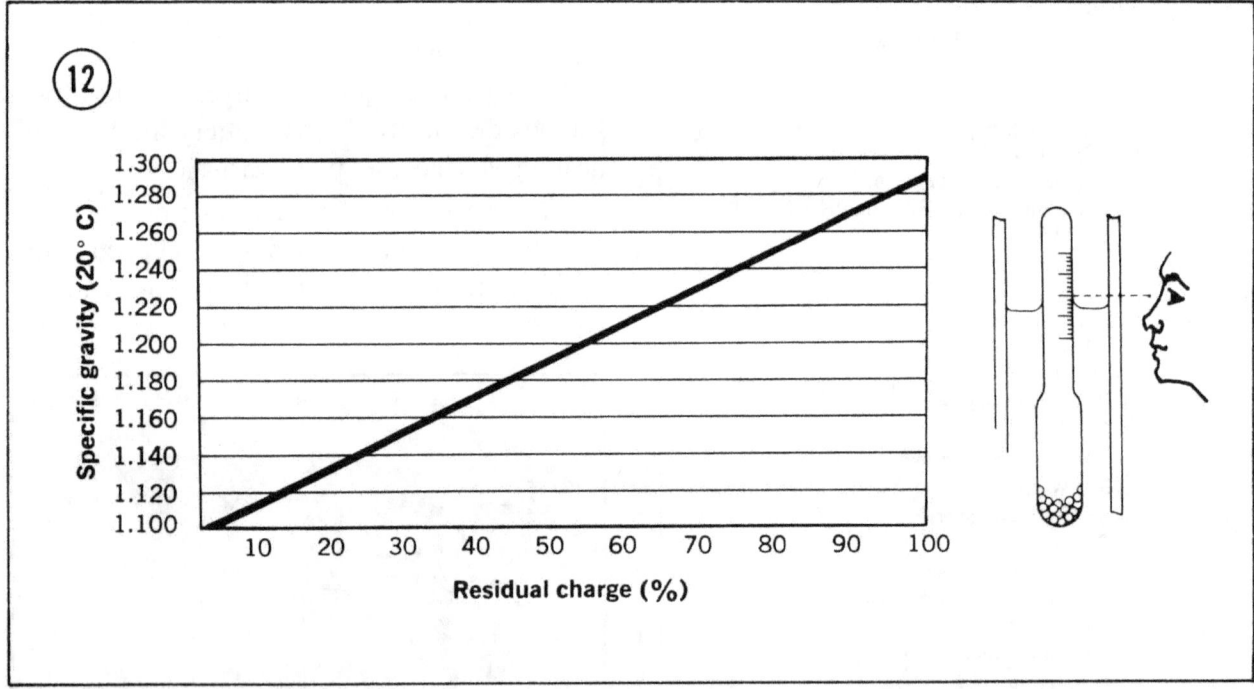

gravity is within the standard range of 1.26 to 1.28. If the reading remains constant for more than an hour, the battery is charged.

Installation

1. Make sure the battery terminals, cable clamps, and case are free of corrosion. Silicone spray or Vaseline can be applied to the terminals to retard this process.

2. When replacing the battery, be careful to route the vent tube so that it is not crimped. Connect the positive terminal first, then the negative one. Don't overtighten the clamps.

New Battery Installation

1. Open sealed end of vent tube.
2. Remove vent plugs and sealing tape.
3. Fill battery cells to the upper level line with sulphuric acid solution with a specific gravity

of 1.260 with a temperature not lower than 60 degrees or higher than 86 degrees F.

4. Let the battery stand for two hours.

5. Charge at 0.4Ah rate for 10 hours, until voltage and specific gravity readings at 3 successive 30 minute intervals are the same.

6. Be sure the battery fluid does not go above 86 degrees during charging. If the charging rate is too high, a taillight bulb in the charging circuit will reduce it (see **Figure 14**).

7. Replace the vent plugs and wash the battery with water before installing.

8. **Be sure to unplug the charger before disconnecting it from the battery. This prevents a spark from igniting the hydrogen gas caused by charging.**

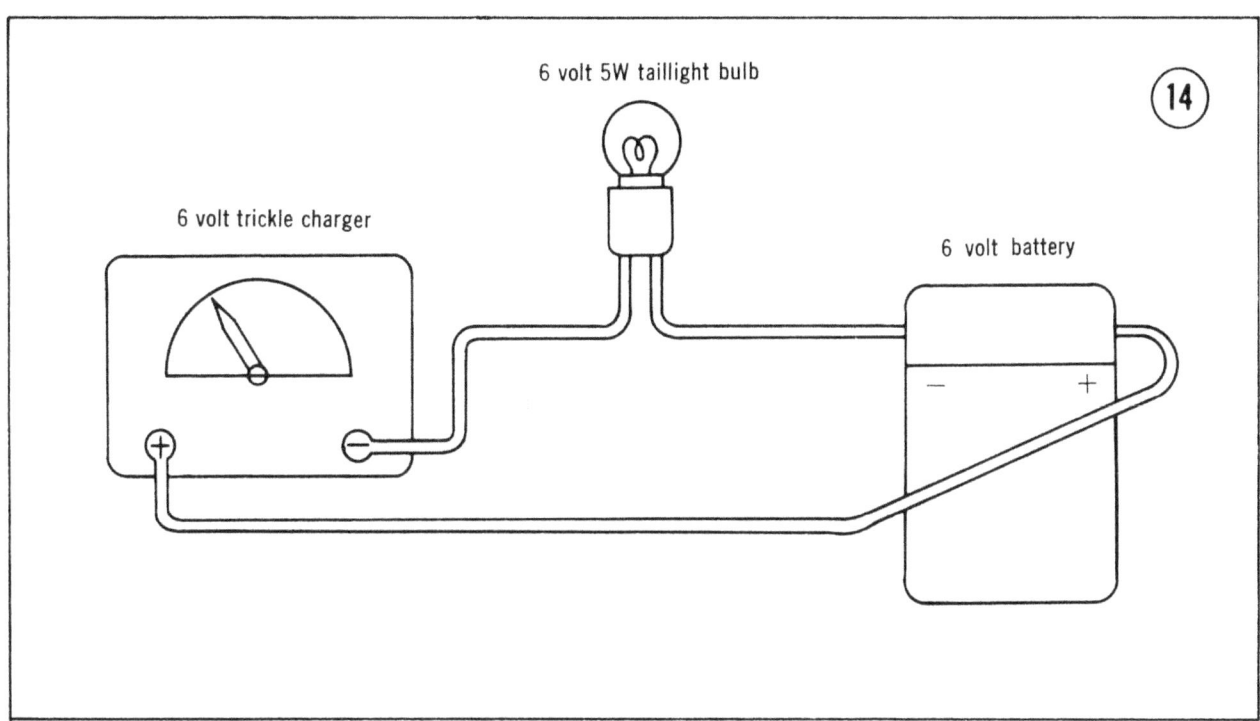

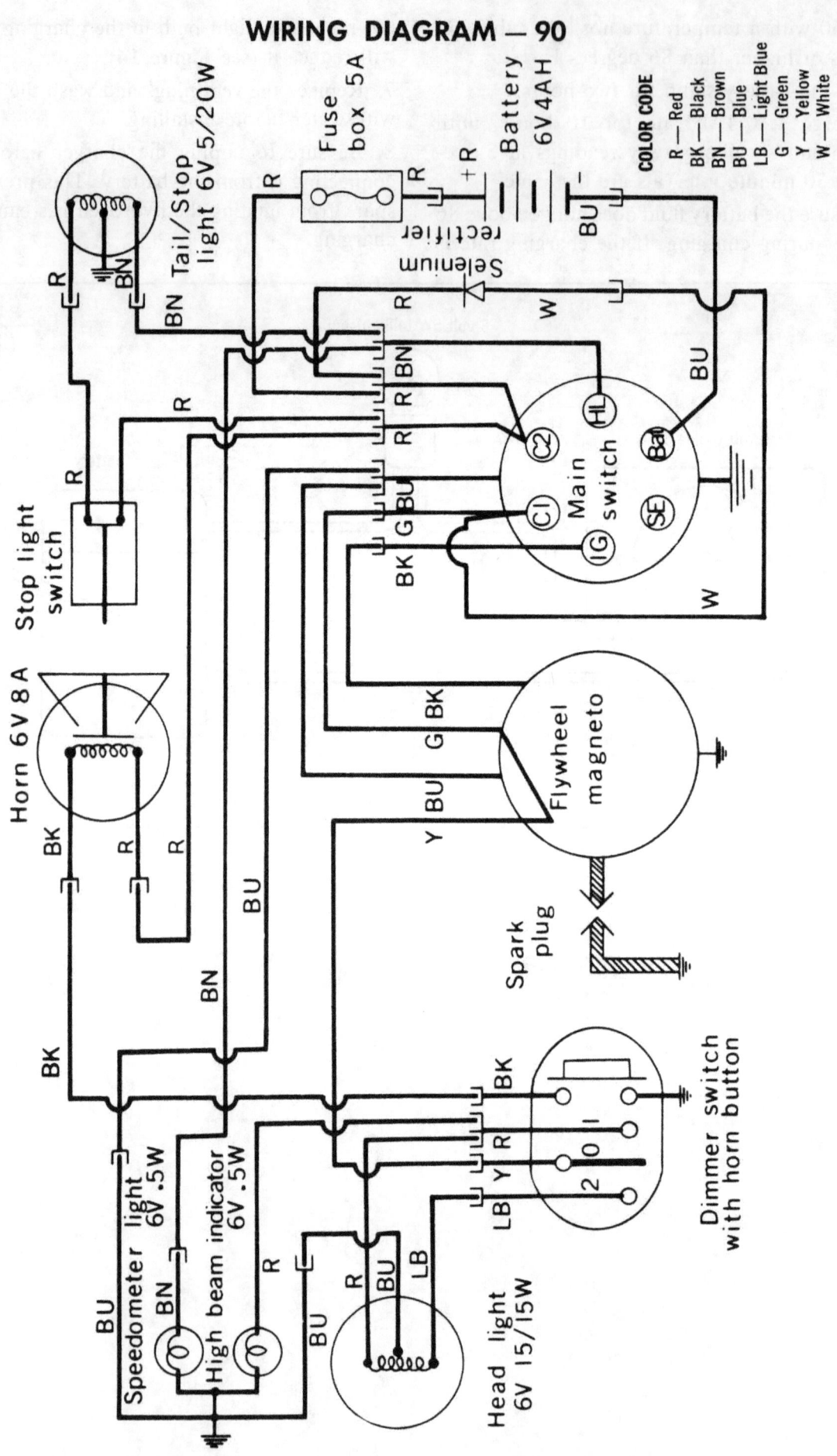

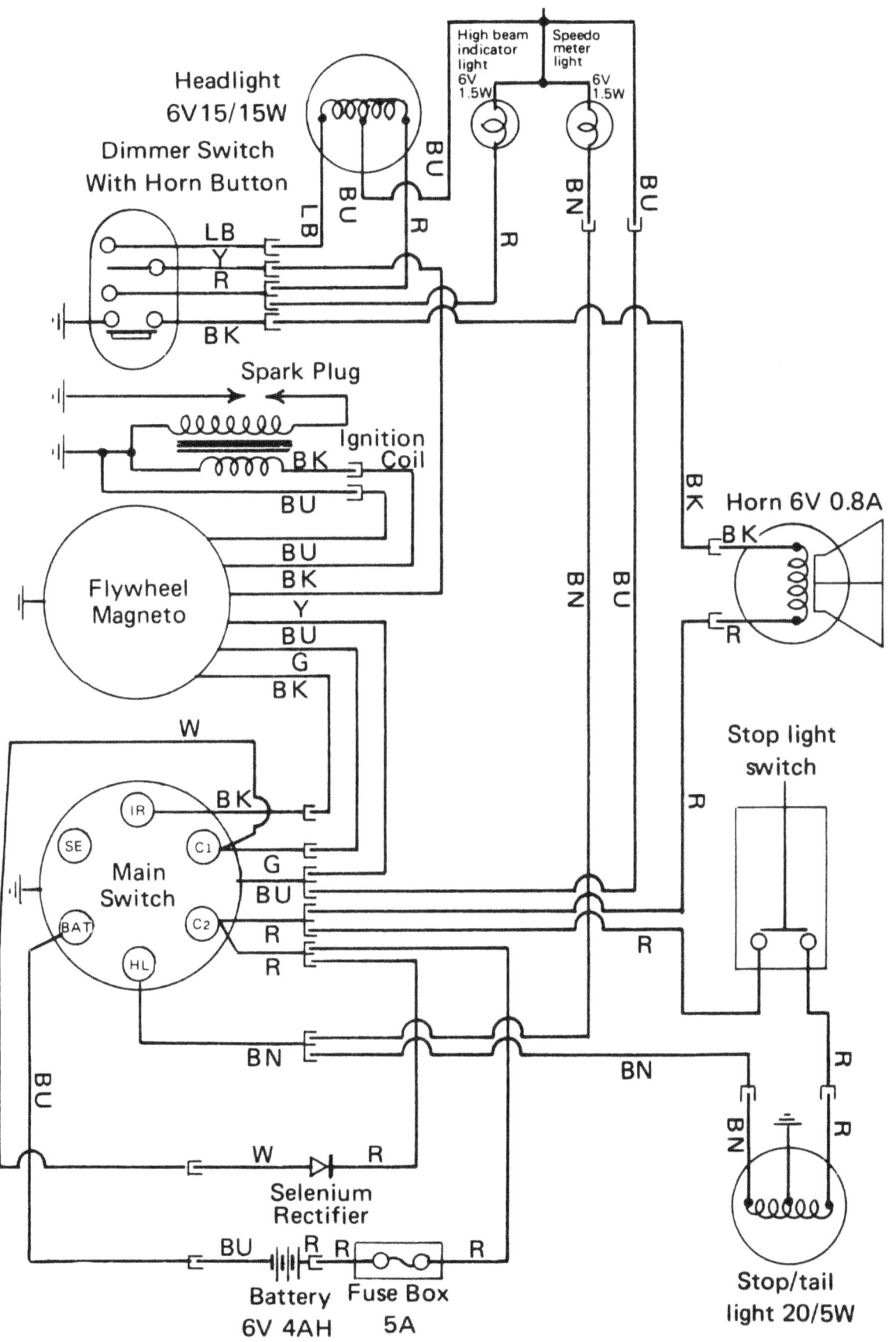

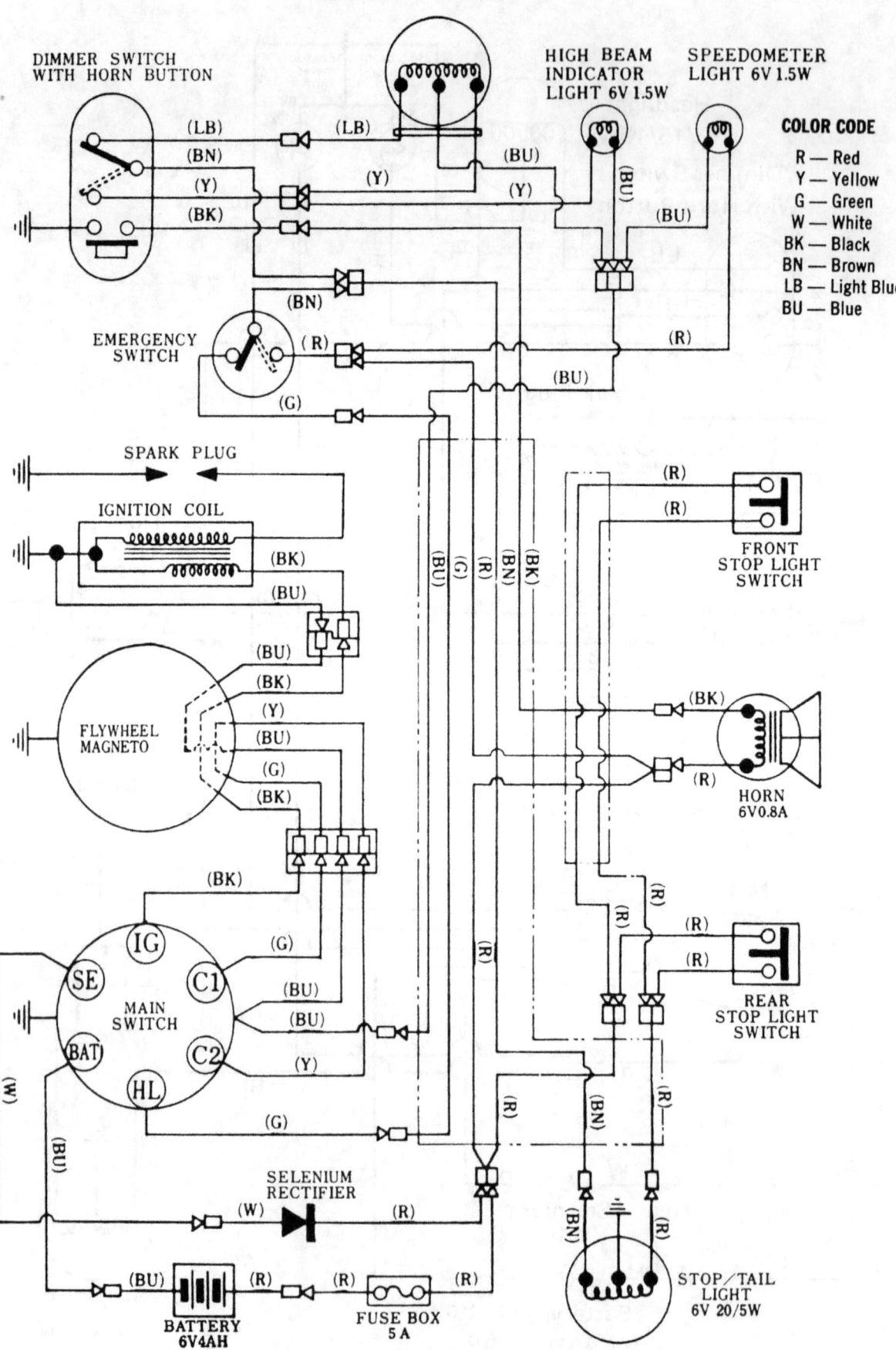

WIRING DIAGRAM — 100
(ALL OFF ROAD MODELS)

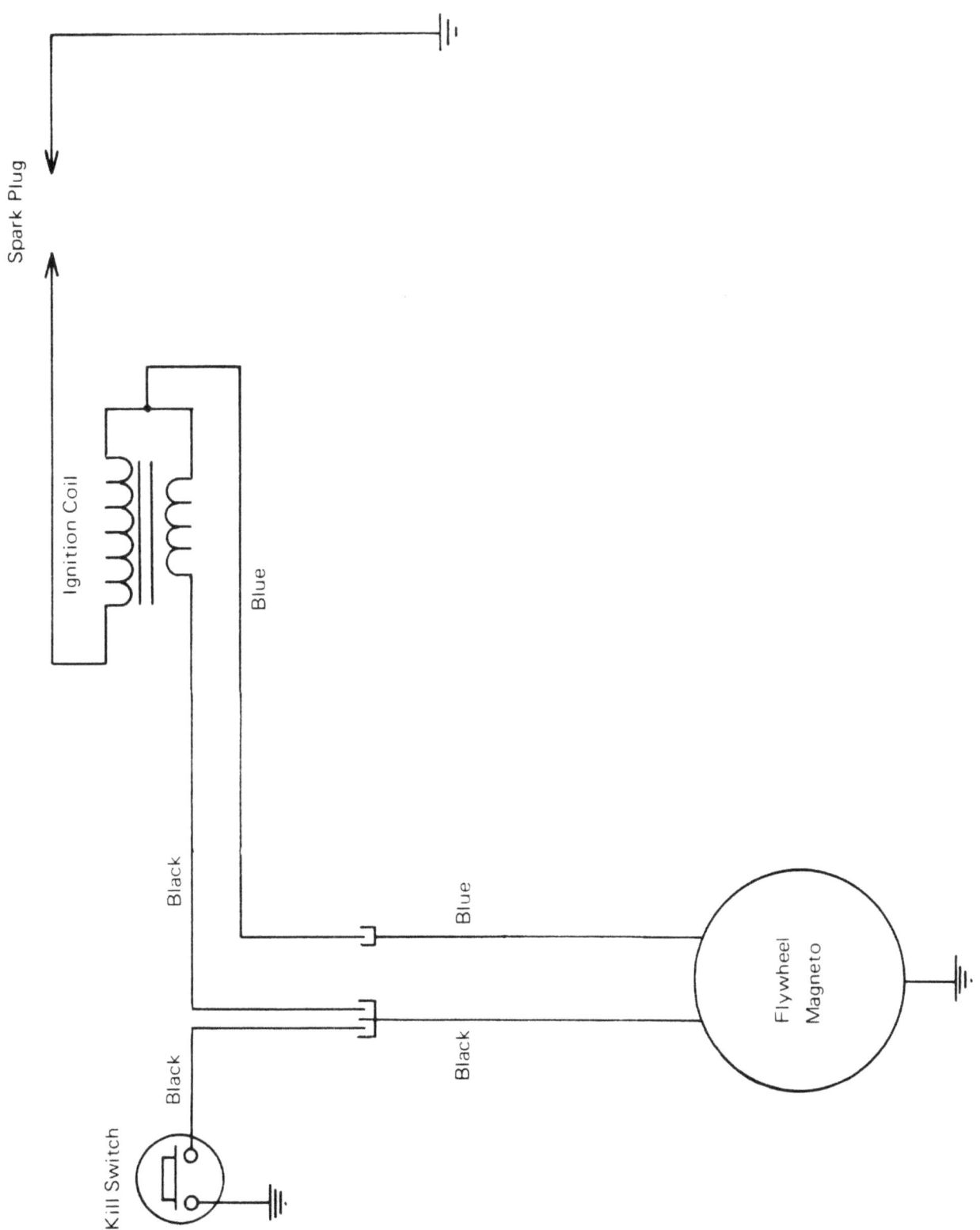

CHAPTER SEVEN

WHEELS, TIRES, AND BRAKES

The front wheel and brake are very critical components on any motorcycle. No matter how well the bike is running, if it can't be ridden safely it is useless.

The front brake must supply more braking effort than the rear to stop in the shortest possible distance. Proper maintenance will assure these operate safely.

Balance and shimmy are more critical on the front wheel than the rear. The front wheel affects all other handling aspects of the bike. The front wheel should be checked for balance, shimmy (side-to-side play), wobble (out-of-round), run-out, and proper tire inflation. Many of these problems go unnoticed at low speeds but become dangerous at highway speeds.

WHEEL REMOVAL

Figures 1 (page 88) **and 2** are exploded views of the front and rear hub assemblies. Refer to them in the following procedures.

Rear Wheel

1. Jack up the machine until the rear wheel is clear of the ground.
2. Put the transmission in first gear to prevent the chain from unwinding off the countershaft sprocket.
3. Remove the master link and remove chain from rear sprocket.
4. Remove the backing plate anchor bolt and knurled adjuster knob on the brake rod.
5. Remove the axle nut and then the wheel assembly from the swing arm.
6. Remove the axle from the hub assembly. Be careful to note the location of the spacer, washer and adjuster.

On some models, the sprocket drive flange will separate from the hub assembly when the axle is removed from the hub. Carefully note the position of the drive flange collar which fits into the drive flange bearing.

7. Remove the backing plate to inspect the brake assembly.

Front Wheel

1. Jack up the machine until the front wheel is clear of the ground.
2. Remove the knurled adjuster nut on the end of the brake cable and remove the assembly from the backing plate.
3. Remove the backing plate anchor bolt.
4. Loosen axle pinch bolt (**Figure 3**) 3 turns and unscrew axle counterclockwise.
5. Disconnect the brake light switch wires on Enduro models.

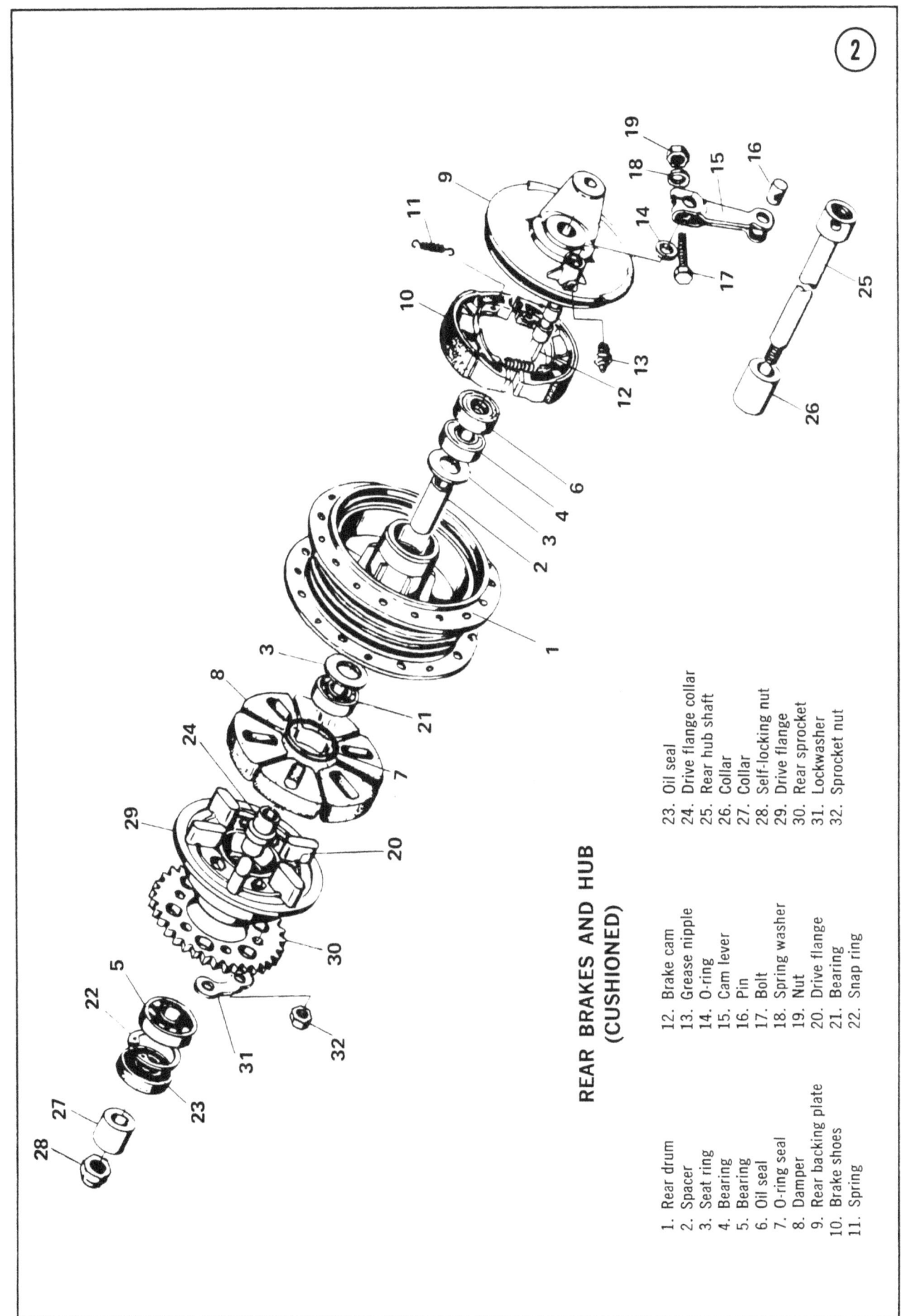

REAR BRAKES AND HUB (CUSHIONED)

1. Rear drum
2. Spacer
3. Seat ring
4. Bearing
5. Bearing
6. Oil seal
7. O-ring seal
8. Damper
9. Rear backing plate
10. Brake shoes
11. Spring
12. Brake cam
13. Grease nipple
14. O-ring
15. Cam lever
16. Pin
17. Bolt
18. Spring washer
19. Nut
20. Drive flange
21. Bearing
22. Snap ring
23. Oil seal
24. Drive flange collar
25. Rear hub shaft
26. Collar
27. Collar
28. Self-locking nut
29. Drive flange
30. Rear sprocket
31. Lockwasher
32. Sprocket nut

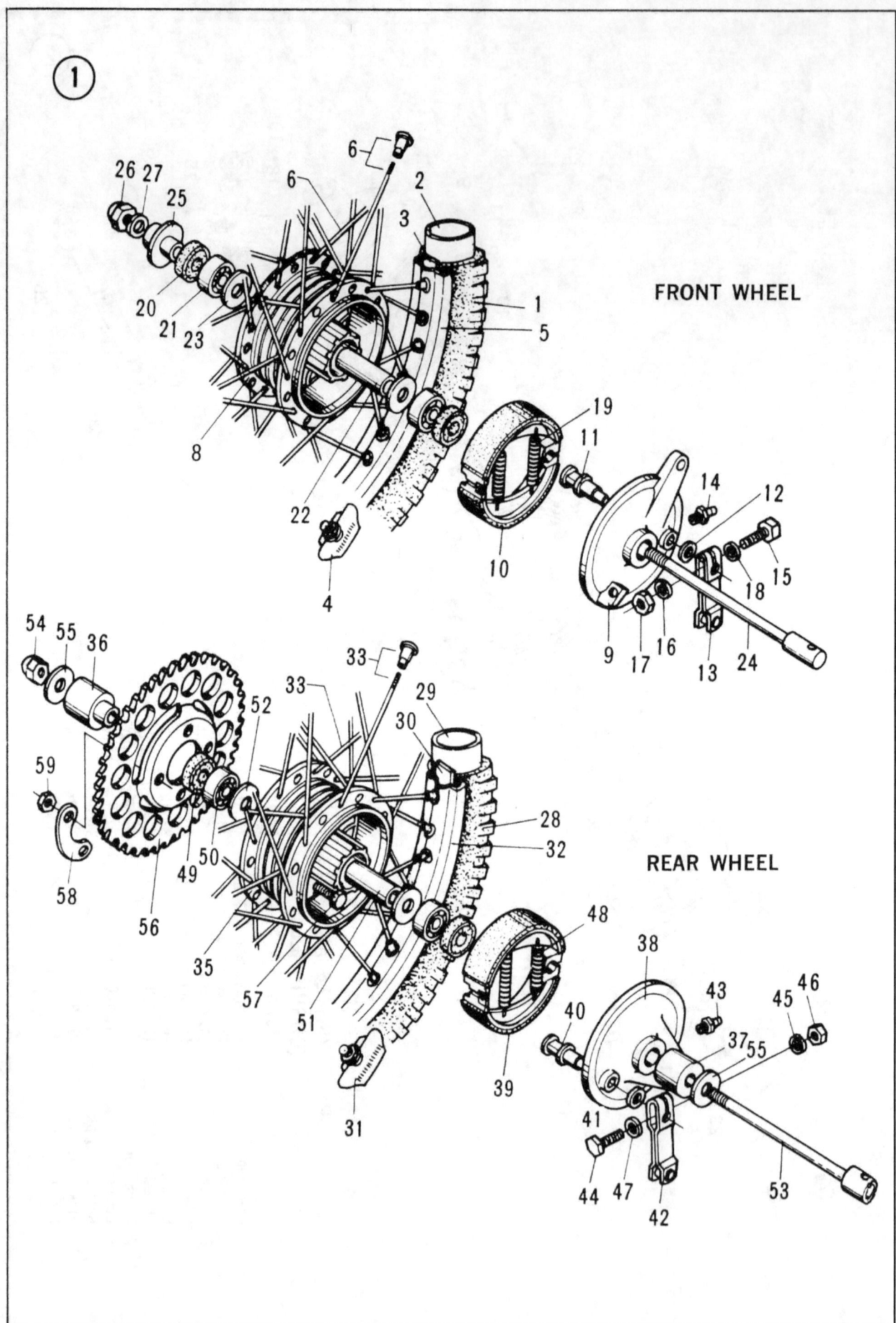

1. Tire
2. Tube
3. Tube protector
4. Tire security bolt
5. Rim
6. Spokes
7. Nipple set
8. Front drum
9. Backing plate
10. Brake shoes
11. Brake cam
12. Brake cam rubber ring
13. Brake cam lever
14. Grease nipple
15. Brake cam lever bolt
16. Spring washer
17. Lever nut
18. Washer
19. Brake shoe spring
20. Drum oil seal
21. Ball bearing
22. Spacer
23. Bearing seat ring
24. Hub shaft
25. Collar
26. Self-locking nut
27. Washer
28. Rear tire
29. Rear tube
30. Tube protector
31. Security bolt
32. Rim
33. Spokes
34. Nipple set
35. Rear drum
36. Bearing spacer
37. Shaft collar
38. Backing plate
39. Brake shoes
40. Cam
41. O-ring
42. Brake cam lever
43. Grease nipple
44. Lever bolt
45. Spring washer
46. Nut
47. Washer
48. Spring
49. Rear drum oil seal
50. Ball bearing
51. Spacer
52. Bearing seat ring
53. Rear hub shaft
54. Self-locking nut
55. Rear hub shaft washer
56. Rear sprocket
57. Sprocket bolt
58. Lockwasher
59. Nut

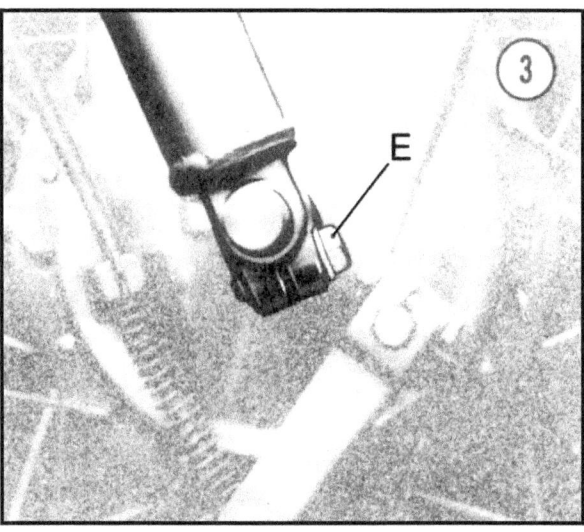

E. Pinch bolt, front axle shaft

6. Remove the axle while supporting the wheel. Note the spacer position.

7. Remove the wheel assembly from the forks.

8. Remove the backing plate to inspect the brake assembly.

Backing Plate Disassembly

1. Remove the brake shoe springs with needle nosed pliers and remove shoes.

2. Remove the cam lever pinch bolt and then the cam lever.

3. Remove the camshaft from the backing plate.

BRAKE INSPECTION AND CLEANING

1. Clean all parts except shoes with solvent and a stiff brush. Dry them with compressed air or a clean cloth.

2. Clean the brake shoes and drums with alcohol or lacquer thinner and dry.

3. Check the drums for wear or damage. If rusty, polish with sandpaper.

4. Check the wheel bearings in the hub for wear or damage.

5. Check the brake linings for wear or damage. Replace if the lining is less than 1/32 in. thick at its thinnest point, if it has oil or grease on it, or if it is badly grooved.

6. Rough up the brake lining surface with sandpaper before installing.

7. Check the backing plate for wear or damage.

8. Check the camshaft and cam lever for wear or damage. Be sure the camshaft rotates freely in the backing plate. Polish with sandpaper if it sticks.

9. Replace the camshaft dirt seals and brake shoe springs with new parts.

10. On models with cushioned rear hubs, replace the O-ring on top of the left side bearing boss. Put a film of grease on the new O-ring. Clean the O-ring seating surface in the sprocket drive flange.

11. Check the neoprene segments in the cushion drive. Replace if cracked, hardened, or worn to allow more than ½ in. travel at the hub rim.

WHEEL REASSEMBLY

Backing Plate

1. Smear a film of grease on the camshaft and brake shoe pivot points (see **Figure 4**).

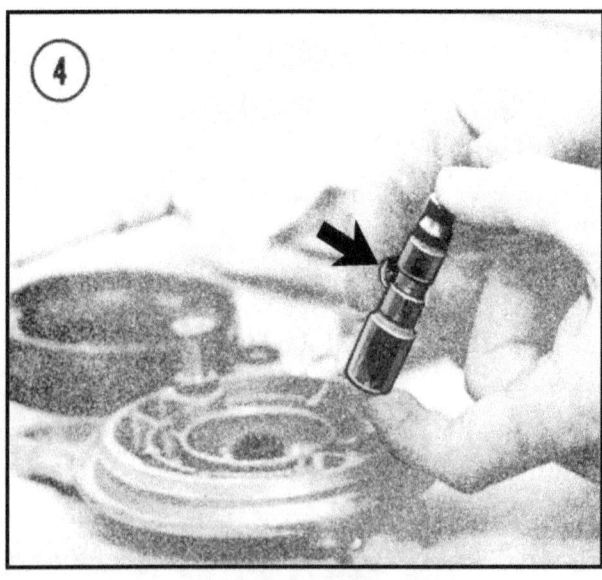

2. Install the camshaft in the backing plate and install a new dirt seal on the outside end of the shaft.

3. Install new springs on the shoes and install on the backing plate.

4. Install the cam lever so it will not swing past a 90 degree angle to the brake rod or cable.

Rear Wheel

1. Install the backing plate assembly in the wheel hub.

2. Install the steel washer, chain adjuster, and stepped spacer (with its stepped end toward the threaded end of the axle) on the axle.

3. Install the axle into the left side of the hub (see **Figure 5**).

F. Steel washers
G. Chain adjusters
H. Stepped spacer
I. Plain spacer
J. Axle nut

4. Install the plain spacer, chain adjuster, steel washer, and axle nut on the right end of the axle.

5. Install the wheel assembly in the swing arm and connect the brake rod.

6. Check to be sure the washers and adjusters are outside the swing arm.

7. Push the wheel all the way forward and install the chain.

8. Check to be sure the chain is aligned and tighten the axle nut lightly.

9. Install the backing plate anchor arm, with a new cotter pin for the nut.

10. Tighten the axle nut securely. Adjust the brake pedal and brake light switch.

11. Recheck chain alignment and tension.

12. On models with cushion drive, be sure the spacer in the sprocket drive flange inserts into the flange bearing and seats its shoulder against it. Be sure to engage the flange driving lugs in the neoprene segments before installing the wheel assembly in the swing arm.

Front Wheel

1. Install the backing plate assembly in the wheel hub.

2. Position the wheel assembly between the fork legs.

3. Install the speedometer drive between the hub and the left fork leg. Be sure the drive teeth engage in the drive slots in the hub.

4. Install the axle in the right fork leg. Lift the wheel hub and push the axle through to the speedometer drive assembly.

5. Install the steel spacer between the speedometer drive and the left fork leg. Push the axle through to the left fork leg and tighten lightly.

6. Check the speedometer drive engagement once more.

7. Install the backing plate anchor bar, using a new cotter pin for the nut.

8. Tighten the axle securely and tighten the pinch bolt on the right fork leg.

9. Install the brake cable assembly and adjust as described in Chapter Two.

10. Connect the brake light switch and adjust.

11. Be sure the speedometer cable has some slack at full extension of the front forks. Install the speedometer drive accordingly.

CHAIN SERVICE

See Chapter Two for details of periodic maintenance and replacement.

WHEEL AND SPOKE INSPECTION

1. Jack up the machine so the wheel is clear of the ground.

2. Spin the wheel and listen for bearing noise. The wheel should rotate smoothly and quietly.

3. Grasp 2 consecutive spokes and squeeze. If they move, tension is not sufficient. Another method for checking is to rap the individual spokes with a wrench or key. A properly tuned spoke will produce a clean ringing sound. A loose spoke will produce a dull thud. Tighten each loose spoke one quarter of a turn at the nipple working around the wheel until all are tight. Tightening each spoke fully at first will cause the wheel to be out-of-round.

4. Measure rim runout with a fixed pointer. It should not be more than 1/16 inch. If it is, true the rim by tightening spokes as detailed later.

5. Measure the eccentricity of the rim with a fixed pointer. If it exceeds 1/16 inch, true the rim by tightening spokes outlined later.

6. If any spoke nipple is tightened more than 2 full turns, remove the tire and tube and file off the protruding spoke end.

WHEEL BEARINGS

Disassembly

1. Remove the wheel from machine and the backing plate from the brake hub.

2. Remove the bearing seals from the hub with a screwdriver.

3. Heat the inside bearing boss with a torch and place the hub with the heated side down on the bench.

4. Tap out the bearing with a hammer and flat ended punch.

5. Set the bearing, spacer, and centering washers to one side.

6. Heat the outer bearing boss and tap out the bearing with the punch through the hub.

Inspection

1. Clean all parts in solvent and dry with compressed air.

2. Wash the hub with solvent and dry with compressed air.

3. Check all parts for wear or damage. Replace if in doubt. Bearings must be replaced as a set.

4. Replace the hub if the bearings fit loosely in their bosses.

Reassembly

1. Pack the bearings with grease. Heat the bearing boss and install the bearing squarely in its seat.

2. Turn the wheel over and install the spacer and centering washers.

3. Heat the other bearing boss and install the second bearing squarely.

4. Be sure the hub is cool before installing grease seals, with the grooved side toward the bearing.

5. Install the wheel on the machine as detailed in this chapter.

WHEEL TRUING

1. Remove the tire, tube, and rim rubber from the wheel.
2. Install the wheel in a truing stand or in the forks. See **Figure 6**.

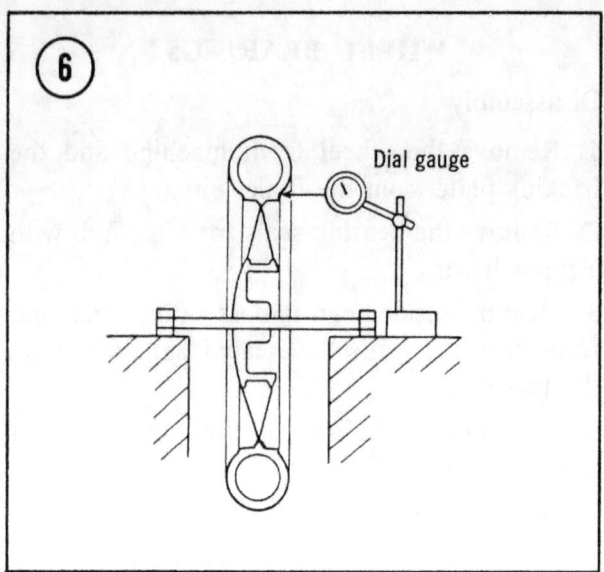

3. Position a dial indicator as shown in Figure 6. A piece of wire, bent to touch the rim at its maximum point of runout, can be used as a substitute for approximate truing.
4. Observe the dial indicator as the wheel is rotated through one complete revolution. Runout for all models should not exceed 0.12 in. (3.0mm).
5. Tighten 3 or 4 spokes on each side of the rim at the high spot to reduce the eccentricity.
6. Spin the wheel and check eccentricity again.
7. If more than 1 or 2 turns are required to lower the high spot, loosen the spokes on the opposite side to prevent flattening the rim.
8. Repeat until eccentricity is 1/64 to 1/32 in.
9. For side to side rim wobble, loosen the spokes on one side and tighten those on the other. Work slowly and evenly.
10. The rim runout should be no more than 1/64 to 1/32 in.

WHEEL LACING

1. To replace the rim only, tape each pair of spokes together and remove the rim. Install the new rim over the spokes and hub.
2. Install the spoke nipples beginning at the valve hole and working around the rim. Turn until 4 threads show at the bottom of the nipple.
3. Tighten each nipple one turn, working around the wheel from the valve hole.
4. When the spokes are fairly tight, true the wheel as detailed before.
5. If hub or spokes require replacing, lay new hub, spokes, and rim on the bench, with 18 A-spokes and 18 B-spokes in separate plies. The hooked ends of the 2 spokes have a different radius (see **Figure 7**).

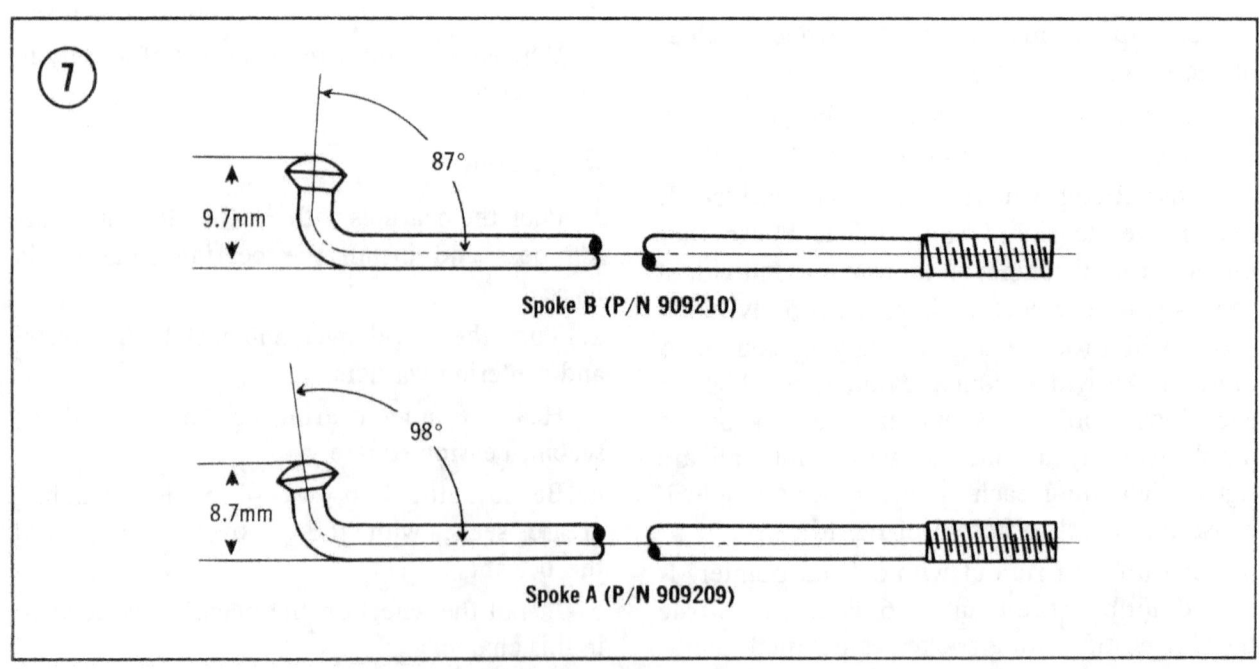

6. Install an A-spoke through a non-chamfered flange hole in the hub. Repeat until 9 A-spokes are installed (see **Figure 8**).

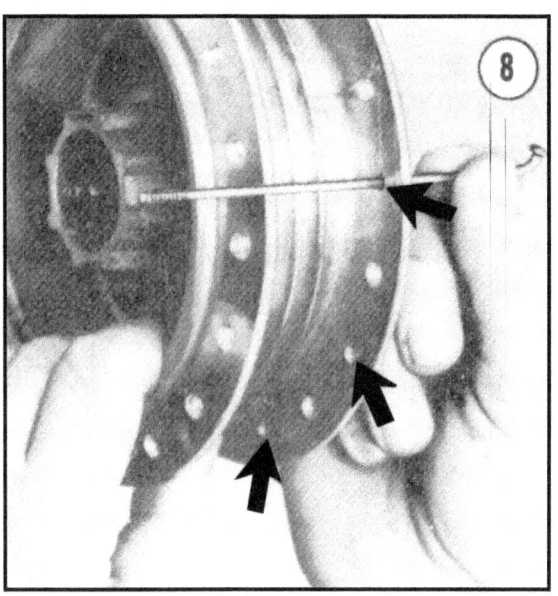

7. Set the hub face down on the bench with the spoke heads seated against the flange and set the rim over the spokes.

8. The rim spoke hole left of the valve hole should be angled up and to the left. Install a spoke in this hole and install the nipple (see **Figure 9**).

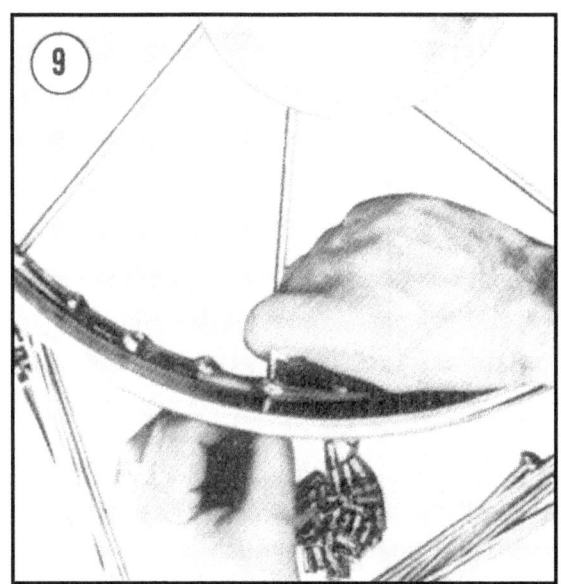

9. Install the next spokes in the fourth hole to the right of the first spoke. Repeat with every fourth hole until the nine spokes are fastened to the rim.

10. Turn the assembly over and install an A-spoke in a non-chamfered hole in the top flange and move the spoke to the right, crossing over 2 spokes in the opposite flange. Install the spoke in the next hole left of a spoke from the opposite flange (see **Figure 10**).

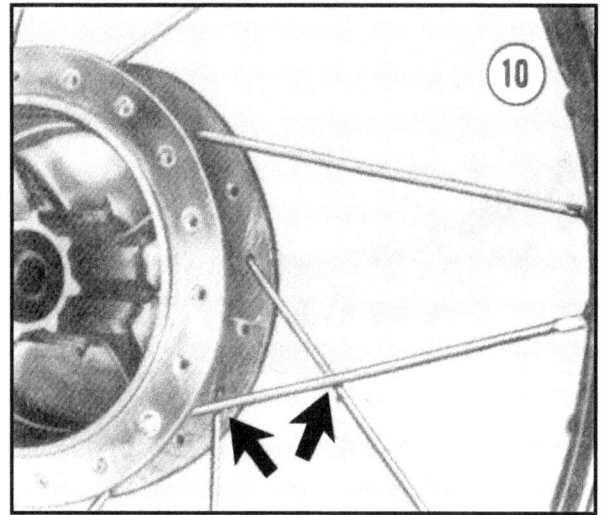

11. Work to the left on the hub, installing the other 8 A-spokes in every other hole in the flange and through the rim hole next left to a spoke from the lower flange.

12. Install a B-spoke in any hole in the top flange and move to the left, crossing over 2 A-spokes (see **Figure 11**) and install in the rim.

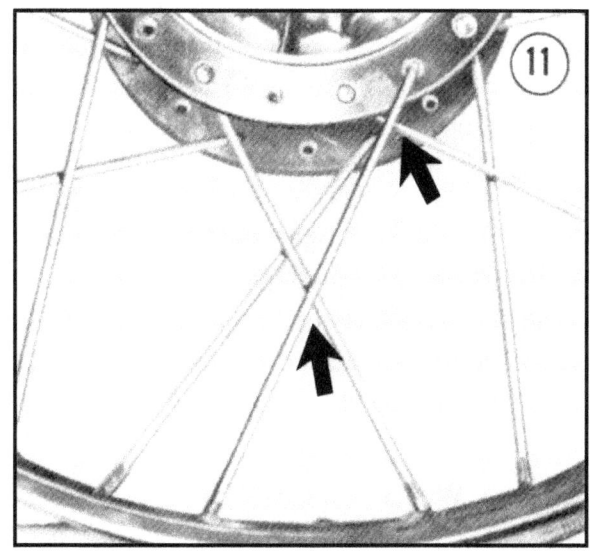

13. Install 9 B-spokes in the holes on this flange.
14. Turn the wheel over and repeat the process on the other side (see **Figure 12**) until all spokes are installed.

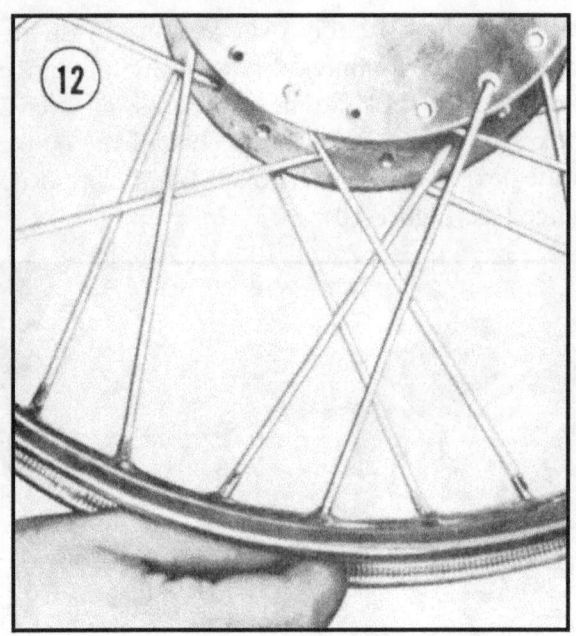

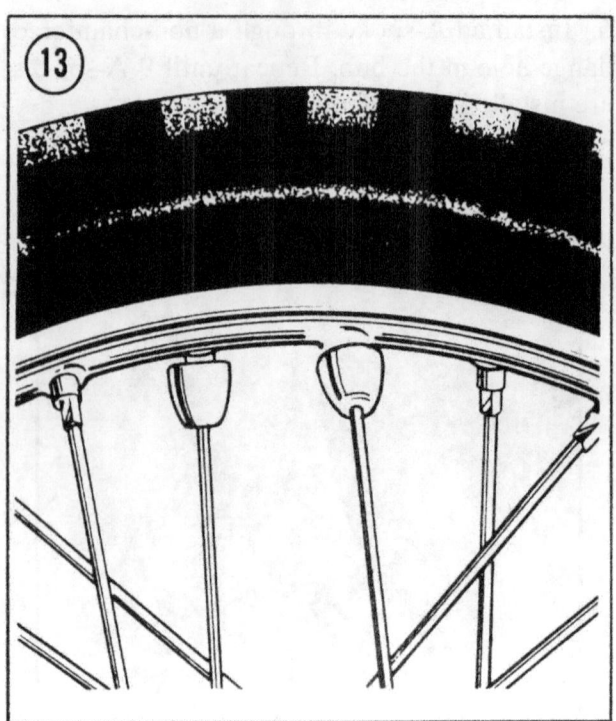

15. Tighten the spoke nipples until 4 threads remain on the spoke. Then tighten each spoke around the wheel one turn until all are tight.

16. True the wheel as detailed in this section.

WHEEL BALANCING

1. The wheels must revolve freely to balance them properly. Loosen the axle nuts and remove the rear chain to eliminate friction.

2. Spin the wheel and let it coast to a stop. Mark the top of the wheel with a piece of chalk. Repeat several times to ensure that this spot is the lightest. A perfectly balanced wheel will stop in random spots.

3. Weights are available to attach to the spokes where the wheel needs balancing. See **Figure 13**. After adding each weight, spin the wheel and proceed as indicated in Steps 1 and 2.

4. Check the tightness of the valve stem. A loose stem, as shown in **Figure 14**, can shift and be torn loose causing the tire to deflate.

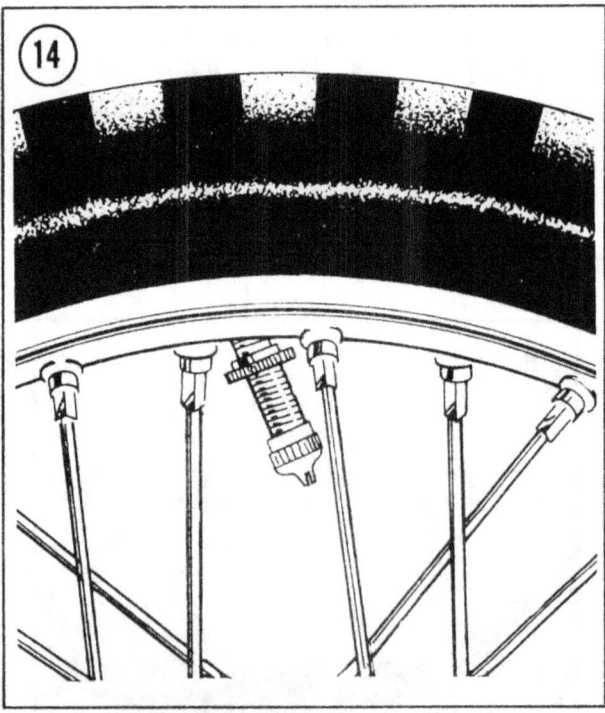

WHEEL ALIGNMENT

1. Measure the width of the 2 tires at their widest points.

2. Subtract smaller dimension from larger.

3. Nail a piece of wood, equal to the figure obtained in Step 2, to a straight piece of wood approximately 7 ft. long. See **Figure 15** (D).

4. Lay the straight edge on blocks 6 in. high and place against the tires. If the wheels are aligned, the board will touch each wheel at 2 points as shown in (B) Figure 15.

5. If the wheels are not aligned as in (A) or (C), Figure 15, the rear wheel must be shifted to correct the situation. The chain adjuster must cause the wheel to move toward the rear on the side shown for the error indicated in Figure 15.

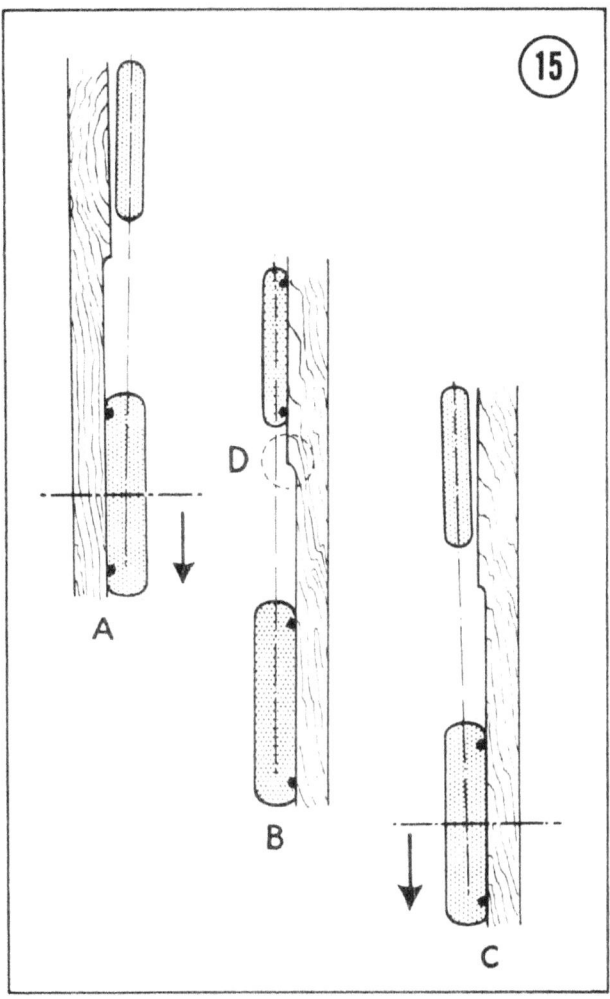

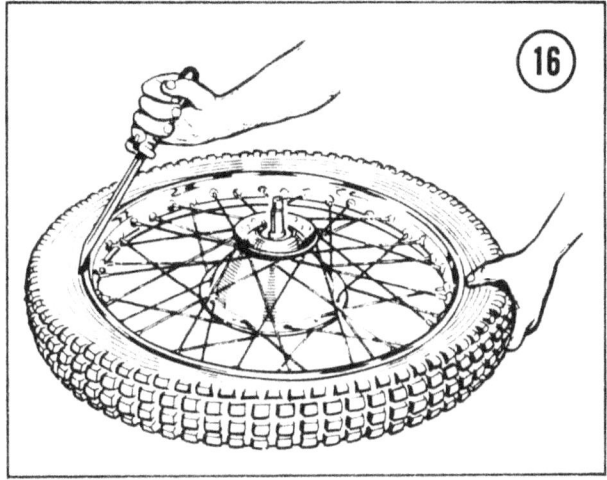

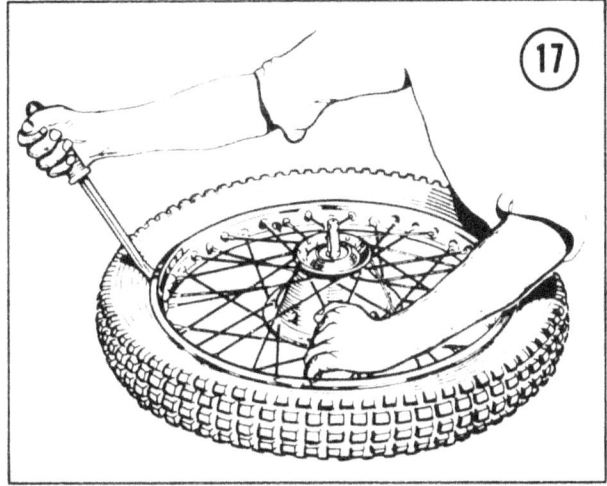

6. If the frame has been bent, this may not correct the misalignment. Replace the frame or have it aligned by an expert.

TIRE CHANGING AND REPAIR

1. Remove the valve core to deflate the tire.
2. Press the entire bead on both sides of the tire into the center of the rim.
3. Lubricate the beads with soapy water.
4. Insert the tire iron under the bead next to the valve. Force the bead on the opposite side of the tire into the center of the rim and pry the bead over the rim with the tire iron (**Figure 16**).
5. Insert a second tire iron next to the first to hold the bead over the rim. Then work around the tire with the first tire iron, prying the bead over the rim (see **Figure 17**). Be careful not to pinch the inner tube with the tire irons.
6. Remove the valve from the hole in the rim and remove the tube from the tire. Lift out and lay aside.

7. Stand the tire upright. Insert a tire iron between the second bead and the side of the rim that the first bead was pried over (see **Figure 18**). Force the bead on the opposite side from the tire iron into the center of the rim. Pry the second bead off the rim, working around as with the first bead.

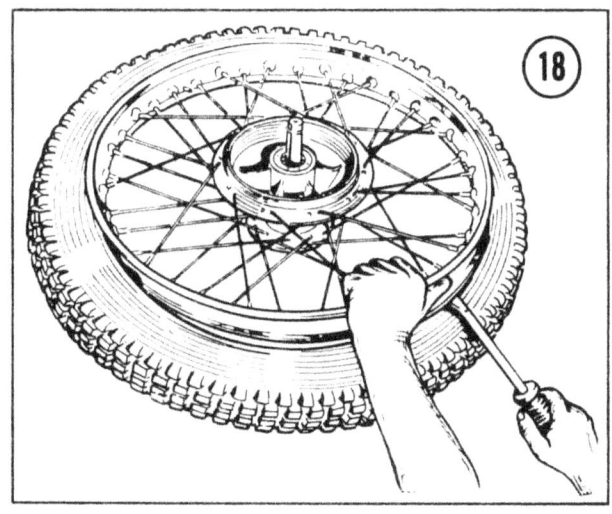

Tire Replacement

1. Carefully check the tire for any damage, especially inside.

2. A new tire may have balancing rubbers inside. These are not patches and should not be disturbed. A white spot near the bead indicates a lighter point on the tire. This should be placed next to the valve or midway between the 2 rim locks if they are installed.

3. Check that the spoke ends do not protrude through the nipples into the center of the rim to puncture the tube. File off any protruding spoke ends.

4. Be sure the rim rubber tape is in place with the rough side toward the rim.

5. Put the core in the tube valve. Put the tube in the tire and inflate just enough to round it out. Too much air will make installing the tire difficult, and too little will increase the chances of pinching the tube with the tire irons.

6. Lubricate the tire beads and rim with soapy water. Pull the tube partly out of the tire at the valve. Squeeze the beads together to hold the tube and insert the valve into the hole in the rim (see **Figure 19**). The lower bead should go into the center of the rim with the upper bead outside it.

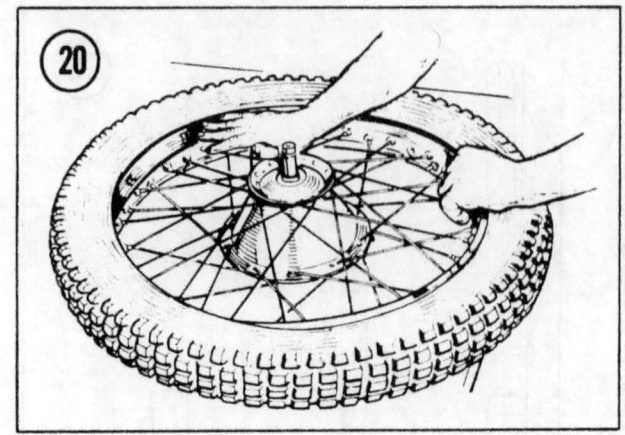

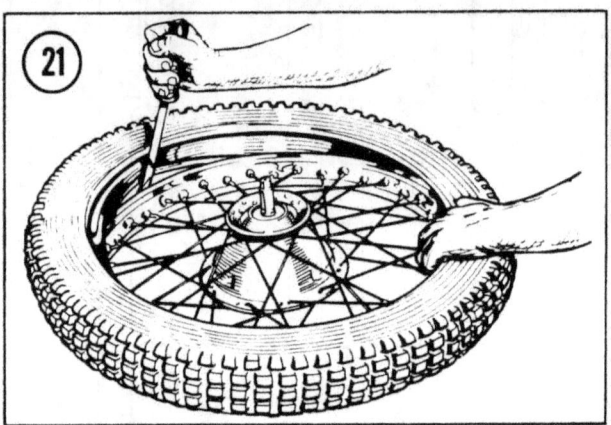

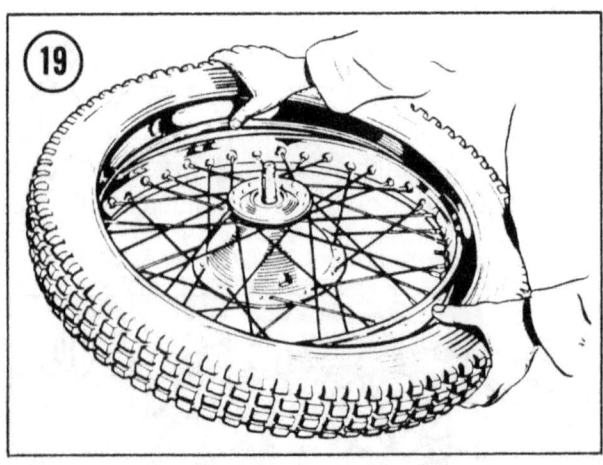

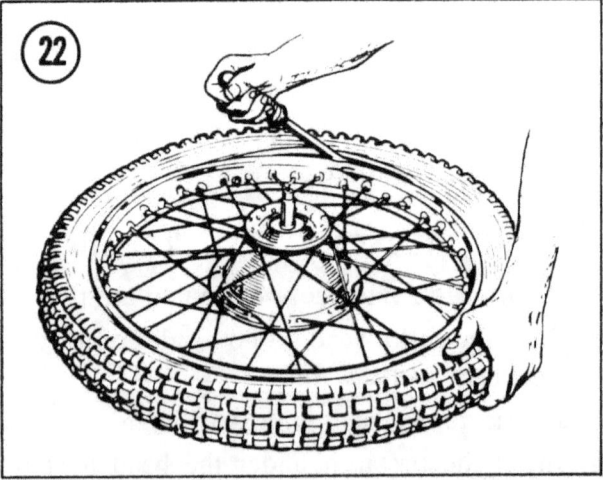

7. Press the lower bead into the rim center on each side of the valve, working around the tire in both directions (see **Figure 20**). Use a tire iron for the last few inches of bead (see **Figure 21**).

8. Press the upper bead into the rim opposite the valve. Pry the bead into the rim on both sides of the initial point with a tire iron, working around the rim to the valve (see **Figure 22**).

9. Wriggle the valve to be sure the tube is not trapped under the bead. Set the valve squarely in its hole before screwing on the valve nut to hold it against the rim.

10. Check the bead on both sides of the tire for even fit around the rim. Inflate the tire slowly to seat the beads in the rim. It may be necessary to bounce the tire to complete the seating. Inflate to the required pressure. Balance the wheel as described previously.

CHAPTER EIGHT

STEERING, SUSPENSION, AND FRAME

The front suspension is a critical part of the motorcycle for the rider's safety. A loose fork stem, worn steering bearings, or bent fork tubes can cause serious steering and handling problems at high speeds. Follow the chart and directions on periodic maintenance outlined in Chapter Two. Refer any problems to the troubleshooting section in Chapter Three.

The frame should never require any type of periodic maintenance other than an occasional spot check near tube junctures for signs of cracking or metal fatigue. If the motorcycle has been involved in an accident, regardless of severity, it should be checked by a shop for bends or fracture. Some damage can be so slight as to escape visual inspection. The only positive method, in some cases, may be magnafluxing (a process using magnetic force fields and iron particles to detect hairline fractures).

FRAME SERVICE

Figure 1 is an exploded view of the frame. Frames on the other models are similar.

1. Check the frame carefully at regular intervals for wear, damage, or metal fatigue.
2. Make repairs by brazing rather than welding.
3. Replace a seriously damaged frame. No alignment jibs are available.
4. Hodaka paint in spray cans is available from dealers for minor touch-up.

STEERING HEAD

Adjustment

1. Jack up the motorcycle so the front wheel is off the ground.
2. Loosen the steering head nut (see **Figure 2**). Loosen the steering head bolt and top triple clamp pinch bolts on models so equipped.

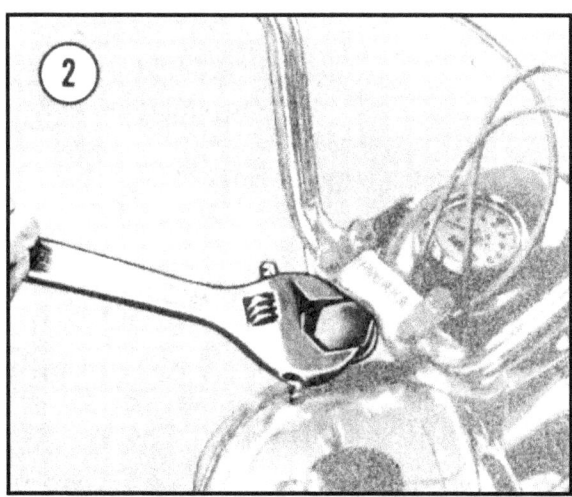

3. Loosen the notched inner nut with a hammer and flat end punch (see **Figure 3**). Loosen the top inner race with the hammer and punch.

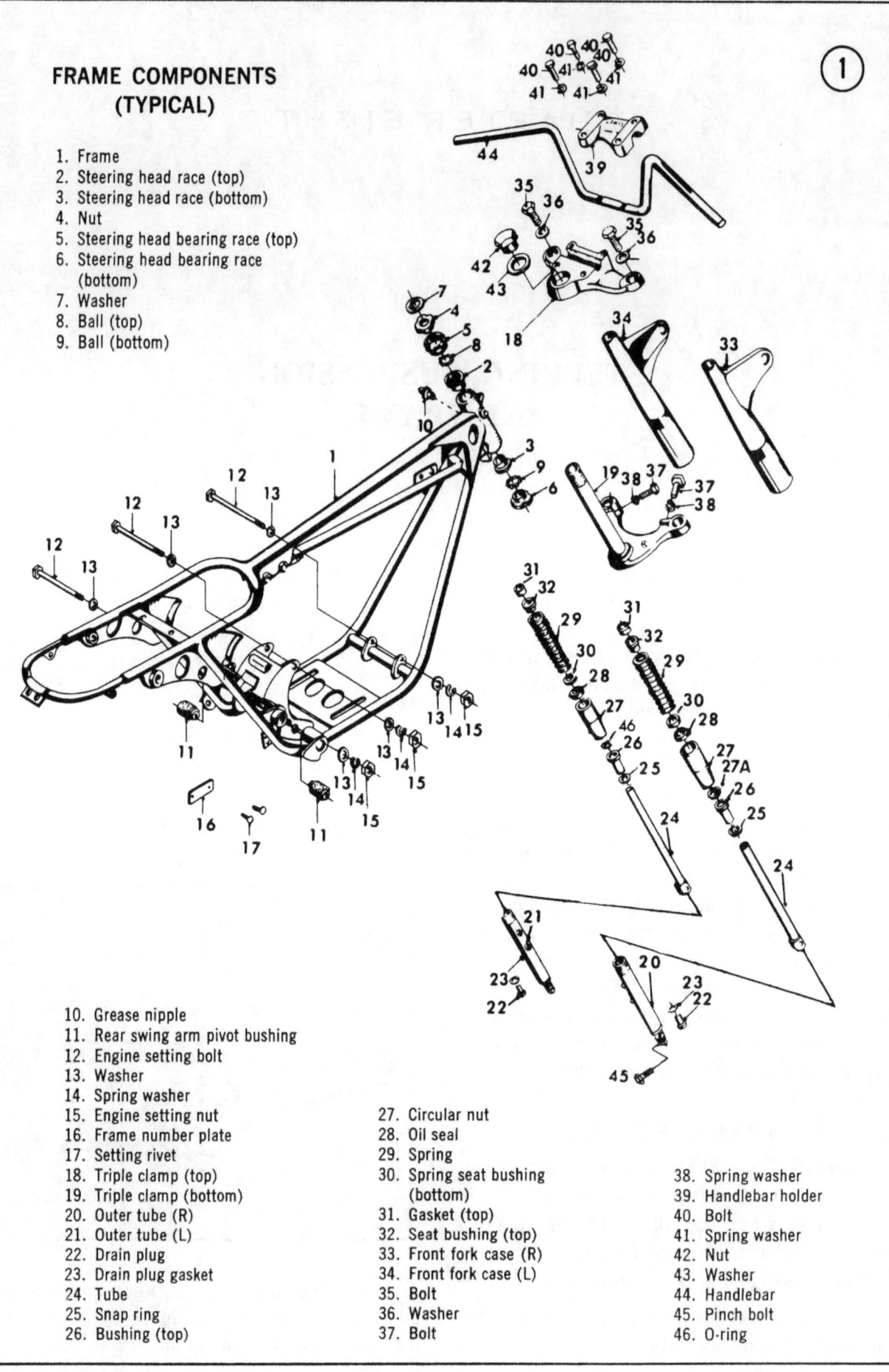

FRAME COMPONENTS (TYPICAL)

1. Frame
2. Steering head race (top)
3. Steering head race (bottom)
4. Nut
5. Steering head bearing race (top)
6. Steering head bearing race (bottom)
7. Washer
8. Ball (top)
9. Ball (bottom)
10. Grease nipple
11. Rear swing arm pivot bushing
12. Engine setting bolt
13. Washer
14. Spring washer
15. Engine setting nut
16. Frame number plate
17. Setting rivet
18. Triple clamp (top)
19. Triple clamp (bottom)
20. Outer tube (R)
21. Outer tube (L)
22. Drain plug
23. Drain plug gasket
24. Tube
25. Snap ring
26. Bushing (top)
27. Circular nut
28. Oil seal
29. Spring
30. Spring seat bushing (bottom)
31. Gasket (top)
32. Seat bushing (top)
33. Front fork case (R)
34. Front fork case (L)
35. Bolt
36. Washer
37. Bolt
38. Spring washer
39. Handlebar holder
40. Bolt
41. Spring washer
42. Nut
43. Washer
44. Handlebar
45. Pinch bolt
46. O-ring

4. Tighten the race until the steering binds slightly. Then loosen until the wheel falls left or right of its own weight.

5. Tighten the inner nut against the race. Tighten the steering head nut or bolt.

Lubrication

1. Lubricate the lower bearing with a grease gun on the nipple (see **Figure 4**).

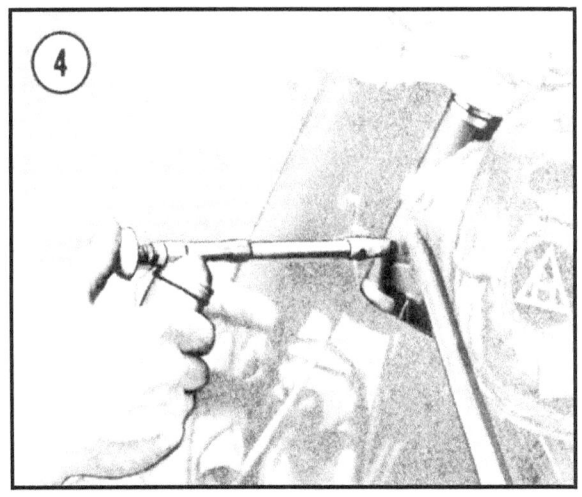

2. Lubricate the top bearing by repacking with grease when the steering head requires overhaul.

Disassembly

1. Remove the handlebar setting bolts (see **Figure 5**) and handlebar holder.

2. Remove the steering head nut and the top triple clamp.

3. Remove the headlight lens from the case and disconnect the wiring harness.

4. Remove inner steering head nut (**Figure 6**).

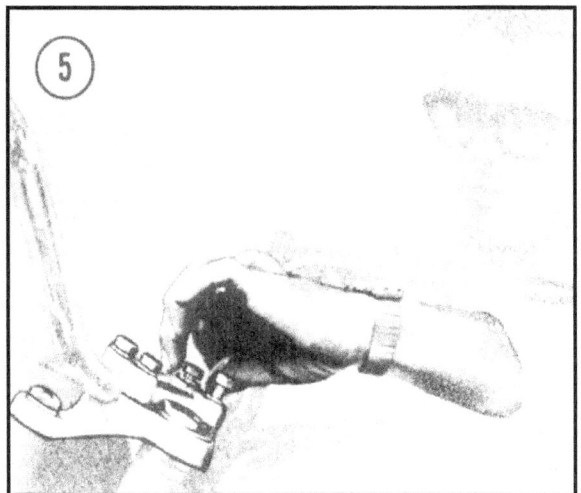

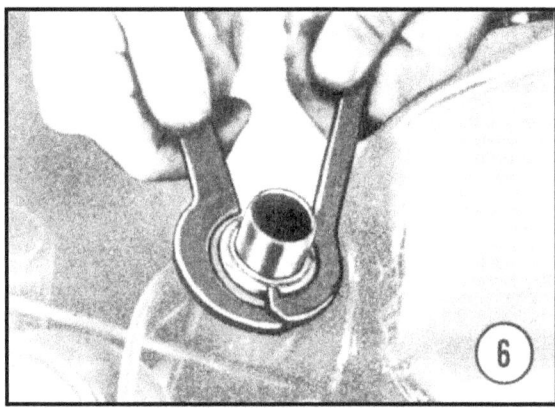

5. Remove the top race and lower the forks from the steering head.

6. Be sure to catch any steel balls that fall out of the races.

Inspection

1. Clean all parts with solvent and dry with compressed air.

2. Clean old grease from the steering head tube and races with cloth and solvent.

3. Check all parts carefully for wear or damage. Replace if necessary. If any bearing is replaced, replace the whole set.

Reassembly

1. Grease the bearing races heavily with chilled wheel bearing grease to hold the balls in place.

2. Pack the 23 large ball bearings in the lower race (see **Figure 7**) and the 25 small bearings in the top race.

3. Install the threaded top inner race on the bearings and install the forks.

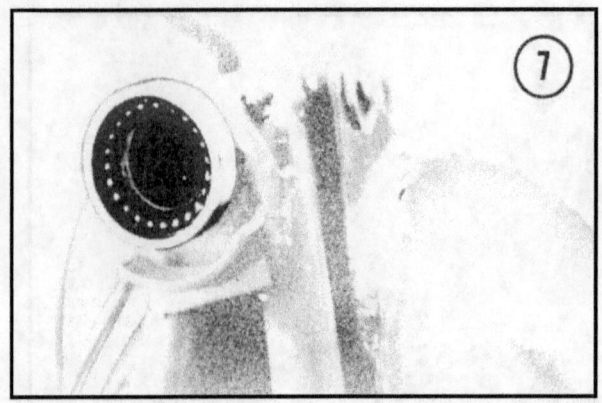

4. Tighten the inner race on the fork assembly threads. Be sure no bearings are lost during this operation.
5. Install the inner and outer nuts and adjust steering as detailed above.
6. Install the other components in reverse sequence.

FRONT FORKS

Figures 8, 9, and 10 are exploded views of the forks used on the Hodaka.

Alignment

1. Loosen the triple clamp pinch bolts.
2. Hold the front wheel between the legs and twist the handlebar to align.
3. Tighten the pinch bolts and check alignment. Wheel alignment is covered in Chapter Seven.

Removal

1. Remove the front wheel assembly as detailed in Chapter Seven.
2. Remove the front fender. Remove the top triple clamp bolts and loosen the bottom triple clamp bolts.
3. Remove the fork assembly and turn upside down to drain.

Disassembly

Refer to Figures 8, 9, and 10.

Enduro Forks:

1. Clamp the lower fork leg in a soft jawed vise.
2. Remove the circular nut with a strap wrench or pipe wrench.
3. Remove the fork tube from the leg and remove the tube bushing.
4. Remove the bushing circlip and circular nut O-ring.
5. Remove the spring cup seal from the circular nut with a punch.

No. 938700 Forks:

1. Remove the internal spring and neoprene dust seal.
2. Clamp the lower fork leg in soft jawed vise.
3. Remove the outer nut with a strap wrench.
4. Remove the fork tube and bushing.

No. 938750 Forks:

1. Replace the spring, spacer, and tube cap after draining oil.
2. Remove the Allen screws in the bottom of the lower fork leg.
3. Remove the cap, spacer, spring, and fork cylinder from the fork tube.

Inspection

1. Clean all parts with solvent and a stiff brush and dry with compressed air.
2. Check all parts carefully for wear or damage. Replace if in doubt.
3. Roll the fork tubes on a sheet of plate glass to check for straightness.
4. Compare the free height of the springs. Change as a set if the difference is ¼ in. or more. The springs must pre-load ½ in. when installed in the forks.
5. Replace the O-rings, oil seals, circlips, and gaskets with new parts.

Reassembly

1. Coat the fork tubes and fork legs with oil.
2. Install the O-rings in the lower circular nut.
3. Install the seals in the upper circular nut and oil the seals.
4. Install the circlips on bushings and install the bushings in the tubes.
5. Install the tubes into the fork legs and seat the bushings.
6. Install the circular nut and tighten securely.

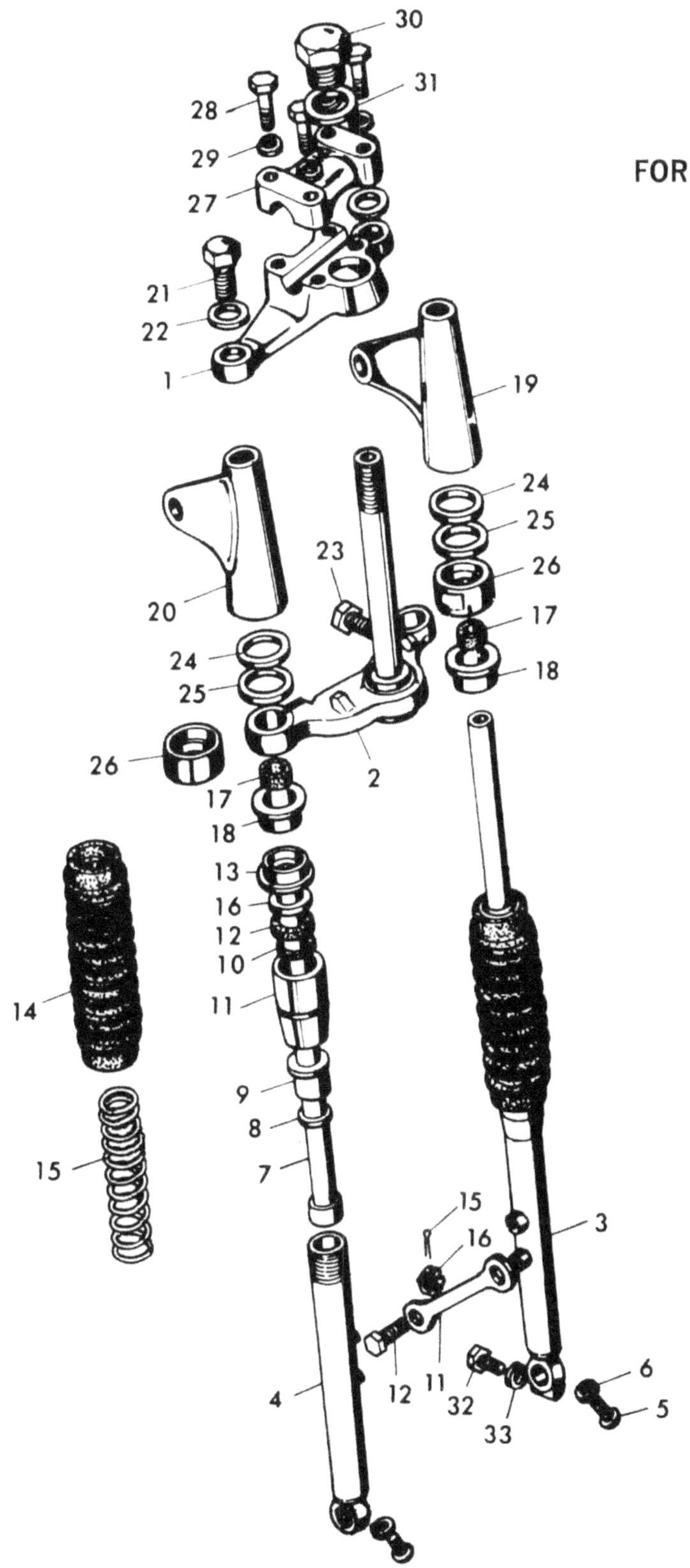

FORKS (ENDURO MODELS ONLY)

1. Handlebar plate
2. Steering fork bracket
3. Outer tube (R)
4. Outer tube (L)
5. Drain plug
6. Gasket
7. Tube
8. Snap ring
9. Bushing (top)
10. O-ring seal
11. Circular nut
12. Oil seal
13. Rubber boots guide
14. Rubber boots
15. Inner spring
16. Spring seat bushing (bottom)
17. Gasket
18. Spring seat bushing (top)
19. Front fork case (R)
20. Front fork case (L)
21. Setting bolt
22. Washer
23. Bolt
24. Fork cover seat
25. Gasket
26. Fork bracket cover
27. Handlebar holder
28. Bolt
29. Spring washer
30. Nut
31. Washer
32. Pinch bolt
33. Spring washer

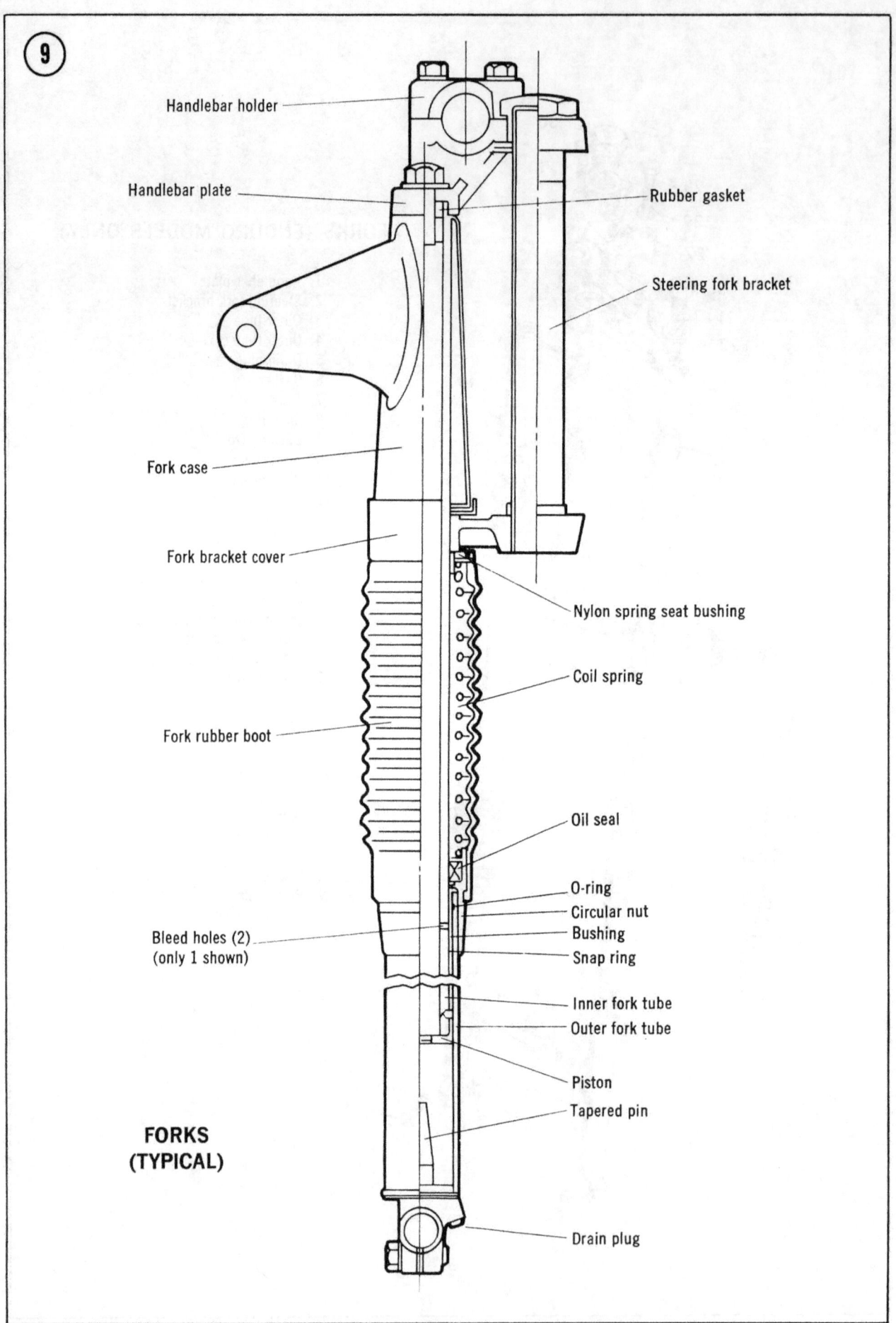

FORKS (OFF-ROAD AND COMPETITION MODELS ONLY)

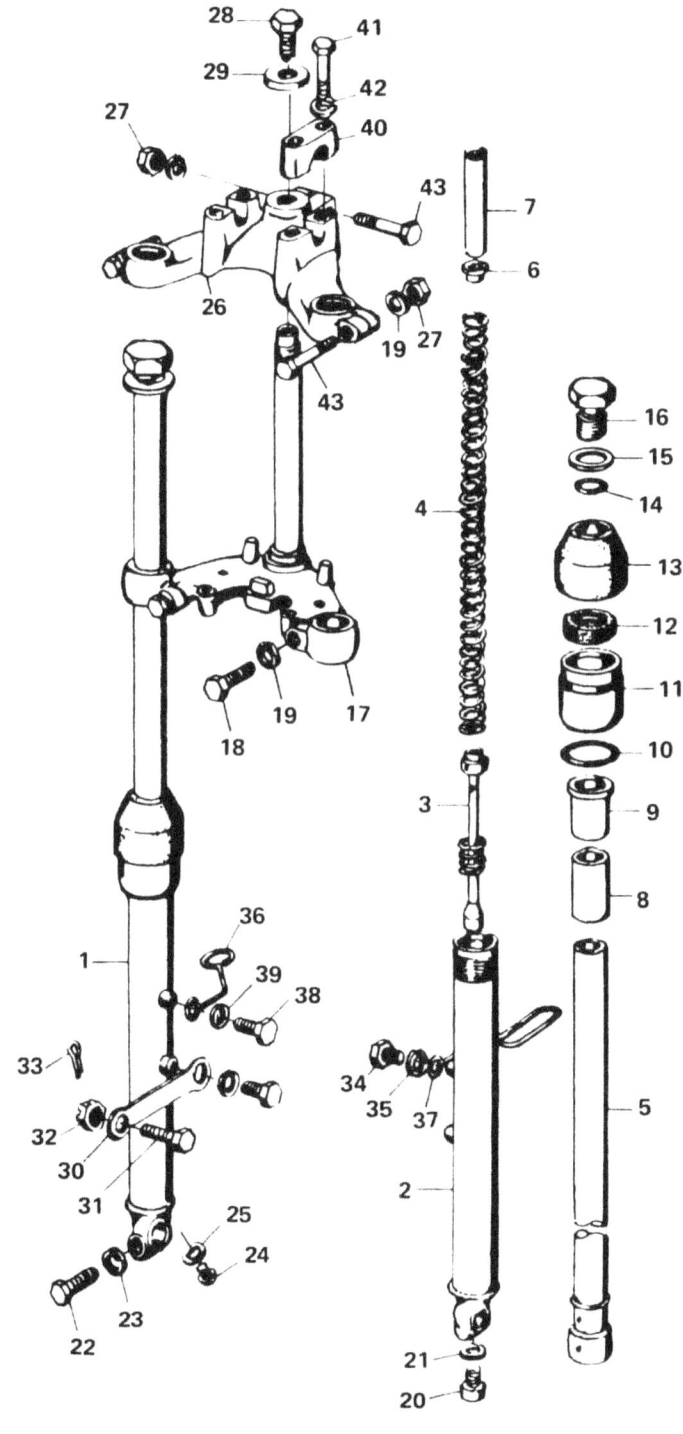

1. Right outer fork tube
2. Left outer fork tube
3. Cylinder, complete
4. Spring
5. Inner fork tube
6. Spring guide
7. Spacer (top)
8. Spacer (bottom)
9. Sliding bushing
10. O-ring seal
11. Outer nut
12. Oil seal
13. Dust seal
14. O-ring seal
15. Cap washer
16. Cap
17. Steering fork bracket
18. Bolt
19. Spring washer
20. Bolt
21. Gasket
22. Pinch bolt
23. Spring washer
24. Drain plug
25. Gasket
26. Handle plate
27. Nut
28. Steering head bolt
29. Washer
30. Bracket
31. Bolt
32. Castellated nut
33. Cotter pin
34. Bolt
35. Spring washer
36. Front brake guide (bottom)
37. Speedometer cable guide (bottom)
38. Bolt
39. Spring washer
40. Handlebar holder
41. Bolt
42. Spring washer
43. Handle plate bolt

7. Install the steel spring seat bushings, springs, and nylon bushings over the fork tubes.

8. Install the rubber seals in the tube tops.

9. On No. 938700 forks, install the fork spring, guide, spacer, and cap to hold the fork cylinder against the bottom of the fork leg.

10. Install Allen screws and tighten securely.

Installation

1. On Enduro models, pull the fork tube into position with a T-handled tool (see **Figure 11**). Note that the top inner race must remain in contact with the bearings during reassembly. See **Figure 12**.

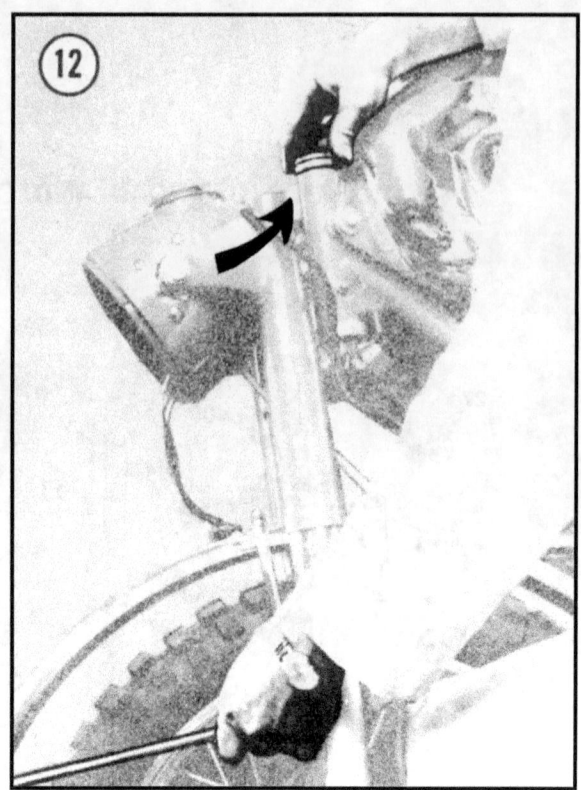

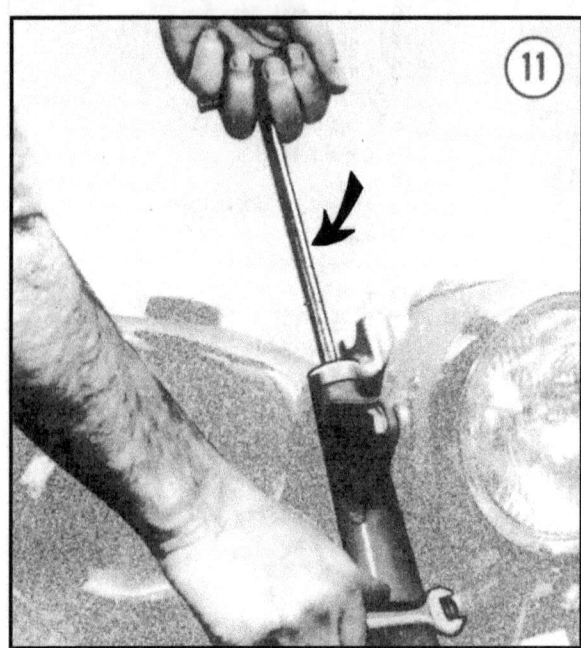

2. On off-road models, install the fork tubes in the triple clamps.

3. Fill each fork tube with SAE 20 oil. The correct amount is shown in the *Quick Reference Data* at the beginning of the book.

4. Install the top caps or triple clamp holding bolts and tighten.

5. Install the front fender and front wheel assembly.

REAR SUSPENSION SERVICE

Figure 13 illustrates a typical rear suspension assembly.

1. Check shock absorbers for wear or damage. Replace if necessary. They are not repairable.

2. Check the swing arm for wear or damage. Replace if necessary.

3. Replace swing arm bushings every 10,000 miles, or more often if the machine is used for racing.

FENDER SERVICE

A typical front fender is shown in **Figure 14**.

1. Check all parts for wear or damage. Replace if necessary with the new plastic fenders. These will last longer than stock.

2. Replace the rubber washers every 10,000 miles or once a year, if worn or cracked.

SEAT

1. The seat cover can be replaced with another one from a dealer.

2. Remove the seat and the metal clips holding the cover to the base (**Figure 15**).

3. Remove the old cover and work the new one to make it pliable.

4. Stretch the new cover over the cushion and fasten the clips (see **Figure 16**).

5. Work from both ends toward the middle, compressing the foam for a good fit.

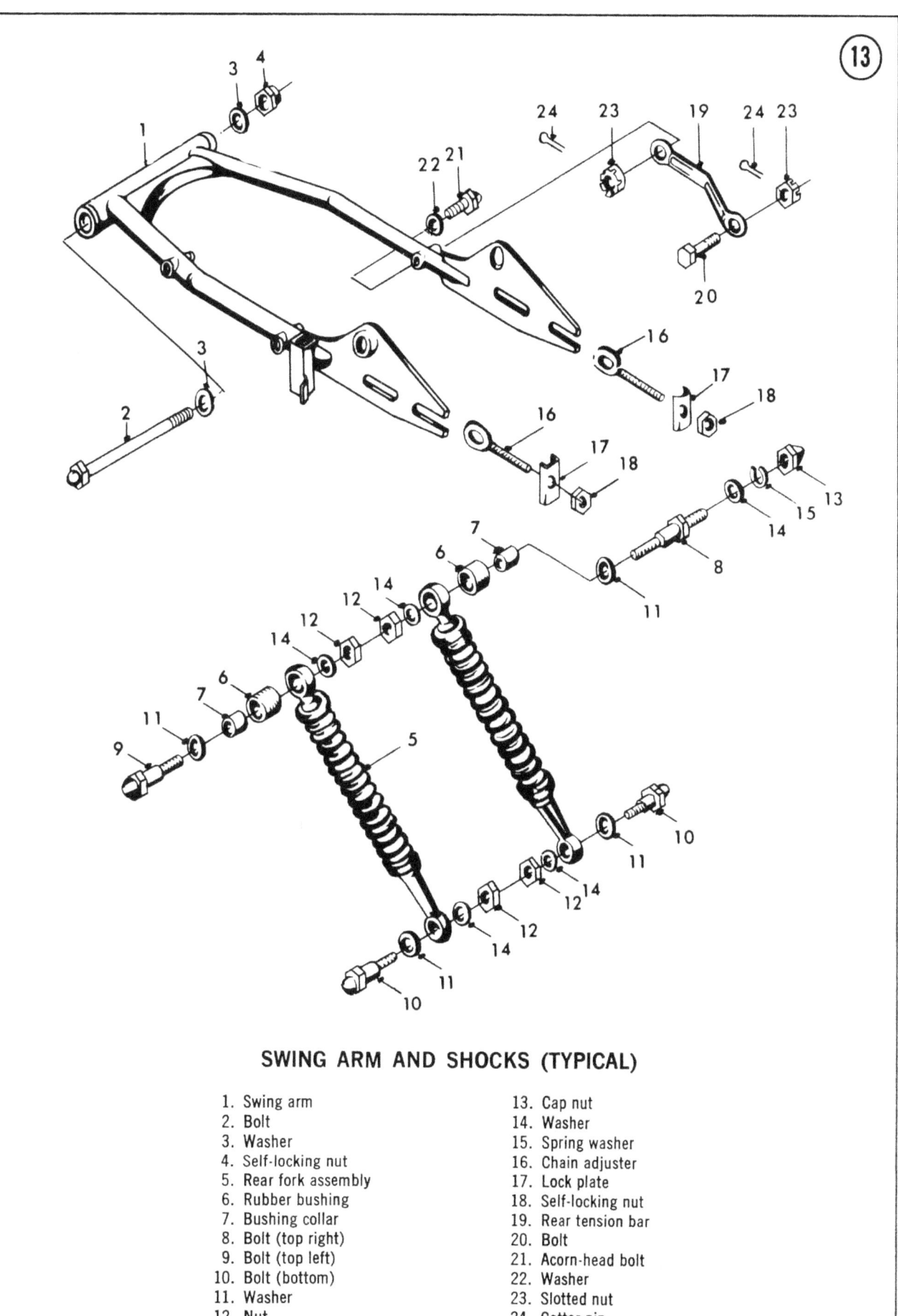

SWING ARM AND SHOCKS (TYPICAL)

1. Swing arm
2. Bolt
3. Washer
4. Self-locking nut
5. Rear fork assembly
6. Rubber bushing
7. Bushing collar
8. Bolt (top right)
9. Bolt (top left)
10. Bolt (bottom)
11. Washer
12. Nut
13. Cap nut
14. Washer
15. Spring washer
16. Chain adjuster
17. Lock plate
18. Self-locking nut
19. Rear tension bar
20. Bolt
21. Acorn-head bolt
22. Washer
23. Slotted nut
24. Cotter pin

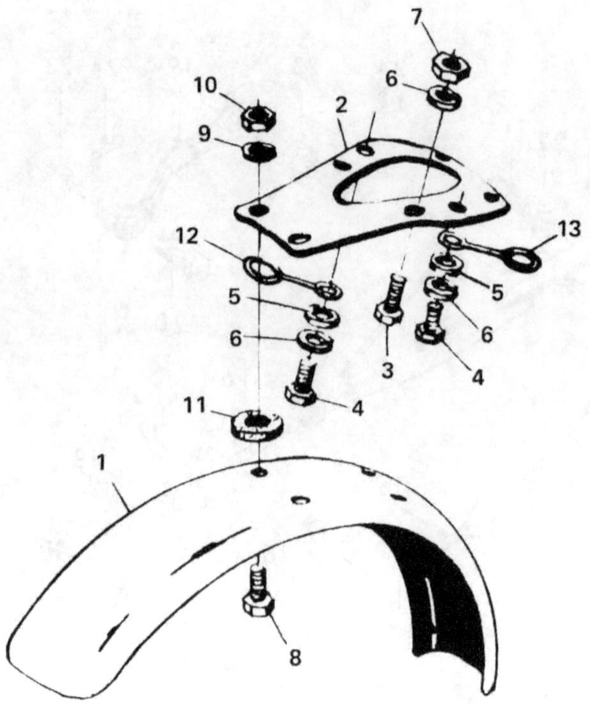

FRONT FENDER

1. Front fender
2. Bracket
3. Bolt
4. Bolt
5. Washer
6. Spring washer
7. Nut
8. Bolt
9. Spring washer
10. Nut
11. Rubber seat
12. Front brake cable guide
13. Front brake cable guide

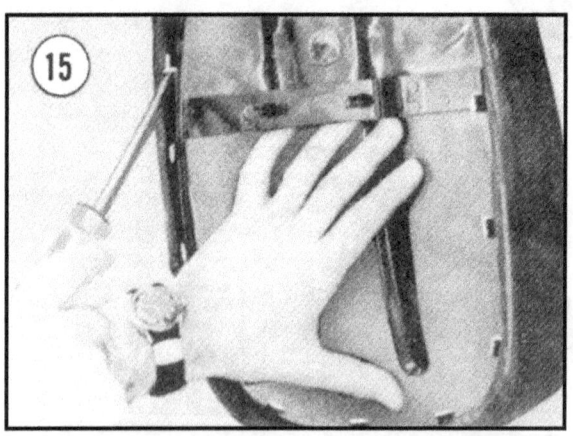

BRAKE PEDAL SERVICE

An exploded view of the brake pedal is given in **Figure 17**.

1. Check all parts for wear or damage. Replace if necessary.

2. To replace the pedal rubber, cut off the old rubber with a knife. Install the new rubber with contact cement.

3. Lubricate the friction points as detailed in Chapter Two.

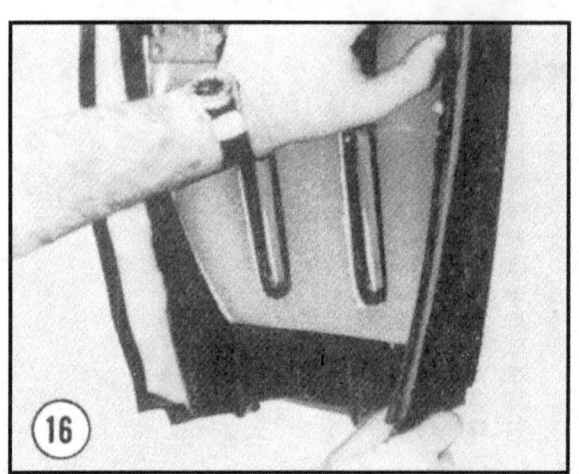

FOOT PEG ASSEMBLY

Figure 18 is an exploded view of typical foot pegs used on the Hodaka.

1. Check all parts for wear or damage. Replace if necessary.

2. Minor bends can be straightened, but major bends indicate replacement.

3. Replace the rubbers with contact cement inside the new ones. For competition use it may be desirable to replace these with serrated metal accessory pegs.

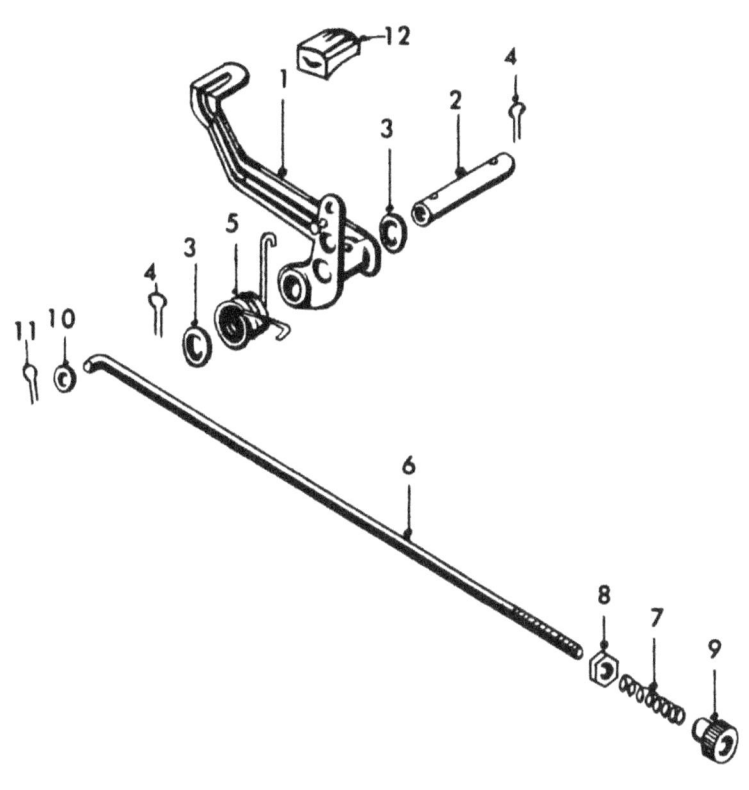

BRAKE PEDAL

1. Brake pedal
2. Pedal shaft
3. Washer
4. Cotter pin
5. Return spring
6. Brake rod
7. Spring
8. Stop nut
9. Adjusting nut
10. Washer
11. Cotter pin
12. Brake pedal rubber

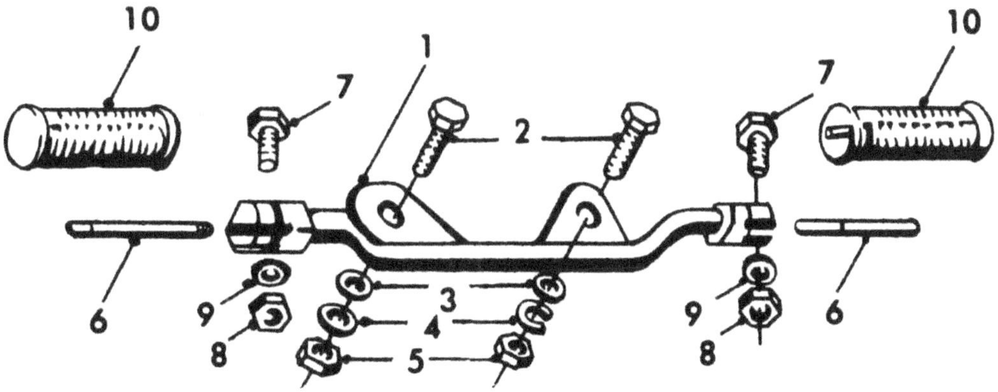

FOOT PEDAL

1. Foot rest bracket
2. Bolt
3. Washer
4. Spring washer
5. Nut
6. Foot rest bar
7. Bolt
8. Nut
9. Spring washer
10. Foot rest rubber

BATTERY BRACKET

Battery bracket for the 100-B is shown in **Figure 19**. Other brackets are similar.

1. Check all parts for wear or damage. Replace if necessary.
2. Immediately wash off any battery acid spillage using baking soda and water.
3. Replace rubber strap if it shows deterioration.

SIDE STAND

1. Remove the nut and bolt (**Figure 20**) with the stand folded, and remove from the machine.

2. Lubricate all friction points as detailed in Chapter Two.
3. Reassemble in reverse sequence.

TOOL BOX

Figure 21 illustrates a typical tool box. Removal and installation are self-explantory.

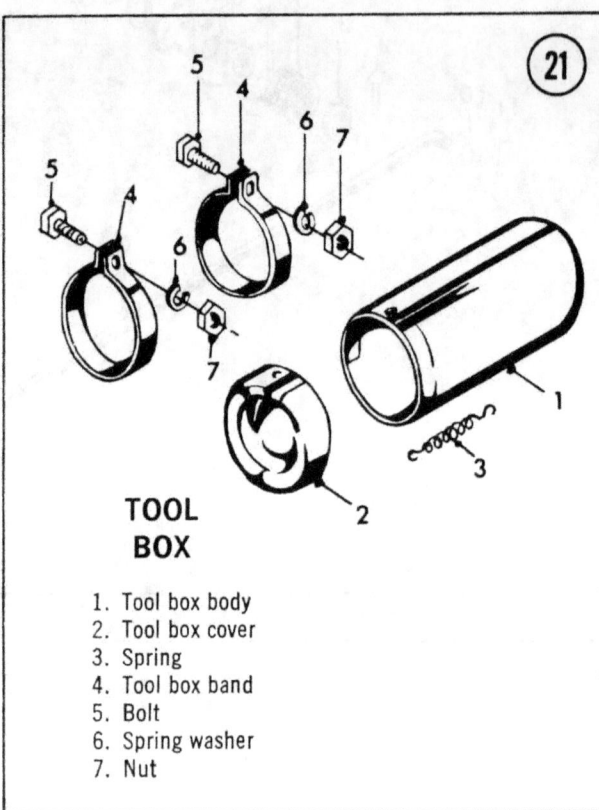

TOOL BOX

1. Tool box body
2. Tool box cover
3. Spring
4. Tool box band
5. Bolt
6. Spring washer
7. Nut

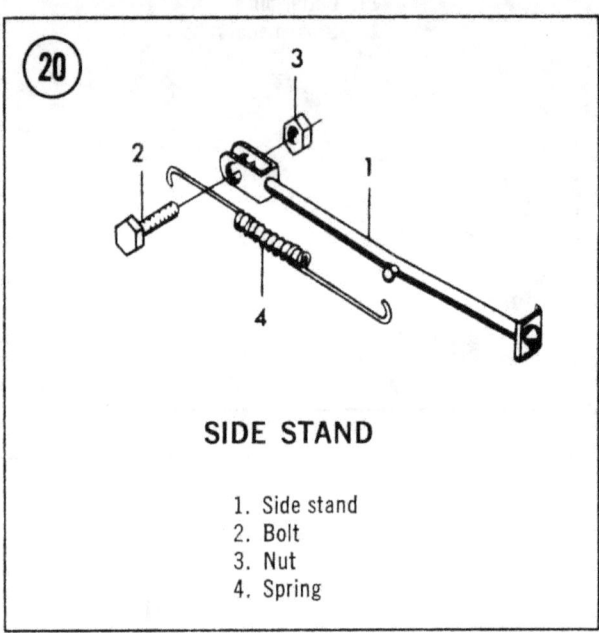

SIDE STAND

1. Side stand
2. Bolt
3. Nut
4. Spring

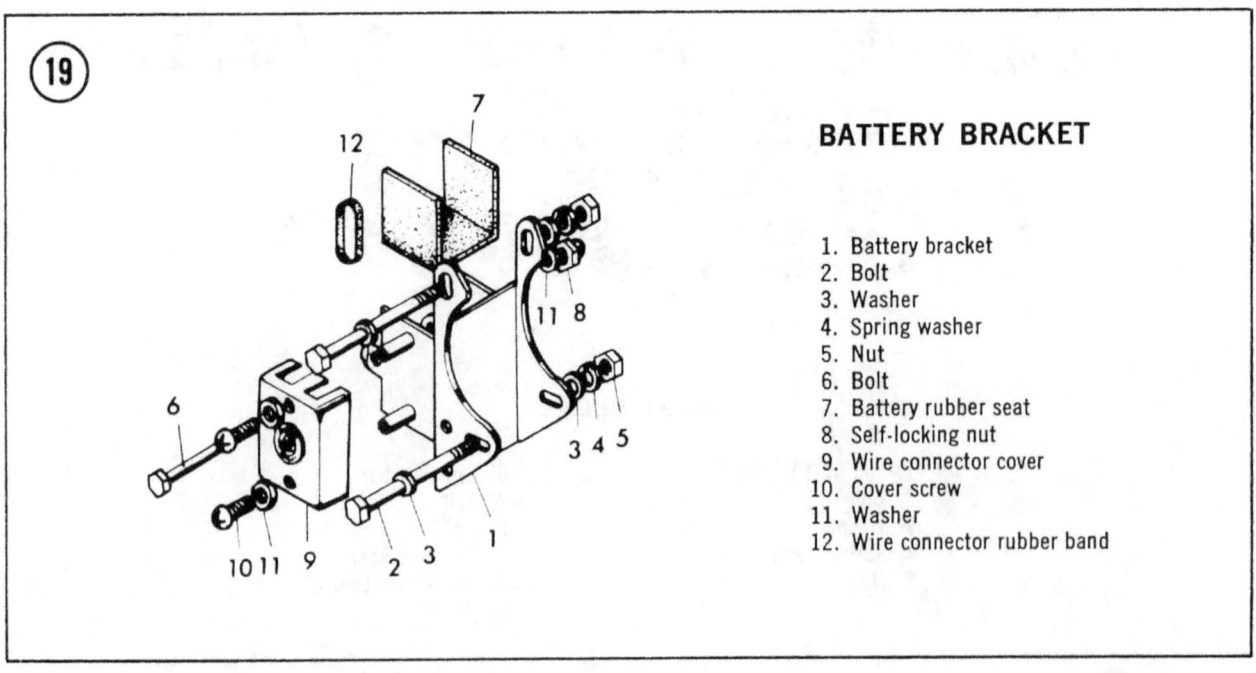

BATTERY BRACKET

1. Battery bracket
2. Bolt
3. Washer
4. Spring washer
5. Nut
6. Bolt
7. Battery rubber seat
8. Self-locking nut
9. Wire connector cover
10. Cover screw
11. Washer
12. Wire connector rubber band

CHAPTER NINE

COMPETITION PREPARATION

In basic trim the Hodaka is capable of winning both desert and motocross races. With a few modifications, it can be used for flat track, TT, trials, enduros, scrambles, road racing, and, of course, motocross. Modifications should be made only to equipment that is in new or top condition. Modifying a tired old machine is futile. Engine modifications should be made exactly as described, since they are from engines of known performance, and the alteration of any specification or component will change the combination. Become familiar with your engine before you attempt to modify it and then proceed with caution.

ROAD RACING

The Hodaka engine modified for road racing has a usable power band from 7,000 to 11,500 rpm. The engine's performance falls off below 7,000 rpm requiring more use of the throttle and gearbox. It will easily exceed its red-line of 11,500 rpm in first and second and will reach 10,200 rpm in the higher gears, so beware of the temptation to over-rev.

Since the engine tends to be "peaky," there will be the tendency to surpass the red-line, so a good, accurate tachometer is a must. The recommended instruments and hardware are:

1. 12,000 rpm, 4:1 Ratio, Clockwise Rotation Smith's Tachometer, P/N RN 1104/02
2. Anti-Vibration Mounting Ring, PN/ MS 1003/00
3. Cable Assembly, P/N DF 1111/15 (40 in.)
4. Tachometer Gear Box, 4:1 Ratio, Reversing, Ball Bearings, P/N BG 1507/03

The above listed parts are available from:

Nisonger Corporation
5220 West Jefferson Boulevard
Los Angeles, California 90016

In addition to Smith's equipment, you'll need the following Hodaka parts to complete the installation (see **Figure 1**).

1. Rear shock bolt, P/N 929139
2. Tool box spring, P/N 909038
3. Magneto nut, P/N 903001

Remove the engine from the frame. Disassemble and clean all parts that will be used.

You can lay aside the following:

1. Cylinder head
2. Piston
3. Flywheel
4. Lighting coil

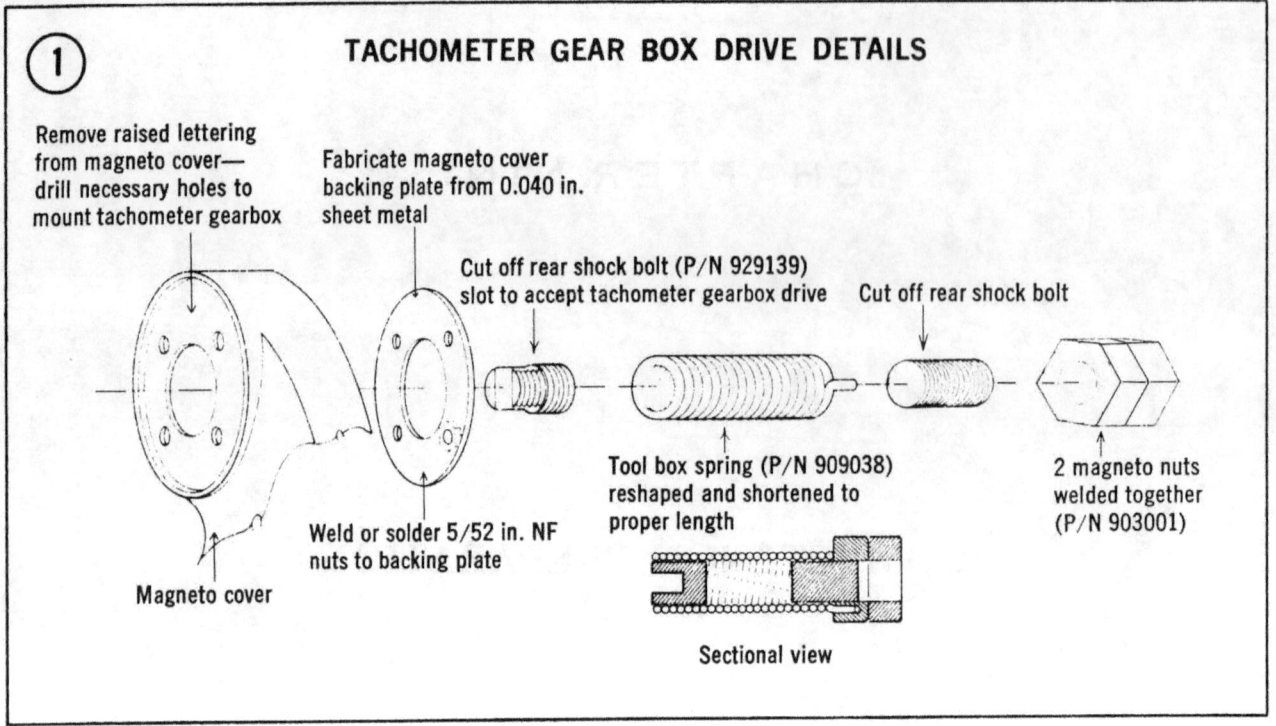

5. Primary exciting coil
6. Breaker points
7. Carburetor
8. Air cleaner assembly
9. Manifold
10. Primary gears
11. Kickstarter mechanism
12. Wide-ratio transmission gear set

Separate the crankshaft and remove the connecting rod for blading and polishing. Use extreme care not to remove fillet metal where the shank joins the eye. Reassemble the crankshaft. There is one deviation from the normal assembly procedure: rod side clearance for racing should be 0.010 in. Use cork to stuff holes in the crank wheels. Contact cement will hold them in place. Place the kick crank shaft passageway in the crankcases with a pair of kickstarter stop rubbers (P/N 901506)—one at either end of the passage. Use contact cement to hold these in place.

Modify the cylinder according to the timing diagram (**Figure 2**). Exercise care in reshaping these ports and stop often to check your progress. If you go too far, too fast, you'll find it impossible to replace the metal removed. Do not leave any square cornered ports as they invite fractures. A minimum radius of 1/8 in.

should be left, a shape best attained with a small round file. Bevel the horizontal edges of the ports where they open out into the cylinder to prevent the ring from snagging on edge of the ports. See Figure 2 for depth and angle of bevel.

Polish ports and passages in the cylinder to ease gas flow and retard carbon buildup. Since a larger than stock carburetor is used, the inlet passageway will have to be opened up to match the manifold (depending on which carburetor option is chosen, the manifold will either be fabricated from stock or reworked from an existing casting). Here shape is more important than shine. Avoid wavy contours or rough junctures.

While the cases are separated, match the transfer passage openings in crankcase halves to those in the cylinder. Other than matching and polishing the juncture, do not alter the transfer passage shape. The exhaust port passageway may be opened up somewhat, however, but do not disturb the "step" in bottomside of port. Finish the cylinder with a light honing operation.

Two carburetor choices are offered. The first (and favored) calls for using an Amal GP-2 (1-5/32 in. venturi) set up as follows: Standard needle (second notch), No. 107 needle jet, No. 5½ slide, No. 30 pilot jet, No. 0.125 air correction jet. Main jet range—No. 300 to 370.

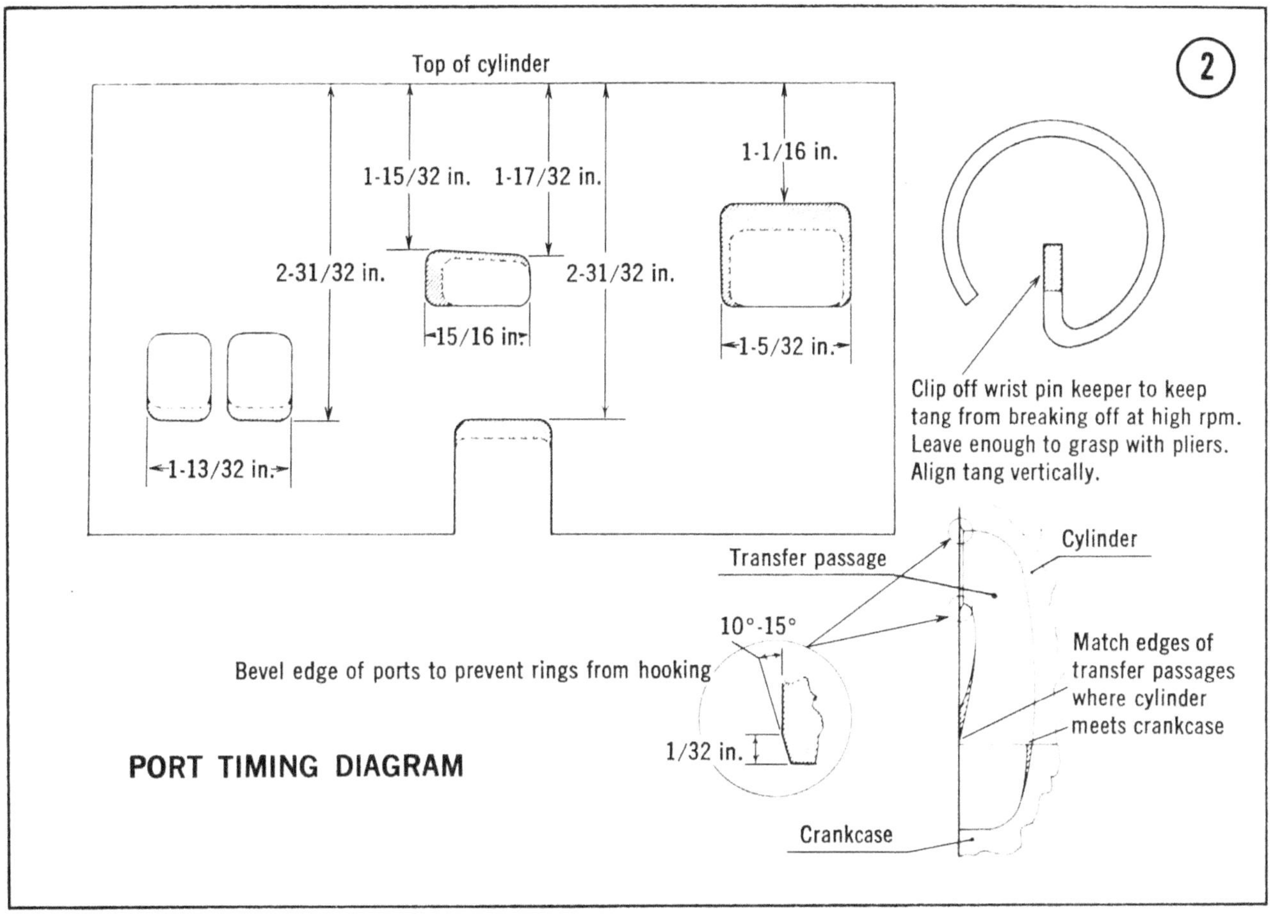

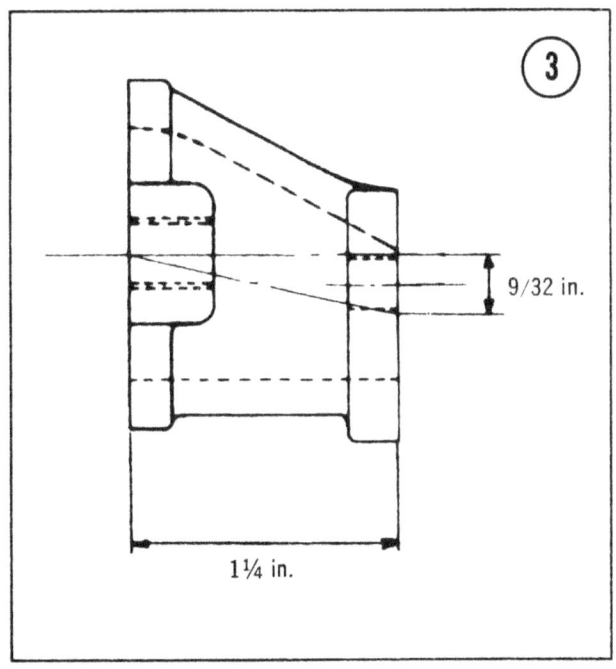

PORT TIMING DIAGRAM

Start with a No. 340 jet. Cut off the stock air horn ¾ in. behind bell end and epoxy it onto the carburetor body. The end of the air horn should be flush with the body.

Blend the inner edges of the horn into the body with a rotary file. Fabricate a manifold as per **Figure 3**, blend the passageway into alignment with the cylinder and carburetor. Avoid any wavy contours in the inlet tract.

Amal GP-2 carburetors are sometimes available used from BSA dealers. The model needed having been standard equipment on the 1966 Mark II (650cc). When you purchase your carburetor, make sure to include cables of adequate length and an air correction control lever in your order.

The second carburetor choice calls for using a Spanish Amal GP (1-3/16 in. venturi) set up as follows: "D" needle (second notch), No. 4½ slide, No. 109 needle jet, No. 20 pilot jet. Main jet range—No. 300 to 450. Start with a No. 340 jet. Use Hodaka TOA 101 accessory manifold in conjunction with this carburetor. Blend the manifold passageway to cylinder and carburetor passages with a rotary file. Use the shortest air bell obtainable from an English Amal carburetor.

NOTE: *Do not substitute other carburetors for the above specifications.*

Recommended fuel mixture for racing: 32:1 premium grade gasoline and Blenzall castor oil (1 pint to 4 gal.).

Regardless of carburetor used, a phenolic heat block must be used between the carburetor and manifold. Inner edges of the heat block should be matched to the inlet tract. A remote float chamber with a built-in anti-foaming device is necessary. A unit from a Yamaha TD1 racer works very well.

Modify the Dykes ring racing piston by removing 0.040 in. from the bottom of the inlet side of the skirt. For added oil retention the piston skirt can be grooved.

Reassemble the engine using the following performance parts:

1. High compression cylinder head, P/N 932501R
2. Straight cut primary gear, P/N 914506R
3. Straight cut pinion gear, P/N 914003R
4. Dykes ring racing piston (standard), P/N 9301500R
5. Dykes ring (standard), P/N 9302500R
6. Battery ignition point cam, P/N 913007R
7. Battery ignition coil, P/N 913009R
8. Coil mounting bracket, P/N 913029R
9. Heavy duty points, P/N 913016R
10. Close ratio transmission gear set, P/N 914600R
11. Gasket set, P/N 922510
12. Accessory manifold (optional—for Spanish Amal only) TOA-101

(Parts listed above are available from your Hodaka dealer.)

In setting up the engine, use standard clearances, settings, and tolerances unless specifically instructed otherwise.

For battery ignition, the magneto stator frame must be slotted to allow the plate to rotate somewhat. Set the point gap at 0.010 in., then rotate the stator plate to achieve a 25° BTDC firing point. (See **Figure 4** for wiring harness details and stator plate slotting.)

Battery ignition requires a fully-charged battery before each race. Charging the stock Hodaka battery at a rate of more than 0.8Ah can ruin the battery. Allow 2 to 4 hours charging time.

Fabricate an expansion chamber according to **Figure 5**. Follow each dimension carefully, using

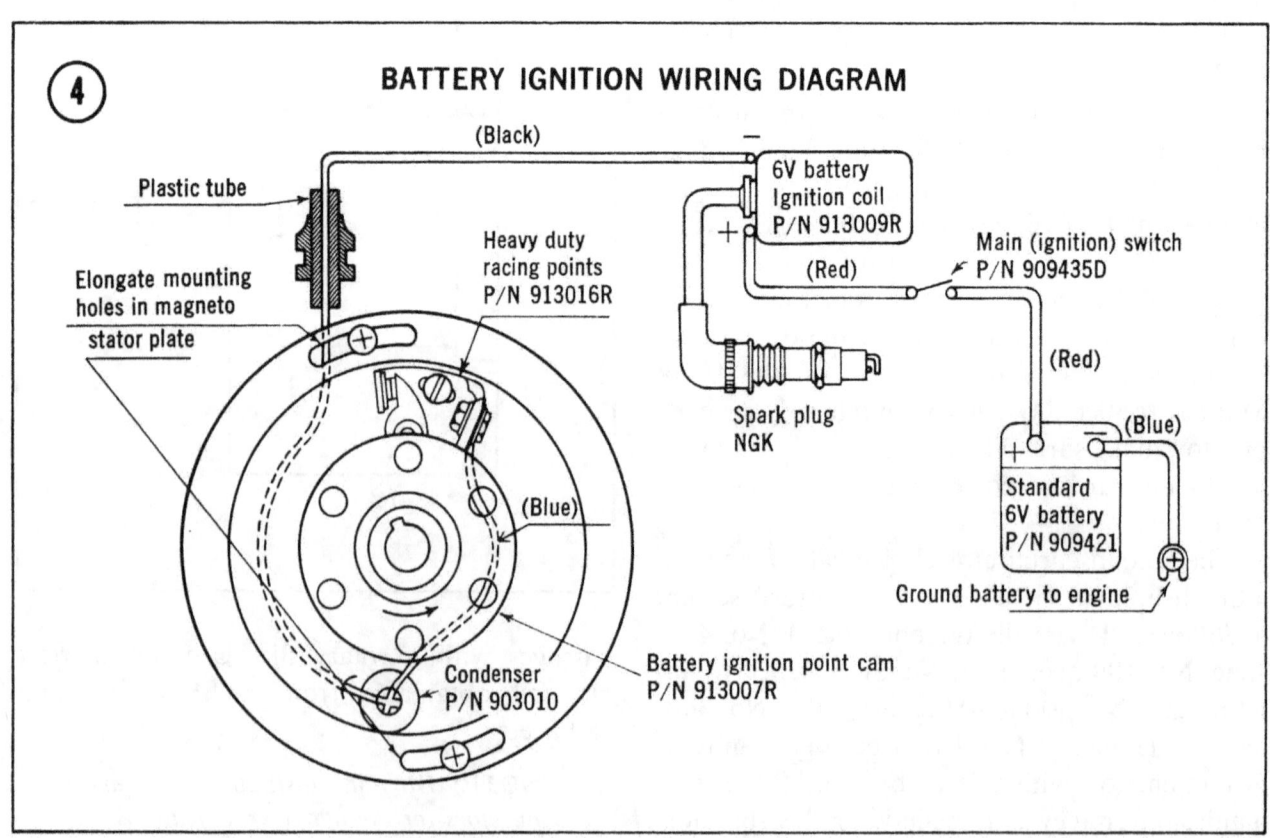

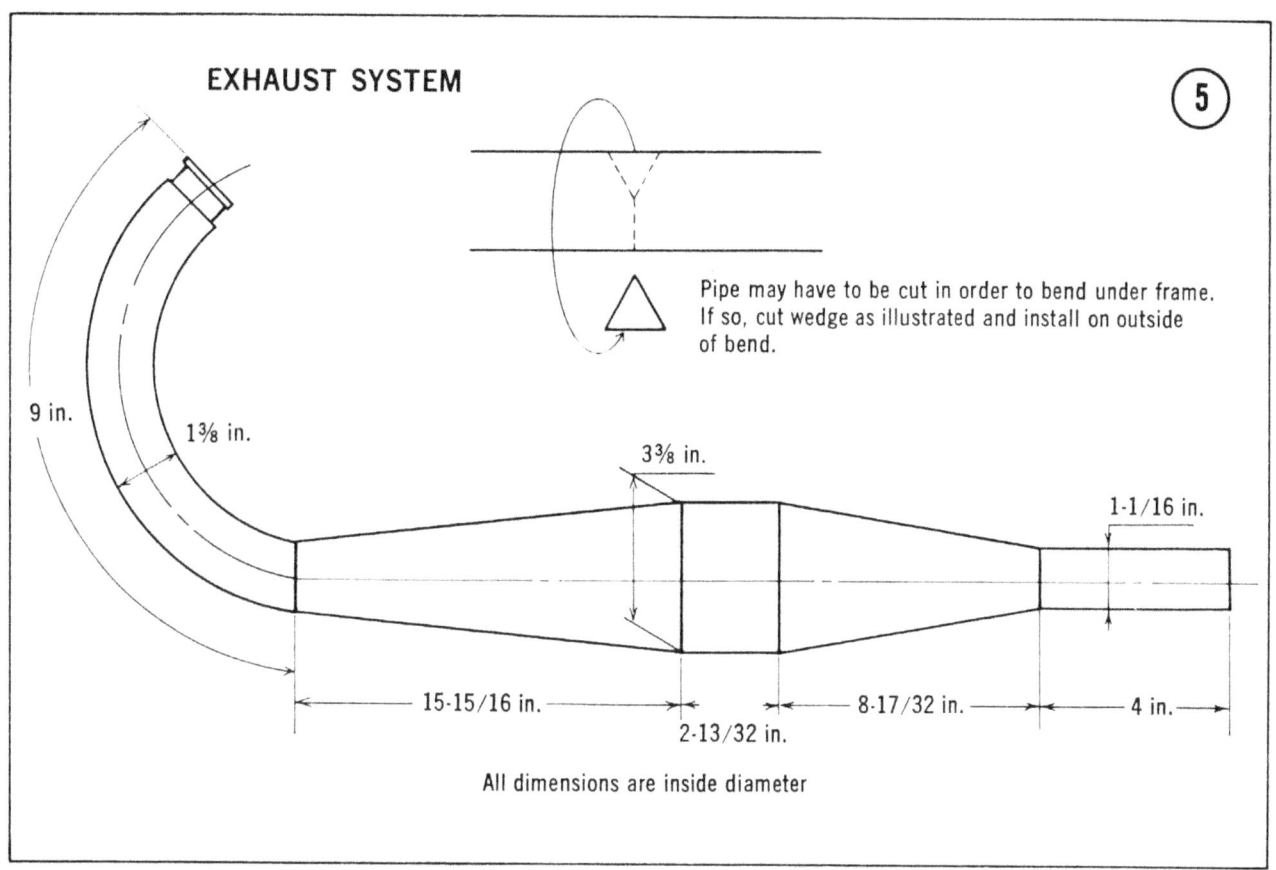

EXHAUST SYSTEM

Pipe may have to be cut in order to bend under frame. If so, cut wedge as illustrated and install on outside of bend.

All dimensions are inside diameter

light gauge sheet steel for the chamber. When welding, take care not to allow globs of weld to protrude into the chamber's inner surface. Most important, don't let yourself be talked out of using the pipe specification given; it's matched to the modification program.

NGK spark plugs are recommended in these heat ranges: NGK B9HN (hot), B10HN (normal), B11HN (cold). You can order them from your Hodaka dealer.

Transmission oil level should be maintained at a minimum level on the oil gauge. Use a SAE 20W non-detergent oil—service MM or MS. To relieve pressure and heat, fabricate a large volume transmission breather by screwing a short length of ½ in. pipe (threaded on one end) into the transmission filler hole. Slip a length of plastic tubing atop the pipe nipple, extending it up and rearwards at least 24 in.

FRAME

Disassemble the chassis down to the bare frame. Remove any superfluous brackets and fabricate front fairing and tachometer mounts. Make-up rear set foot rests and foot controls next. Before welding in place, carefully check the riding posture so as to ensure a comfortable position and free use of the controls. To duplicate this set-up, you'll need the following Hodaka parts:

1. Weld on foot peg assemblies: (includes peg, peg rubber, mount base, swivel bolt and nut; 2 required), P/N 919110R
2. Foot shift shaft (2 required), P/N 902005
3. Foot shift shaft snap ring (2 required), P/N 902014
4. Foot shift lever (2 required), P/N 902030
5. Foot shift rubber, P/N 902032
6. Lever setting bolts (2 required), P/N (10) 0622
7. Lockwashers (2 required), P/N (63) 06015
8. Front brake cable, P/N 908931C
9. Front brake cable spring, P/N 908932
10. Front brake cable adjusting nut, P/N 908933
11. Cable adjusting bolt, P/N 908903

12. Cable adjusting nut, P/N 908904
13. Front backing plate, P/N 909218

Notice that this set-up converts the rear brake to cable operation. The front backing plate, however, must have the built-in axle spacer machined away to allow the backing plate assembly to slide completely into the brake drum. It is necessary to modify the end of the foot shaft to accept the cable end. The cable must also be shortened. The remote shift linkage uses ¼ in. clevis and rod to connect up with abbreviated stock shift lever.

The swing arm should be cross-braced. Standard rear shocks are adequate in most cases although heavier damped shocks such as Girlings can be used. If you prefer this route, order Girling shock P/N GS2141 from your Hodaka dealer. The standard spring rate is 88 lb. but an optional 100 lb. spring is available.

A rear fender is not used on the road racer; however, a sheet aluminum bulkhead should be installed between the rear frame downtubes. This prevents carburetor spit-back from coating the rear tire with oil. To prevent accumulated oil from dripping, cement ½ in. thick foam rubber onto the bulkhead.

The battery will have to be relocated to clear the carburetor and remote float chamber. Use Hodaka's racing kit battery for this job. Order P/N 919040R from your dealer.

If your racing association's rules permit, exchange the stock fuel tank for a long, narrow tank of the "bread loaf" variety.

The standard seat should be replaced with a fiberglass "road-racing" type. Double check riding posture before permanently attaching the seat.

Handlebars should be of the "clip-on" variety and a "quick-turn" twistgrip throttle control should be fitted.

A fiberglass racing fairing is a must item. After obtaining the fairing, tailor it to the bike and yourself. This may involve a bit of cutting and shaping, but it's necessary work. In essence, the rider must become part of the streamlining while in the racing crouch. Shroudwork should be glassed into the fairing so as to duct air around the cylinder. This measurably improves engine cooling. In addition, a sheet aluminum panel should be fitted between the expansion chamber and the bottom of the engine. This prevents expansion chamber heat from reaching the engine and gearbox.

As a general rule, safety wire, cotter pin, or Loctite every nut and bolt. Road and engine vibrations at racing speeds will loosen all types of hardware.

GEARING

A 17T countershaft sprocket and 32T wheel sprocket is suitable for most short courses. Longer tracks require a 31T or possibly even a 30T wheel sprocket. The 17T and 32T sprockets are stock Hodaka parts—available from your dealer. The 30T and 31T wheel sprockets must be fabricated from blank sprockets.

1. 17T countershaft sprocket, P/N 042017
2. 32T wheel sprocket, P/N 909237

BRAKES, WHEELS, AND TIRES

If racing other than AMA sanctioned events, a larger than stock front brake may be used. The twin leading shoe assembly from a 175 Honda works well. Sandblasting the brake drum and backing plate surfaces and then spraying them with a light coat of flat black enamel helps to dissipate heat. Stock brake lining material should be replaced with Velvet Touch or other similar "racing" linings. Air scoops should be added to provide a constant flow of cool air across the linings.

Rim size should be WMO width and 18 in. in diameter. Alloy rims work best for road racing and are available from accessory supply houses or can be ordered through your dealer. New spokes will also be required, so order them at the same time.

Tires must be changed to road racing type. At present, Dunlop tires seem to work best. Optimum tire sizes are 2.25 to 2.50 x 18 in. Larger sizes cut down top speed without improving cornering ability. Balancing is a must—an out-of-balance wheel at high speed is dangerous. Although tire pressures vary with tire type, road conditions, and so forth, 24 to 26 psi can be taken as an average beginning point.

MOTOCROSS

The flat track or TT bike is extremely similar to the road racer in many respects. If your interests lie in riding on cow trails, then you should take heed and avoid turning the forgiving Hodaka into a Jekyll and Hyde machine. High-revving motocross engines are useless anywhere except on a race track.

The engine modifications included in this text will result in a peaky operating range from 6,000 to 10,000 rpm. Below this, the power will definitely fall off. Another deterring factor for anything short of competition is the noise that accompanies a high-revving 2-stroke with tuned exhaust.

Any modifications should be made only to equipment that is in top condition. Hopping up a worn engine is futile. The methods described here have been proven time and again on highly successful racing engines and modifying them can only result in a power loss.

If you want to tinker and feel that this method isn't the ultimate, then wait until you become familiar with the engine's characteristics.

Remove the engine from the frame, disassemble it and clean all of the components thoroughly. The following parts can be discarded: cylinder head, piston, flywheel, primary gears, manifold, air cleaner, carburetor, breaker points, primary coil, and lighting coil.

The cylinder should be modified according to **Figure 6**. Exercise extreme care in reshaping the parts, stopping often to inspect progress. If you go too far, you'll find it impossible to replace any metal that has been removed. Don't leave any sharp corners, since these are an invitation to cracking and fractures. A minimum radius of 1/8 in. can be maintained with a small round file. Bevel the horizontal edges of ports where they open out into the cylinder to prevent the piston ring from hooking the edge of the ports. Polish the ports and passages in the cylinder to ease the gas flow and retard carbon buildup.

Since a larger than stock carburetor is used on the TT engine, the inlet passageway must be opened to match the manifold. Here the final shape is more important than a smooth surface. Avoid any wavy contours or rough surfaces that

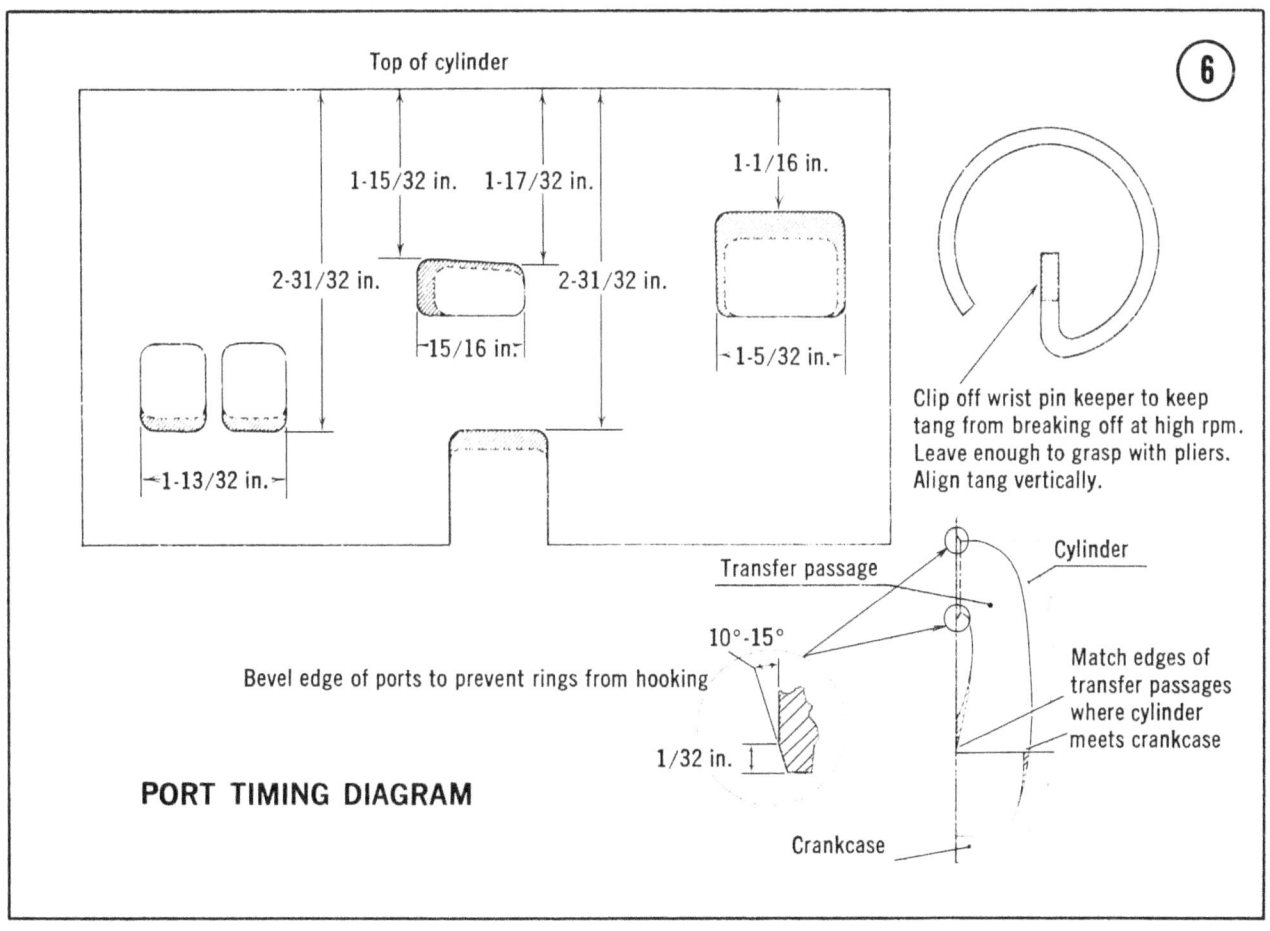

might disrupt the flow of gases. While the cases are separated, match the transfer passage openings in the cases to those in the cylinder.

Fabricate an expansion chamber according to the illustration, and follow each dimension carefully. Use light gauge sheet steel and, when welding, take care not to allow blobs of metal to protrude into the chamber's inner surface. Reassemble the engine using the following parts:

1. High compression cylinder head, P/N 932501R
2. Straight cut primary gear, P/N 914506R
3. Straight cut pinion gear, P/N 914003R
4. Dykes ring racing piston (standard), P/N 9301500R
5. Dykes piston ring (standard), P/N 9302500R
6. Battery ignition point cam, P/N 913007R
7. Battery ignition coil, P/N 913009R
8. Coil mounting bracket, P/N 913029R
9. Heavy duty points, P/N 913016R
10. Manifold assembly, P/N TOA 101

(Parts listed above are available from your Hodaka dealer.)

If the battery ignition is to be used, then the magneto stator plate must be slotted enough to allow the plate to rotate slightly. Set the point gap at 0.02 in., then rotate the stator to achieve 25° BTDC firing point. **Figure 7** is included to show the slot configuration.

The standard handlebars aren't up to the rigors of competition, so they should be replaced with accessory cross-braced bars. Sit on the seat and try to imagine the most comfortable position for you to assume and pick a set of suitable bars. The parts are:

1. Front number plate assembly, P/N 919300R
2. Cross-braced handlebars, P/N AC 100

A special tank is made by Hodaka for TT racing that is extremely light. Order TT tank, P/N AZ 100.

A TT seat's extra length allows you to crouch down on straights and the lip on the back will prevent you from sliding off. Order TT seat, P/N D 102.

The stock front suspension units are adequate for TT racing provided the correct grades and

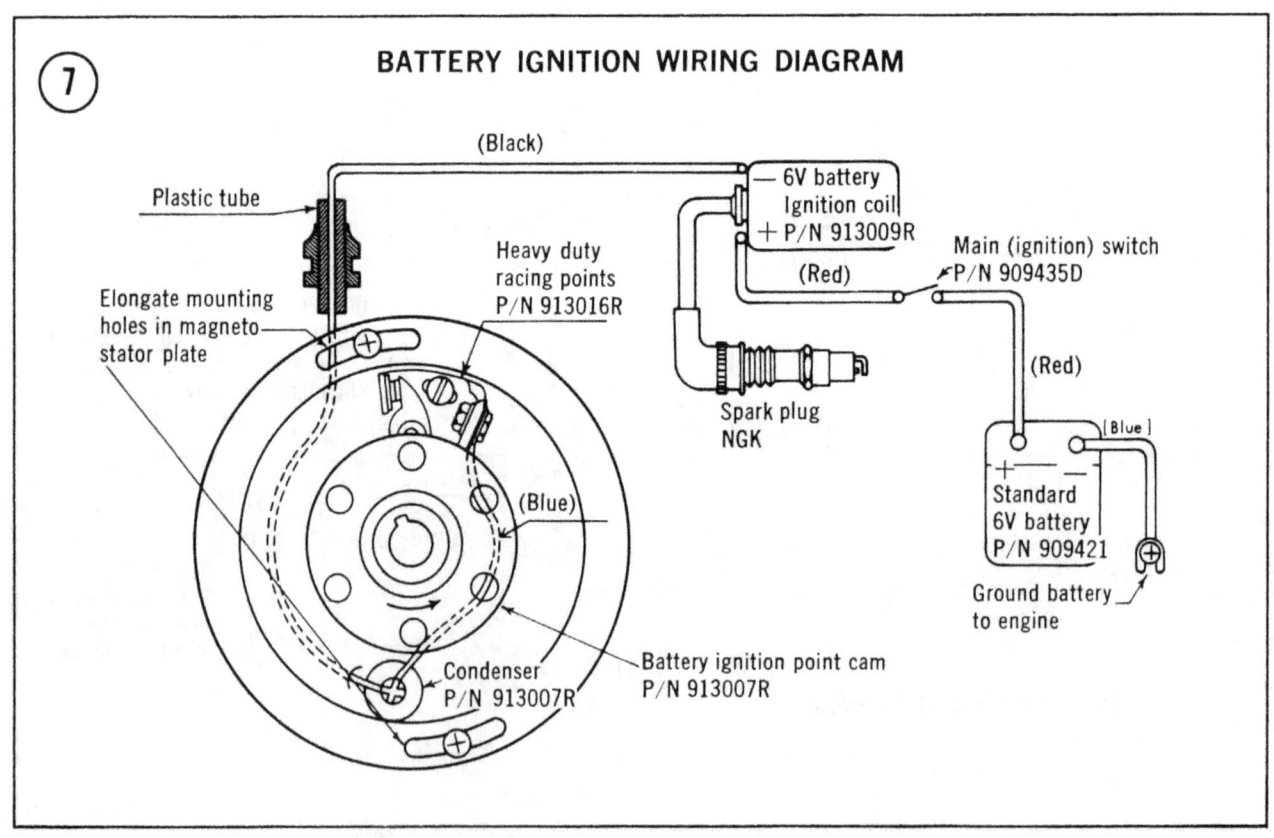

weights of oil are used. For serious racing the rear units should be replaced with adjustable Girling shock absorbers. The standard spring on the Girling shock is 88 lb., but one of a 100 lb. spring is available as an option. You will need Girling shock No. GS 2141.

The gearing you choose will depend a lot on the condition and length of the track, but you can start with the stock 15T X 50T and go from there.

The stock steel wheels are more than adequate for racing provided that they are kept true and tight. As a note to the weight conscious builder, aluminum rims can save about one pound per wheel. The steel rims must be outfitted with rim locks to prevent tire slip. Tred sizes and patterns are strictly a matter of personal choice and should relate to your local track conditions. It is important, however, not to use a larger size than is absolutely necessary. Tire sizes larger than 3.25 require a good deal of horsepower to turn. Tire pressures are an item of personal preference. A well proven combination has been the use of Dunlop K-70's 3.00 X 17" inflated to 18 pounds.

A total-loss battery-type ignition system requires a fully charged battery before each race to function properly. If a stock battery is used, then don't exceed 0.8 amps per hour of charging rate or you'll ruin it. Allow 2 to 4 hours to charge the battery. If the battery won't hold a charge, then check for short circuits or electrolyte in the battery. It's possible that two or more plates could be shorting out.

Use NGK B9HN (hot), B10HN (normal), B11HN (cold) or an equivalent Champion plug. The transmission oil level should never drop below the minimum level on the dipstick at any time. Use only SAE 20W *non-detergent* oil-service MM or MA.

You can fabricate a large volume transmission breather easily enough by screwing a short length of ½" pipe (threaded on one end) into the transmission filler hole. Slip a length of suitable plastic tubing onto the pipe extending it up and back to exhaust past the rear wheel. This large breather is necessary to relieve pressure and heat in the transmission case.

The carburetor specifications for the TT engine are as follows: 1-3/16" Amal Monobloc fitted with a "D" needle set on the 2nd notch, No. 4½ slide, No. 109 needle jet, and No. 20 pilot jet. The main jet range will fall between numbers 300 to 400. Start with a No. 320 jet and work from there as dictated by the condition of the spark plug. Be sure to use a heat block, as supplied with the TOA 101 manifold (see **Figure 8**), between the carburetor and mani-

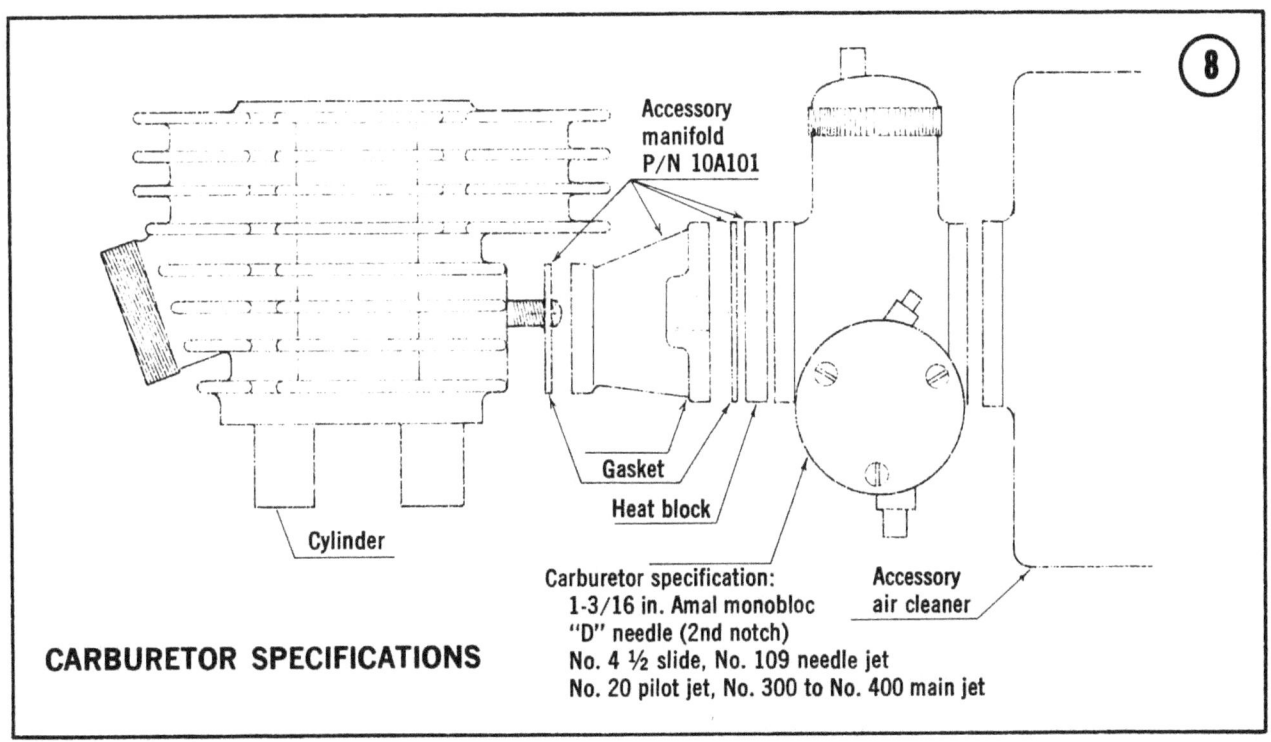

fold. The only other carburetor that we would recommend is the pumper type as sold by Kendick Engineering.

An efficient large capacity air filter, such as the foam type sold by Filtron, should be used on either carburetor to protect the engine without adversely affecting the performance.

The oil-to-fuel mix for racing is considerably less than the normal 20:1 ratio. The mixture should be approximately 16:1 using premium grade gasoline, and SAE 30W two-cycle oil.

If you intend to run minus front brakes, usually required in flat track racing, then replace the brake shoe and backing plate assembly with a stepped spacer such as used on the rear axle. Install the spacer (P/N 909232) with the stepped end toward the wheel bearing. An accessory front hub shaft collar (P/N 918910R) is available to replace the stock speedometer drive unit. Apply a light coat of silver paint to protect the brake drum from rust and to enhance the appearance of the bike.

A front fork brace is a necessity to prevent the forks from twisting under racing conditions. A well-equipped shop should stock a lightweight, factory-designed fork brace that will be suitable for racing or order P/N 918731R.

Since flat track or TT racing is professional as well as semi-professional, you'll need an AMA approved number plate. Your Hodaka dealer should be able to obtain the plate complete with brackets and hardware to make it a bolt-on item.

TRIALS

Trials is a form of competition that requires a great deal of skill and moderate amount of machine preparation. Making alterations as you need them, and practice, will put the burden of proof on the rider. Modifications should be made only to equipment in top condition. Should your Hodaka need work, bring it up to specs before attempting any modifications. This manual is a helpful guide to all maintenance of the bike.

Engine

A well tuned stock engine will perform very well in Trials competition. Modifications to the engine are minimal, consisting of an exhaust system change, waterproofing, and an optional carburetion change.

In setting up your engine, use the standard clearances, torque settings, timing specifications.

Exhaust System

The Ace 90 Muffler responds better at lower rpm than the Ace 100 and is therefore more desirable. Adding 4 to 6 inches of header pipe to the Ace 90 muffler adds even more low end response. Tucking the system in closer to the bike will give a slimmer profile and prevent burning of the leg while holding it in close during competition.

Waterproofing

Strict attention should be given to waterproofing a Trials bike. Be sure to seal all vent holes in the magneto cases and the one behind the point backing plate. A non-hardening cement such as 3-M Adhesive will work best for this purpose. On the Ace 90 models, a vent pipe must be installed, and a hose run to a high point on the machine. The Ace 100 needs no magneto case vent because of an externally mounted high tension coil. Both models will require a vent hose attached to the transmission vent located under the carburetor and just off center toward the clutch side of the engine. The original vent should be drilled out and a tube mounted with a hose running to a high point on the machine. This will prevent water from entering the gearcase. After sealing the magneto case, a strong adhesive tape should be put over the mating edges of the magneto cover and engine case. The carburetor air intake should be moved to a higher position to allow for deep water crossings. Larger capacity air cleaners are available from Webco, Filtron and others.

Carburetion

Retaining the standard 20mm carburetor will give good low end response. The main jet may be dropped in size to a No. 85 for cleaner running at low end and the needle can be lowered.

NOTE: *The needles should be lowered for slow Trials riding only.*

An optional reed valve induced system using a ⅞-inch Amal Monobloc carburetor with standard needle, number four and one-half slide and 160 main jet will increase low and mid-range power and give amazingly smooth throttle response. Amal carburetors can be obtained from several outlets, Hap Jones, BSA or Triumph dealers.

Longer manifold studs will be required to allow the carburetor to extend past the top rear engine mount. To prevent occasional crankcase fuel flooding from stalling the engine, fit a fuel petcock to the carburetor float chamber. In this manner the engine may be quickly leaned out allowing the engine to run clean. This will also allow the carburetor float chamber to be drained if water has entered.

On both sides of the standard 20mm carburetor is a vent hole for the float chamber. These should have a small metal tube (such as the overflow tube at the bottom of the float bowl) inserted into them and a 10 in. hose connected to prevent water from entering.

Ignition

Suggested spark plug heat range for Trials work is NGK-7 (hot) to NGK B-9 (normal). NGK plugs are available from your Hodaka dealer. A waterproof spark plug cover should be used, such as a Sparky or waterproof Lodge.

The battery and battery bracket assembly will have to be removed to provide room for other than stock air cleaner assemblies. If you desire to keep the lighting system intact, remove the tool box and relocate the battery high in the frame using the racing kit battery bracket (P/N 9190400R). If the lighting system is removed entirely, it is advisable to remove the lighting coil from the magneto. A blank coil core must be installed in place of the lighting coil, and these are also available from your dealer (P/N 9130034).

Tires and Wheels

Tire size and tread pattern are largely a matter of personal choice and should be related to local conditions. Tire security bolts (rim locks) are a must item especially with the low pressures often required. Two are recommended for the rear and one for the front (P/N WSB 2—please state rim size). If the Speedo-Headlight assembly is removed, the drive unit should be replaced with a spacer (P/N 918910R). The headlight can be replaced with Hodaka's front number plate.

Items that may be changed:

Small seat—accessory companies

Small tank—PABATCO TT tanks No. AZ-100

Sealed wheel bearings—(local bearing sales)

Hodaka front number plate—P/N 919300R

Frame

The steering lock can, and should, be increased by cutting the stops down a little at a time. This should be done in stages to ensure that the fork bracket does not hit the gas tank when fully turned. Steering lock can be further increased by installing PABATCO's TT Tank (P/N 919300R). If an 18-inch rear wheel is fitted to the machine the loop above the rear wheel may have to be heated and bent upwards approximately ¾" in order to provide sufficient clearance.

To achieve better balance, plus better rear wheel traction, fit a pair of rear-set foot pegs. This of course, eliminates the stock foot rest assembly. Fabricate mounting gussets from ¼" steel plate and weld to the frame. Use care not to block lower engine mounting bolt access with too generous a gusset. Brake pedal and foot shift lever will have to be shortened. The kick crank lever must be re-angled by cutting off and re-welding. Remove half the kick crank stop rubber allowing the crank to come even further forward. Pegs should swing back and up at a 45 degree angle. This also allows the front wheel to be raised for log crossing and such activities. Weld-on foot peg assemblies include peg, peg rubber, mount base, swivel bolt and nut (P/N 919110R).

GEARING AND SUSPENSION

Beware of gearing the machine too low. While largely a matter of personal preference, gearing the bike too low is just as bad as too high. Start with a 14-tooth primary and 50-tooth rear sprocket and then alter to suit local conditions. For serious Trials competition, Girling rear shock absorbers are available to replace the stock units. Hodaka dealers carry the correct length and size to fit your machine. The standard spring is 88 lb. Other spring rates are available and springs should be changed to suit the individual. Suspension should be soft enough to absorb the rough terrain at very slow speeds. If your suspension does not bottom upon occasion during a Trials, it is too stiff. If you are using rear shock absorbers that are adjustable, the adjusters may be removed to further soften the suspension. Extended travel front forks kits are available, if you prefer, from accessory manufacturers such as Roehr Bros., Steens Inc., Hanco Sales and others. The Girling rear shock is P/N GS 2141 (two required).

- Recommended lubricant: SAE 30W 2-cycle oil
- Fuel/oil mixture for Trials—20-1
- Front fork oil—3½ oz. each leg—mixture of 70% SAE 30 and 30% SAE 70 non-detergent oil

REED VALVE CONVERSION

Following the procedure outlined earlier, remove the carburetor, exhaust system, cylinder head, cylinder, and piston. Wash the cylinder and piston in clean solvent and air dry. Remove the piston rings. Step-by-step instructions are as follows.

The main tools you will need to put booster ports in your engine are dividers, auto body cloth, felt pen, small files, electric drill, 5/16" bit, polishing mandrel, grinding stone, rotary files and hand grinder. You will also need some fine abrasive cloth, a couple of pieces of wood or plastic to protect barrel and piston and a bench vise.

CYLINDER

1. Insert the piston into the cylinder from the bottom. Push the piston up the bore until the *transfer* ports are *almost* closed. With a fine-line pen, using the top of the piston as straight edge, draw a line from the top of one transfer port to the other on the intake side of the cylinder.

2. Sit down in front of a work bench. Lay the cylinder so that the intake port is lying down on the bench and you are looking at the top of the cylinder. You are ready to mark in the port location and shape. Take a good look at **Figure 9**. Start a line 1/16" in from the outside of the intake port. Draw this line straight up to the horizontal line indicating transfer port height.

3. Mark the other side of the booster port. Using dividers, make a mark 5/8" in from the outside of the intake port (toward the intake bridge). Just a dot is enough. From the dot mark a line that aims directly at the cylinder stud hole. Remember that the cylinder is lying on the bench and you are looking at the top, and the intake port is down. Check it again—the right intake port aims at the right stud hole. The left intake port aims at the left stud hole (see **Figure 10**). Now that the booster ports are marked, you have what looks roughly like an inverted "V".

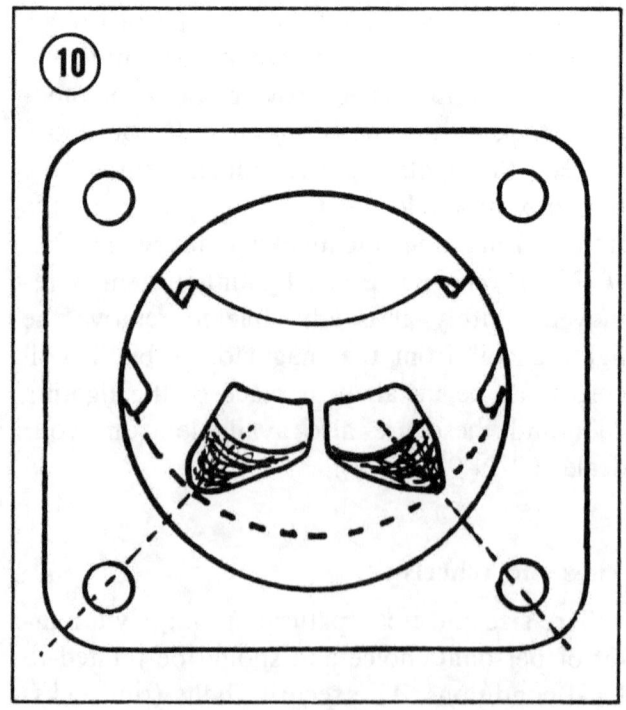

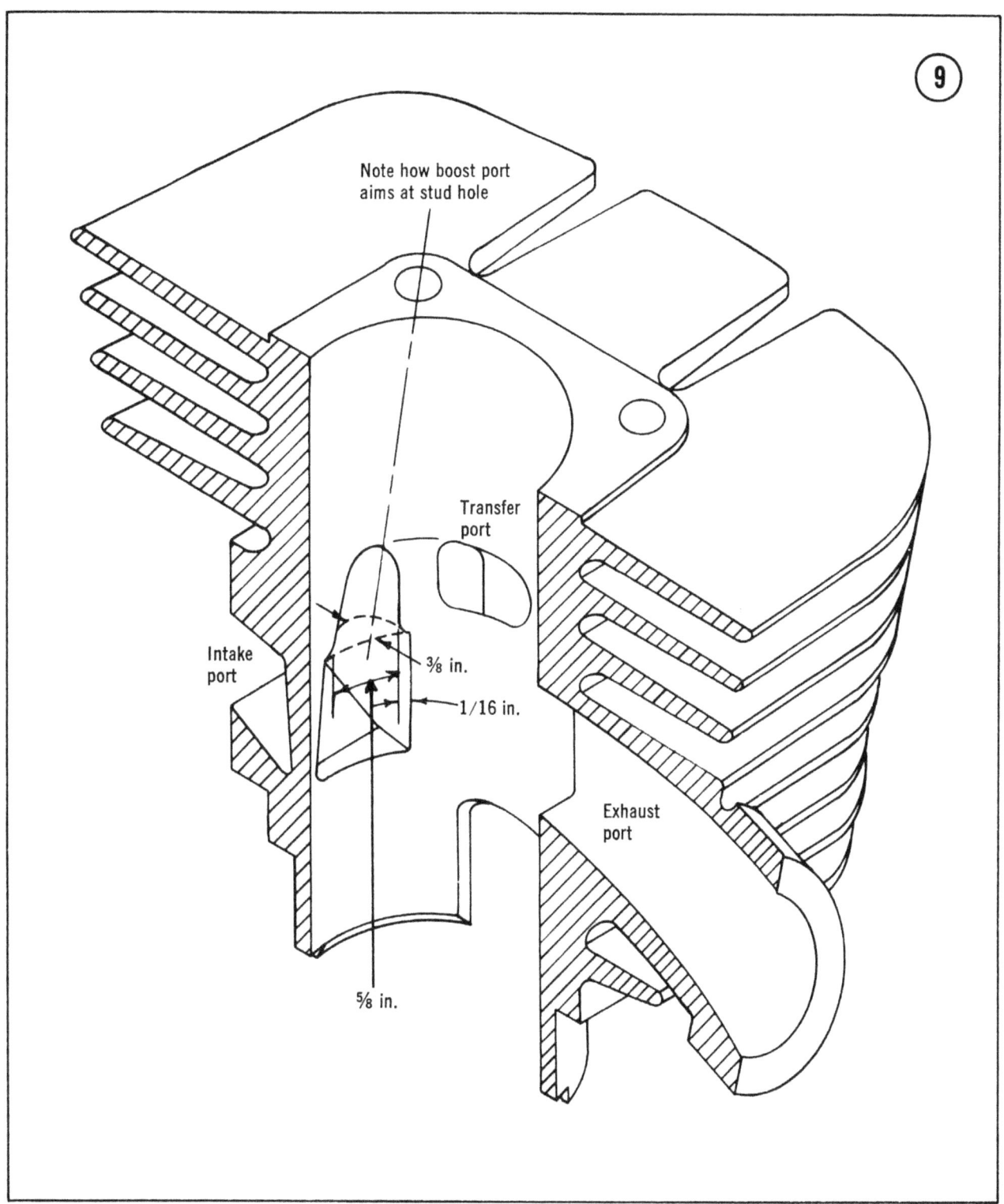

4. Before you attempt to follow all these marks and grind in the booster ports, first grind the rough casting marks out of the exhaust port. Do not remove much metal, just smooth the port. Use a piece of ¼" bare welding rod and ¼" bolt, 3" long, and hacksaw a slot in one end about ½" deep. Chuck this rod into the grinder. For polishing the port use some "auto body cloth roll" 1" or 1½" wide (available from your local auto parts store); 180 or 200 grit is ideal. Tear off 6" of the abrasive cloth. Tear again lengthwise so that the piece is about ½" wide. Fit one end of this piece into the slot and roll on to the rod. Check the grinder rotation to see which way to roll the cloth, and start polishing.

5. Use a grinding stone that is ½" in diameter, 1¼" long, with a ¼" shank and chuck it in the grinder. Very carefully, place the cylinder in a vise—(use wood or plastic to protect the fins)—as it was before, with the port down. Work from the top of the cylinder. Go slowly while grinding and look at the diagram frequently. Grind slowly so that the booster port is approximately ⅜" deep and taper it out to the cylinder wall surface at the transfer height scribe line.

6. Polish these ports using the same technique as you did with the exhaust port.

7. Remove the cylinder from the vise and use a small round hand file to radius the sharp edge from the top of intake into new booster ports.

8. Now is a good time to set the reed manifold on the carburetor mounting studs. Scribe a line around the inside of the reed manifold throat onto the face of the mounting surface of the cylinder. Grind out the scribed area on the manifold side of intake port to match the reed manifold opening. Try to duct as much fuel flow down toward the crankcase as possible.

It will be necessary to use several small rotary files and stones to complete this port. Don't forget to polish this port too as described before.

Piston

1. Follow **Figure 11** and mark the window openings on intake side of the pistons—watch for locating pin.

2. Place the piston in the vise between two pieces of wood or plastic. Hold the piston by the top and bottom, not the sides (you could collapse it). Use an electric drill to make a 5/16" hole in the center of each of the four scribed windows.

3. Use a ¼" round coarse file and hand file the piston windows to the diagram specifications.

4. Follow the diagram for the piston skirt radius. Use a grinder or a file. Be careful not to bear too heavily on the piston.

5. Very carefully deburr or round all sharp edges with a fine file and abrasive cloth.

6. Completely wash the piston in clean solvent and reassemble the engine as described in Chapter Four.

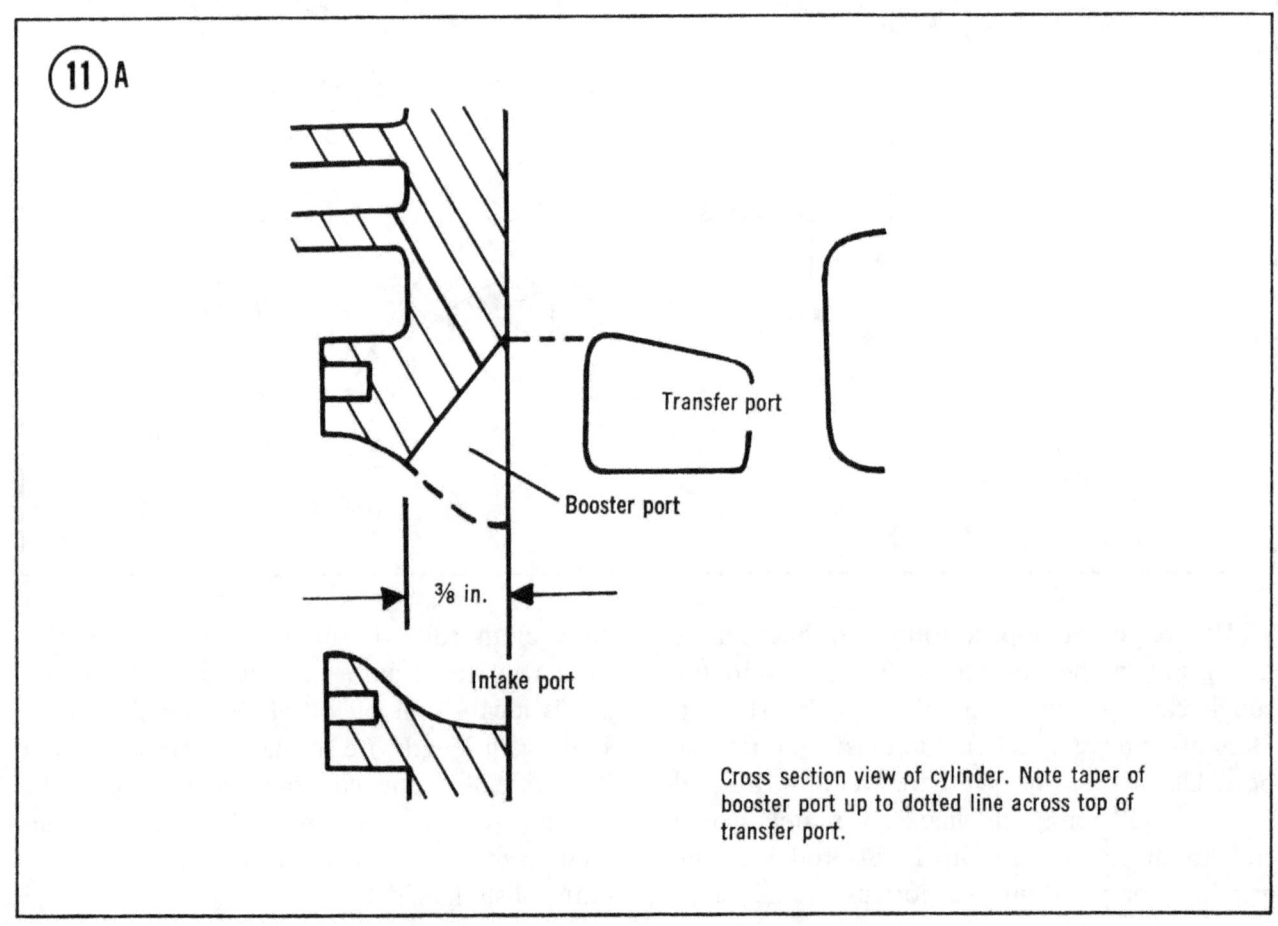

Cross section view of cylinder. Note taper of booster port up to dotted line across top of transfer port.

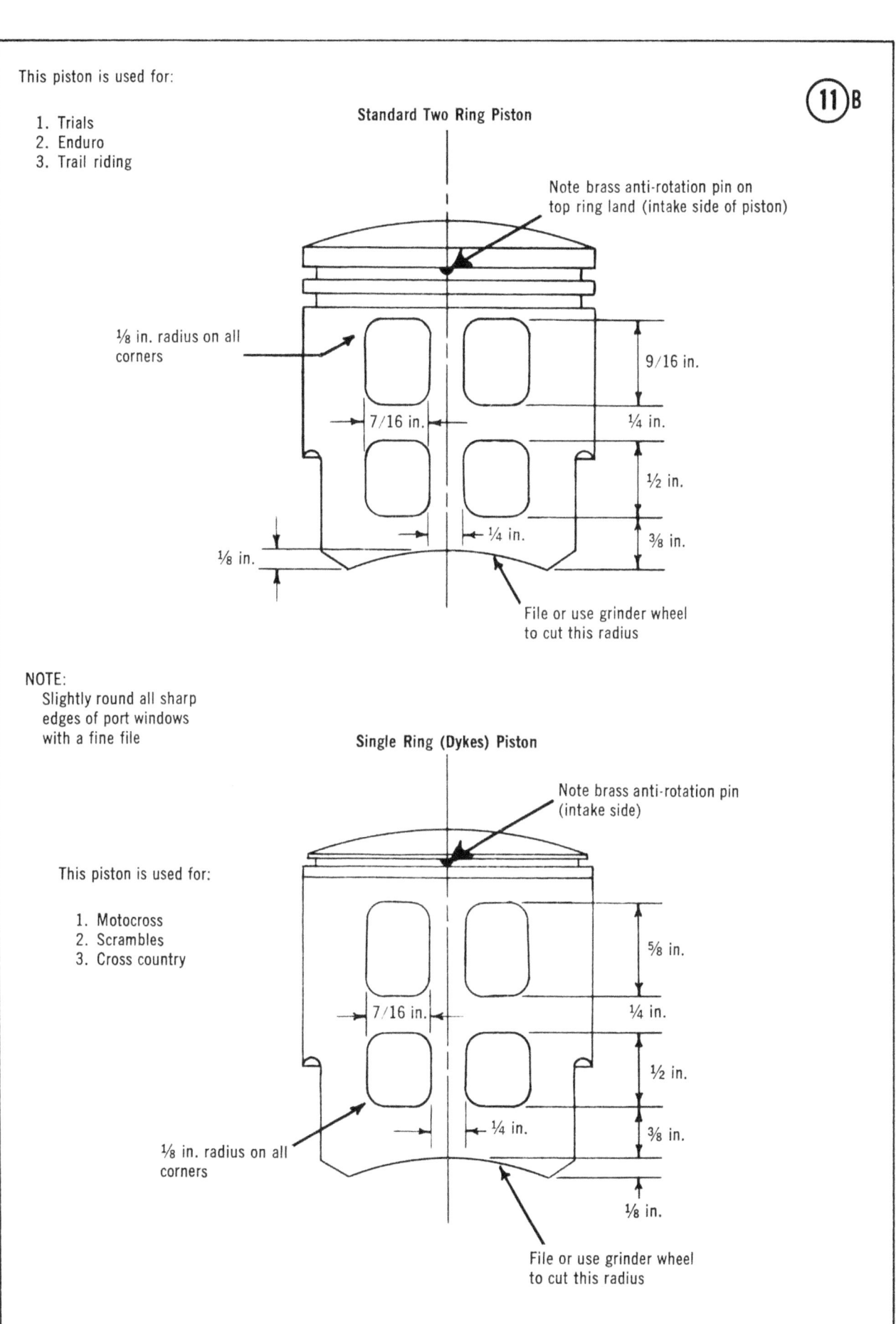

CHAPTER NINE

GENERAL SPECIFICATIONS AND DATA

> This chapter contains specifications and performance figures for the various Hodaka models covered by this book. The tables are arranged in order of increasing engine size.

SPECIFICATIONS, ACE 90

ENGINE

Type	25° inclined single cylinder, two stroke/cycle air cooled, loop scavenged, piston port induction
Rated horsepower	8.2 at 7500 rpm
Maximum torque	5.1 ft.-lb. at 5500 rpm
Bore	48mm (1.89")
Stroke	50mm (1.97")
Piston displacement	90cc (5.5 C.I.)
Compression ratio	9.5 : 1
Exhaust duration	160°
Transfer duration	128°
Inlet duration	122°
Lubrication system	Fuel/oil mix
Fuel mixture	16:1-first 500 miles
	20:1-thereafter
Recommended engine lubricant	SAE 30 W 2 cycle oil
Starting system	Kickstarter

CARBURETOR

Type	Horizontal mounted Mikuni carburetor with sliding throttle and needle valve
Model	VM 20-SH 10
Main jet	#85 (std.)
Venturi	20mm
Needle jet	#N6
Jet needle	#4F6
Needle clip position	3rd notch (middle) std.
Pilot jet	#25
Idle screw	#2
Idle screw adjustment	1¼ turns from closed
Throttle slide	#2.0
Float valve seat	#1.5
Starting carburetor jet	#40
Air cleaner	Washable poly-foam element type

MAGNETO/ALTERNATOR

Type	Flywheel type Kokusan Electric Co. unit.
Model	FA-87
Lighting coil	18 Watt rated
Lighting coil output	5.8 volts at 2500 rpm / 8.5 volts at 8000 rpm (with 25 watt circuit load)
Lighting coil resistance	.2 ohm
Lighting coil air gap	Fixed
Ignition coil:	
Primary resistance	.8 ohm
Secondary resistance	4800 ohms
Power test	Steady fire over 6mm gap at 500 rpm
	Steady fire over 8mm gap at 3000 rpm
Spark plug	NGK B-7 (std.)
	NGK B-8 (cold)
Condenser capacitance	.25 to .27 Mf. (+ or − 10%)

(continued)

SPECIFICATIONS, ACE 90 (continued)

MAGNETO/ALTERNATOR (continued)

Magneto drive	Engine crankshaft
Contact breaker gap	.012" to .014" (.3mm to .4mm)
Spark plug gap	.024" to .027" (.6mm to .7mm)
Firing point (ignition timing)	25° (.114" or 2.90mm) B.T.D.C.
Ignition coil air gap	.010" (.25mm)

CLUTCH

Type	3-plate wet type crankshaft mounted, spring tensioned
Clutch spring free length:	
Inner spring	.67" (17mm)
Outer spring	.79" (20mm)
Clutch lever free play	3/32" (2.4mm)
Clutch lever adjustment	By spacer
Spacers available	.2mm - .3mm - .5mm
Friction plate thickness (new)	.078" (2mm)

PRIMARY DRIVE

Type	Helical cut gears
Pinion gear	19T
Primary (mainshaft) gear	69T
Primary ratio	3.63 : 1
Gear module	1.5

TRANSMISSION

Type: 4-speed constant mesh with foot operated gearchange. Straight cut gears. (Pat. #495715)

Gear ratio, overall:

		(32T X 15T)	(46T X 15T)
Low	29.53	(11T X 42T)	42.57
2nd	17.86	(16T X 37T)	25.74
3rd	12.37	(20T X 32T)	17.83
Top	9.04	(24T X 28T)	13.03

Gear module	1.5
Foot change shaft end play	.008" to .012" (.2mm to .3mm)
Foot change shaft end play adj.	By washer
Washers available	.2mm - .3mm
Shifter arm adjustment	1.697" (43mm) from shifter sliding pin to magneto cover base surface
Shifter arm adjustment method	Eccentric bolt
Shifter guide side play	.003" to .005" (.1mm to .15mm)
Shifter guide adjustment	By spacer
Spacers available	.2mm - .3mm

FINAL DRIVE

Type	Chain and sprockets
Chain	½" X ¼" #420 Japanese Standard Chain
Rear wheel sprocket(s)	32T (road) 46T (trail)
Countershaft sprocket	15T
Final drive ratio(s)	2.13 : 1 (32T)
	3.07 : 1 (46T)

(continued)

SPECIFICATIONS, ACE 90 (continued)

KICKSTARTER	
Kick shaft end play	.002" to .004" (.05mm to .1mm)
End play adjustment	By washer
Washers available	.2mm · .3mm · .5mm
LIGHTING SYSTEM	
Headlight	14,000 c/pwr., 5" dia., dual sealed beam Josai Electric unit
Bulb data:	
Headlamp	6V 15W/15W
High beam indicator	6V 1.5W
Speedometer lamp	6V 1.5W
Stop & tail lamp	6V 20W/5W
Dimmer switch	3 position · high, low, and off
Main switch	3 position · off, ign., and ign./lights
Battery	6 volt, 4 ampere hr., 3 cell, visible level, GS MV2-6 unit
Rectifier	Selenium type, single plate, 6 volt, 5-SH-E unit
FRAME	
Type	Duplex (twin tube) .109 wall, steel tube arc welded frame
FRONT SUSPENSION	
Type	Oil dampened, spring cushioned, ferrous iron bushed, telescopic fork
Trail	2.737"
Caster angle	64°
Rake angle	26°
REAR SUSPENSION	
Type	Pivoted swing arm with multi-rate springs on single action hydraulic shock absorbers. Short wheelbase position provided for in swing arm
WHEEL RIMS	
Type	Chromed, WMO width, drop center steel rims
Spokes	11 ga. spring steel
TIRES & TUBES	
Tires	2.50 X 17" front, 2.75 X 17" rear, traction tread, 4 ply nylon cord IRC tires
Tubes	IRC butyl rubber tubes
Tire pressures	22psi front, 25psi rear (driver only) / 25psi front, 28psi rear (driver & passenger)

(continued)

SPECIFICATIONS, ACE 90 (continued)

BRAKES

Type	Drum type with single leading shoe front & rear
Shoes	Die cast aluminum with bonded friction material
Drums	4.3" (110mm) diameter aluminum full hub drums with cast iron friction surface
Total lining area	18.9"

DIMENSIONS & WEIGHT

Wheelbase	48"
Overall length	71"
Height at handlebars	49.4"
Height at saddle	31"
Width at footpegs	18"
Width at handlebars	33.3"
Weight (dry)	155 lb.
Weight (fuel, lubricants, tools)	173 lb.
Ground clearance	8"

TORQUE SETTINGS

Cylinder head nuts	105 in.-lb. (1.2 kg. m.)
Flywheel nut	170 in.-lb. (2 kg. m.)
Clutch nut	250 in.-lb. (2.9 kg. m.)

CAPACITIES

Fuel tank	2¾ U.S. gallons (10.4 liters)
Transmission	1¼ pints (581cc or .6 liters)
Front forks	4.5 oz. (135cc) per fork leg

CLEARANCES

Max. cylinder wear (taper)	.008" (+.2mm) maximum
Piston to cylinder	.004" (.1mm) total
Piston ring end gaps:	
Top ring	.006" to .014" (.15mm to .35mm)
Bottom ring	.004" to .012" (.10mm to .30mm)
Piston ring side play:	
Top ring	.0004" to .0024" (.01mm to .06mm)
Bottom ring	.0008" to .0024" (.02mm to .06mm)
Piston pin to piston	.00008" (.002mm)
Piston pin to connecting rod bushing	.0005" (.013mm)
Connecting rod to crank pin	.0005" (.013mm)
Connecting rod side play	.002" to .004" (.05mm to .1mm)

COMPRESSION PRESSURE

Normal compression pressure	80 to 150 lbs.

PERFORMANCE

Maximum speed	56 mph
Climbing ability	30°
Fuel consumption	155 mpg at 31 mph (level road)

(continued)

SPECIFICATIONS, ACE 90 (continued)

TIMING SPECIFICATIONS

ACE 90 Ignition Timing

(0.071") 19°41' B.T.D.C.
(0.075") 20°14' B.T.D.C.
(0.079") 20°50' B.T.D.C.
(0.083") 21°19' B.T.D.C.
(0.087") 21°50' B.T.D.C.
(0.091") 22°22' B.T.D.C.
(0.094") 22°52' B.T.D.C.
(0.098") 23°22' B.T.D.C.
(0.102") 23°50' B.T.D.C.
(0.106") 24°20' B.T.D.C.
(0.110") 24°47' B.T.D.C.
(0.114") 25°15' B.T.D.C. - STD.
(0.118") 25°44' B.T.D.C.
(0.122") 26°10' B.T.D.C.
(0.126") 26°36' B.T.D.C.

ACE 90 Transfer Port Timing

(1.54") 39mm 64°10' STD.
(1.50") 38mm 67°00'
(1.46") 37mm 69°44'
(1.42") 36mm 72°23'

ACE 90 Exhaust Port Timing

(1.30") 33mm 79°58' STD.
(1.26") 32mm 82°23'
(1.22") 31mm 84°46'
(1.18") 30mm 87°07'
(1.14") 29mm 89°57'

ACE 90 Inlet Port Timing

(2.80") 71mm 61°10' STD.
(2.83") 72mm 63°28'
(2.87") 73mm 65°44'
(2.91") 74mm 67°59'
(2.95") 75mm 70°13'
(2.99") 76mm 72°27'
(3.03") 77mm 74°41'
(3.07") 78mm 76°55'

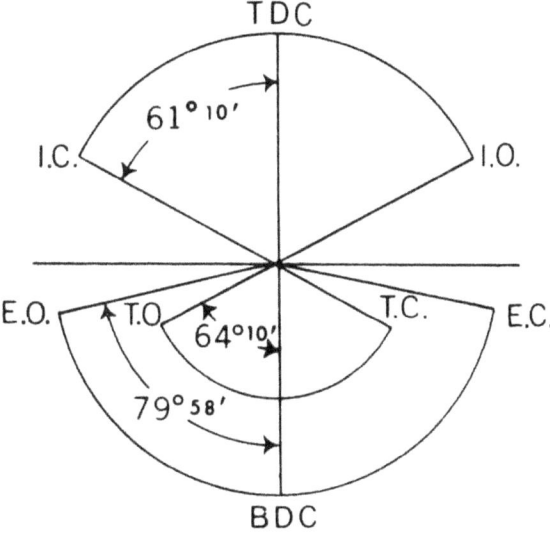

ACE 90 Stock Engine Port Timing Diagram
(total duration)

Inlet: 122°20'
Exhaust: 159°56'
Transfer: 128°20'

SPECIFICATIONS, ACE 100

ENGINE

Type	25° inclined single cylinder, two stroke/cycle air-cooled. Loop scavenged, piston port induction
Rated horsepower	9.8 at 7,500 rpm
Maximum torque	6.7 ft.-lb. at 5,500 rpm
Bore	50mm (1.97")
Stroke	50mm (1.97")
Piston displacement	98cc (5.99 C.I.)
Compression ratio	10 : 1
Exhaust duration	164°
Transfer duration	128°
Inlet duration	131°
Lubrication system	Fuel/oil mix
Fuel mixture	16:1 - first 500 miles 20:1 - thereafter
Recommended engine lubricant	SAE 30W 2 cycle oil
Starting system	Kickstarter

CARBURETOR

Type	Horizontal mounted Mikuni carburetor with slide throttle and needle jet system
Model	VM 20-SH 10
Main jet	#95 (std.)
Venturi	20mm
Needle jet	#N6
Jet needle	#4F6
Needle clip position	4th notch (std.)
Pilot jet	#25
Idle screw	#2
Idle screw adjustment	1¼ turns from closed
Throttle slide	#2.0
Float valve seat	#1.5
Starting carburetor jet	#40
Air cleaner	Washable poly-foam element type

MAGNETO/ALTERNATOR

Type	Flywheel type Kokusan Electric Co. unit with external HT coil
Model	FA-119
Lighting coil	18 watt rated
Lighting coil output	5.8 volts at 2,500 rpm 8.5 volts at 8,000 rpm (with 25 watt circuit load)
Lighting coil resistance	.2 ohm
Lighting coil air gap	.010" (.25mm)
Ignition coil:	
Primary resistance	0.75 ohm
Secondary resistance	6.0 ohms
Power test	Steady fire over 6mm gap at 500 rpm Steady fire over 8mm gap at 3,000 rpm

(continued)

SPECIFICATIONS, ACE 100 (continued)

MAGNETO/ALTERNATOR (continued)

Primary exciting coil output	8 volts at 2,500 rpm (Measured with ignition
	15 volts at 8,000 rpm coil in circuit)
Primary exciting coil resistance	.63 ohm
Primary exciting coil air gap	.010" (.25mm)
Spark plug	NGK B-8 (std.)
	NGK B-9 (cold)
Condenser capacitance	.25 to .27 Mf. ($\pm$ 10%)
Magneto drive	Engine crankshaft
Contact breaker gap	.012" to .014" (.3mm to .4mm)
Spark plug gap	.024" to .027" (.6mm to .7mm)
Firing point (ignition timing)	25° (.114" or 2.90mm) B.T.D.C.

CLUTCH

Type	4-plate wet type, crankshaft mounted
Clutch spring free length:	
Inner spring	.67" (17mm)
Outer spring	.70" (20mm)
Clutch lever free play	3/32" (2.4mm)
Clutch lever adjustment	By spacer
Spacers available	.2mm -.3mm -.5mm
Friction plate thickness (new)	.078" (2mm)

PRIMARY DRIVE

Type	Helical cut gears
Pinion gear	19T
Primary (mainshaft) gear	69T
Primary ratio	3.63 : 1
Gear tooth module	1.5

TRANSMISSION

Type: 5-speed, wide-ratio constant mesh with foot-operated gear change. Straight cut gears (Pat. #495715)

Gear ratio overall:

	(36T x 15T) road gear	(50T x 15T) trail gear
Low	30.49	42.39
Second	18.64	25.92
Third	13.07	18.17
Fourth	10.37	14.41
Fifth	8.71	12.11

Transmission Gears

	Mainshaft		Countershaft		Ratio
Low	10T	X	35T	=	3.5:1
Second	14T	X	30T	=	2.14:1
Third	18T	X	27T	=	1.5:1
Fourth	21T	X	25T	=	1.19:1
Fifth	23T	X	23T	=	1:1

(continued)

SPECIFICATIONS, ACE 100 (continued)

TRANSMISSION (continued)

Gear tooth module	1.75
Foot change shaft end play	.008" to .012" (.2mm to .3mm)
Foot change shaft end play adj.	By washer
Washers available	.2mm - .3mm
Shifter arm adjustment	1.382" (35.1mm) measured from shifter sliding pin to inside cover surface in third gear position
Shifter arm adjustment method	Eccentric bolt
Shifter guide side play	.003" to .005" (.1mm to .15mm)
Shifter guide side play adj.	By spacer
Spacers available	.2mm - .3mm

FINAL DRIVE

Type	Chain and sprockets
Chain dimensions	½ x ¼" #420 Japanese Standard Chain
Rear wheel sprocket(s)	36T (road) 50T (trail)
Countershaft sprocket	15T
Final drive ratios	2.4:1 (36T)
	3.33:1 (50T)

KICKSTARTER

Kick gear	35T
Kick shaft end play	.002" to .004" (.05mm to .1mm)
Kick shaft end play adjustment	By spacer
Spacers available	.2mm - .3mm - .5mm

LIGHTING SYSTEM

Headlight	14,000 c/pwr., 5" dia., dual sealed beam Josai Electric unit
Bulb data:	
Headlamp	6V 15W/15W
High beam indicator	6V 1.5W
Speedometer lamp	6V 1.5W
Stop and taillamp	6V 20W/5W
Dimmer switch	3 position - high, low, and off
Main switch	3 position - off, ign., and ign./lights
Battery	6 volt, 4 ampere hr., 3 cell, visible level, GN4-2A unit
Rectifier	Selenium type, single plate, 6 volt, 5-SH-E unit

FRAME

Type	Duplex (twin tube) .109 wall, steel tube arc welded frame

(continued)

SPECIFICATIONS, ACE 100 (continued)

FRONT SUSPENSION

Type	Oil damped, spring cushioned, ferrous iron bushed, telescopic forks
Trail	2.737"
Castor angle	64°
Rake angle	26°

REAR SUSPENSION

Type	Pivoted swing arm with multirate springs on single action hydraulic shock absorbers. Short wheelbase position provided for in swing arm bracket.

WHEEL RIMS

Type	Chrome plated steel, WM1 width, drop center rims. 36 spoke holes
Spokes	10 ga. spring steel

TIRES AND TUBES

Tires	2.75 x 17" front, 3.00 x 17" rear traction tread, 4 ply nylon cord Nitto tires
Tubes	Nitto butyl rubber tubes
Tire pressures	22 psi front, 25 psi rear (rider only)
	25 psi front, 28 psi rear (rider and passenger)

BRAKES

Type	Drum type with single leading shoe front and rear
Shoes	Die cast aluminum with bonded-on friction material
Drums	4.3" (110mm) dia., die cast aluminum full hub drums with cast iron friction surface
Total lining area	18.9"

DIMENSIONS AND WEIGHT

Wheelbase	48"
Overall length	72.8"
Height at handlebars	39.4"
Height at saddle	32.5"
Width at footpegs	18"

(continued)

SPECIFICATIONS, ACE 100 (continued)

DIMENSIONS AND WEIGHT (continued)

Width at handlebars	33.3"
Weight (dry)	170 lbs.
Weight (fuel, lubricants, tools)	188 lbs.
Ground clearance	8.07"

TORQUE SETTINGS

Cylinder head nuts	105 in.-lb. (1.2 kg. m.)
Flywheel nut	170 in.-lb. (2 kg. m.)
Clutch nut	250 in.-lb. (2.9 kg. m.)
8mm rear sprocket bolts	250 in.-lb. (2.9 kg. m.)
10mm rear sprocket bolts	250 in.-lb. (2.9 kg. m.)

CAPACITIES

Fuel tank	2¾ US gallons (10.4 liters)
Transmission	1¼ pints (581cc or .6 liters)
Front forks	4.5 oz. (135cc) per fork leg

CLEARANCES

Max. allowable cyl. taper (wear)	.008" (+.2mm)
Piston to cyl. clearance	.004" (.1mm)
Piston ring end gaps:	
Top ring	.006" to .014" (.15mm to .35mm)
Bottom ring	.004" to .012" (.10mm to .30mm)
Piston ring side play:	
Top ring	.0004" to .0024" (.01mm to .06mm)
Bottom ring	.0008" to .0024" (.02mm to .06mm)
Piston pin to piston	.00008" (.002mm)
Piston pin to connecting rod bearing	.0003" to .0006" (.007mm to .014mm)
Connecting rod to crank pin	.0005" (.013mm)
Connecting rod side play	.002" to .004" (.05 to .1mm)

COMPRESSION PRESSURE

Normal compression pressure	80 to 150 lbs.

PERFORMANCE

Maximum speed	62 mph (road gear)
Climbing ability	30°
Fuel consumption	155 mpg at 31 mph (level road)

(continued)

SPECIFICATIONS, ACE 100 (continued)

TIMING SPECIFICATIONS

ACE 100 Ignition Timing

(0.071")	19°41'	B.T.D.C.
(0.075")	20°14'	B.T.D.C.
(0.079")	20°50'	B.T.D.C.
(0.083")	21°19'	B.T.D.C.
(0.087")	21°50'	B.T.D.C.
(0.091")	22°22'	B.T.D.C.
(0.094")	22°52'	B.T.D.C.
(0.098")	23°22'	B.T.D.C.
(0.102")	23°50'	B.T.D.C.
(0.106")	24°20'	B.T.D.C.
(0.110")	24°47'	B.T.D.C.
(0.114")	25°15'	B.T.D.C. - STD.
(0.118")	25°44'	B.T.D.C.
(0.122")	26°10'	B.T.D.C.
(0.126")	26°36'	B.T.D.C.

ACE 100 Transfer Port Timing

(1.54")	39mm	64°10' STD.
(1.50")	38mm	67°00'
(1.46")	37mm	69°44'
(1.42")	36mm	72°23'

ACE 100 Exhaust Port Timing

(1.30")	33mm	79°58'
(1.26")	32mm	82°23' STD.
(1.22")	31mm	84°46'
(1.18")	30mm	87°07'
(1.14")	29mm	89°57'

ACE 100 Inlet Port Timing

(2.80")	71mm	61°10'
(2.83")	72mm	63°28'
(2.87")	73mm	65°44' STD.
(2.91")	74mm	67°59'
(2.95")	75mm	70°13'
(2.99")	76mm	72°27'
(3.03")	77mm	74°41'
(3.07")	78mm	76°55'

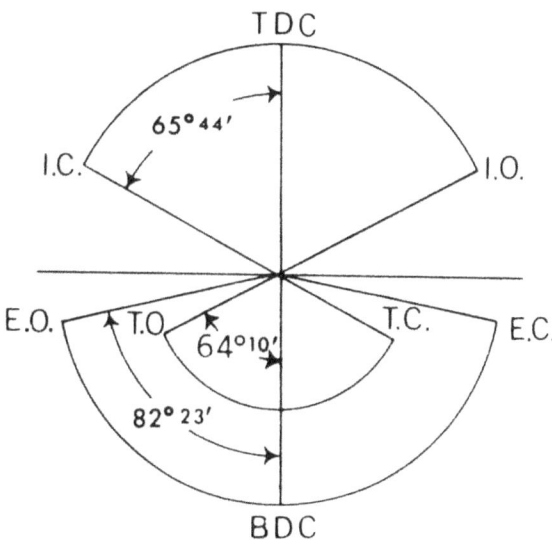

ACE 100 Stock Engine Port Timing
(total duration)

Inlet:	131°28'
Exhaust:	164°46'
Transfer:	128°20'

SPECIFICATIONS, DIRT SQUIRT 100

ENGINE

Type	25° inclined single cylinder, two cycle, air-cooled engine. Loop scavenged, piston port induction
Rated horsepower	@ 7,500 rpm
Maximum torque	@ 5,500 rpm
Bore	50mm (1.97")
Stroke	50mm (1.97")
Piston displacement	98cc (5.99 cu. in.)
Compression ratio	6.7 : 1
Exhaust duration	164°
Transfer duration	128°
Inlet duration	131°
Lubrication system	Fuel/oil mix
Recommended engine lubricant	SAE 30W 2 cycle oil
Fuel mixture	16:1 first 500 miles
	20:1 thereafter
Starting system	Kickstarter

CARBURETOR

Type	Horizontal mounted Mikuni instrument with slide throttle and needle jet system
Model	VM 20-SH 10
Main jet	No. 95 (std.)
Venturi	20mm
Needle jet	No. N6
Jet needle	No. 4F6
Needle clip position	4th notch (std.)
Pilot jet	No. 25
Idle screw adjustment	1¼ turns from closed
Throttle slide	No. 2.0
Float valve seat	No. 1.5
Starting carburetor jet	No. 40
Air cleaner	Washable poly foam element type

MAGNETO / ALTERNATOR

Type	Flywheel type Kohusan Electric Co. unit with external HT coil
Model	FA 119 and FA4309
Lighting coil	21.8 watt rated
Lighting coil output	4.5 volts at 2,500 rpm
	8 volts at 8,000 rpm
	with 25 watt circuit load
Ignition coil	
Power test	Steady fire over 7mm gap at 500 rpm
	Steady fire over 8mm at 5,000 rpm
Spark plug	NGK B-8 (std.)
	NGK B-9 (cold)
Condenser capacitance	.25 to .27 mf. (+ or − 10%)
Magneto drive	Engine crankshaft
Contact breaker gap	.012" to .014" (.3mm to .4mm)
Spark plug gap	.024" to .027" (.6mm to .7mm)
Firing point (ignition timing)	25° (.114" or 2.90mm) BTDC

(continued)

SPECIFICATIONS, DIRT SQUIRT 100 (continued)

TRANSMISSION

Type			5-speed, wide-ratio constant mesh with foot-operated gear change. Straight cut gears. (Pat. No. 495715)	

Gear ratio overall:
- Standard gearing — 14T x 56T
- First — 38.94
- Second — 26.49
- Third — 18.90
- Fourth — 13.81
- Fifth — 11.32

Transmission gears

	Main shaft		Countershaft		Ratio
Low	9T	X	31T	=	3.44 : 1
Second	12T	X	28T	=	2.34 : 1
Third	15T	X	25T	=	1.67 : 1
Fourth	18T	X	22T	=	1.22 : 1
Fifth	20T	X	20T	=	1.00 : 1

- Gear tooth module — 2.0
- Foot change shaft end-play — .008" to .012" (.2mm to .3mm)
- Foot change shaft end-play adj. — By washer
- Washers available — .2mm-.3mm
- Shifter arm adjustment — 1.382" (35.1mm) measured from shifter sliding pin to inside cover surface in third gear position
- Shifter arm adjustment method — Eccentric bolt
- Shifter guide side-play — .003" to .005" (.1mm to .15mm)
- Shifter guide side-play adj. — By spacer
- Spacers available — .2mm-.3mm

CLUTCH

- Type — 4 plate wet type, crankshaft mounted
- Clutch spring free length
  - Inner spring — 17.65mm
  - Outer spring — 17.27mm
- Clutch lever free-play — 3/32" (2.4mm)
- Clutch lever adjustment — By spacer
- Spacers available — .2mm-.3mm-.5mm
- Friction plate thickness (new) — .100" (2.54mm)

PRIMARY DRIVE

- Type — Helical cut gears
- Pinion gear — 23T
- Primary (main shaft) gear — 65T
- Primary ratio — 2.83:1
- Gear tooth module — 1.75

FINAL DRIVE

- Type — Chain and sprockets
- Chain dimensions — No. 423 Japanese standard chain
- Rear wheel sprocket — 56T
- Countershaft sprocket — 14T
- Final drive ratio — 4:1

(continued)

SPECIFICATIONS, DIRT SQUIRT 100 (continued)

KICKSTARTER
- Kick gear: 29T
- Kick shaft end-play: .002" to .004" (.05mm to .1mm)
- Kick shaft end-play adj.: By spacer
- Spacers available: .2mm-.3mm-.5mm

FRAME
- Type: Duplex (twin tube), steel tube arc welded frame

FRONT SUSPENSION
- Type: Telescopic fork
- Trail: 4.2"
- Castor angle: 60.5°
- Rake angle: 29.5°

REAR SUSPENSION
- Type: Swing arm with shock absorbers

WHEEL RIMS
- Type: Chrome plated steel, front WM-1 width x 19", rear WM-2 width x 17"

TIRES AND TUBES
- Tires: 2.75 x 19" front, 3.25 x 17" rear, knobby tread, 4-ply nylon cord Nitto tires
- Tire pressures: 25 psi front, 28 psi rear (rider and passenger)

BRAKES
- Type: Single leading shoe drum type front and rear
- Shoes: Die cast aluminum with bonded-on friction material
- Drums: 4.3" (110mm) front, 5.2" (130mm) rear dia., full hub drums with cast iron friction surface

DIMENSIONS AND WEIGHT
- Wheelbase: 51.5"
- Overall length: 78"
- Height at handlebars: 41.9"
- Height at saddle: 30.23"
- Width at handlebars: 32.28"
- Weight (dry): 185.6 lbs.
- Ground clearance: 8.86"

TORQUE SETTINGS
- Cylinder head nuts: 105 in.-lb. (1.2 mkg)
- Flywheel nut: 170 in.-lb. (2 mkg)
- Clutch nut: 250 in.-lb. (2.9 mkg)
- Sprocket bolts: 250 in.-lb. (2.9 mkg)

(continued)

SPECIFICATIONS, DIRT SQUIRT 100 (continued)

CAPACITIES	
Fuel tank	2.0 U.S. gallons
Transmission	1¼ pints (581cc or .6 liters)
Front forks	5½ oz. (163cc) per fork leg

CLEARANCES	
Max. allowable cylinder taper (wear)	.008" (+.2mm)
Piston to cylinder clearance	.004" (.1mm)
Piston ring end gaps	
Top ring	.006" to .014" (.15mm to .35mm)
Bottom ring	.004" to .012" (.10mm to .30mm)
Piston ring side-play	
Top ring	.0004" to .0024" (.01mm to .06mm)
Bottom ring	.0008" to .0024" (.02mm to .06mm)
Piston pin to piston	.0008" (.02mm)
Piston pin to connecting rod bearing	.0003" to .0006" (.007mm to .014mm)
Connecting rod to crank pin	.0005" (.013mm)
Connecting rod side play	.002" to .004" (.05mm to .1mm)

TIMING SPECIFICATIONS (STD.)		
Ignition timing		
(0.114") 2.4mm	25° 15' BTDC	
Transfer port timing		
(1.54") 3.9mm	64° 10' BTDC	
Exhaust port timing		
(1.26") 32mm	82° 23' BTDC	
Inlet port timing		
(2.87") 73mm	65° 44' BTDC	

SPECIFICATIONS, ACE 100-B

ENGINE

Type	25° inclined single cylinder, two stroke/cycle air cooled. Loop scavenged, piston port induction
Rated horsepower	10.5 at 7,500 rpm
Maximum torque	6.7 ft.-lb. at 5,500 rpm
Bore	50mm (1.97")
Stroke	50mm (1.97")
Piston displacement	98cc (5.99 C.I.)
Compression ratio	10:1
Exhaust duration	164°
Transfer duration	128°
Inlet duration	131°
Lubrication system	Fuel/oil mix
Fuel mixture	16:1 first 500 miles
	20:1 thereafter
Recommended engine lubricant	SAE 30W 2 cycle oil
Starting system	Kickstarter

CARBURETOR

Type	Horizontal mounted Mikuni carburetor with slide throttle and needle jet system
Model	VM20-SH 10
Main jet	#95 (std.)
Venturi	20mm
Needle jet	#N6
Jet needle	#4F6
Needle clip position	4th notch (std.)
Pilot jet	#25
Idle screw	#2
Idle screw adjustment	1¼ turns from closed
Throttle slide	#2.0
Float valve seat	#1.5
Starting carburetor jet	#40
Air cleaner	Washable poly-foam element type

MAGNETO/ALTERNATOR

Type	Flywheel type Kokusan Electric Co. unit with external HT coil
Model	FA-119 & FA-4309
Lighting coil	18 watt rated & 21.8 watt rated
Lighting coil output	18-watt coil:
	5.8 volts at 2,500 rpm) with 25-watt
	8.5 volts at 8,000 rpm (circuit load
	21.8-watt coil:
	Green lead wire:
	2.4 volts at 2,500 rpm) with 25-watt
	6.1 volts at 8,000 rpm (circuit load
	Yellow lead wire:
	4.5 volts at 2,500 rpm) with 25-watt
	8 volts at 8,000 rpm (circuit load

(continued)

SPECIFICATIONS, ACE 100-B (continued)

MAGNETO/ALTERNATOR (continued)

Lighting coil resistance	
18-watt coil	.35 ohm (either lead but checked at coil)
21.8-watt coil	.08 ohm (green lead wire)
	.2 ohm (yellow lead wire)
Lighting coil air gap	.010" (.25mm)
Ignition coil:	
923008 coil primary resistance	.75 ohm
secondary resistance	4,800 ohms
923008A coil primary resistance	1.6 ohms
secondary resistance	5,000 ohms
Primary exciting coil output	8 volts at 2,500 rpm } (ign. coil
	15 volts at 8,000 rpm } in circuit)
Primary exciting coil resistance	.63 ohm
Primary exciting coil air gap	.010" (.25mm)
Spark plug	NGK B-8 (std.)
	NGK B-9 (cold)
Condenser capacitance	.25 to .27 Mf. (± 10%)
Magneto drive	Engine crankshaft
Contact breaker gap	.012" to .014" (.3mm to .4mm)
Spark plug gap	.024" to .027" (.6mm to .7mm)
Firing point (ignition timing)	25° (.114" or 2.90mm) BTDC

CLUTCH

Type	4-plate, wet type, crankshaft mounted
Clutch spring free length:	
Inner spring	17.65mm
Outer spring	17.27mm
Clutch lever free play	3/32" (2.4mm)
Clutch lever adjustment	By spacer
Spacers available	.2mm - .3mm - .5mm
Friction disc thickness (new)	.100" (2.54mm)

PRIMARY DRIVE

Type	Helical cut gears
Pinion gear	19T
Primary (mainshaft) gear	69T
Primary ratio	3.63:1
Gear tooth module	1.5

TRANSMISSION

Type	5-speed, wide-ratio constant mesh with foot-operated gear change. Straight cut gears (Pat. #495715)

(continued)

SPECIFICATIONS, ACE 100-B (continued)

TRANSMISSION (continued)

Gear ratio overall:

	(15T x 36T) road gear	(15T x 50T) trail gear
Low	30.49	42.39
Second	18.64	25.92
Third	13.07	18.17
Fourth	10.37	14.41
Fifth	8.71	12.11

Transmission Gears

	Mainshaft		Countershaft		Ratio
Low	10T	X	35T	=	3.5:1
Second	14T	X	30T	=	2.14:1
Third	18T	X	27T	=	1.5:1
Fourth	21T	X	25T	=	1.19:1
Fifth	23T	X	23T	=	1:1

Gear tooth module	1.75
Foot change shaft end play	.008" to .012" (.2mm to .3mm)
Foot change shaft end play adj.	By washer
Washers available	.2mm - .3mm
Shifter arm adjustment	1.382" (35.1mm) measured from shifter sliding pin to inside cover surface in third gear position
Shifter arm adjustment method	Eccentric bolt
Shifter guide side play	.003" to .005" (.1mm to .15mm)
Shifter guide side play adj.	By spacer
Spacers available	.2mm - .3mm

FINAL DRIVE

Type	Chain and sprockets
Chain dimensions	½ x ¼" #420 Japanese Standard Chain
Rear wheel sprocket(s)	36T (road) 50T (trail)
Countershaft sprocket	15T
Final drive ratios	2.4:1 (36T)
	3.33:1 (50T)

KICKSTARTER

Kick gear	35T
Kick shaft end play	.002" to .004" (.05mm to .1mm)
Kick shaft end play adjustment	By spacer
Spacers available	.2mm - .3mm - .5mm

LIGHTING SYSTEM

Headlight	5" diameter, dual sealed beam Josai (Aiki) or Stanley unit

(continued)

SPECIFICATIONS, ACE 100-B (continued)

LIGHTING SYSTEM (continued)	
Bulb data:	
Headlamp	6V 15W/15W
High beam indicator	6V 1.5W
Speedometer lamp	6V 1.5W
Stop and taillamp	6V 20W/5W
Dimmer switch	2-position: high, low
Mainswitch	3-position: off, ign., & ign./lights
Battery	6V, 4 ampere hr., 3 cell unit
Battery specification number	GS 6n4 - 2A
Rectifier	Selenium type, single plate, 6 Volt, 5-SH-E unit
FRAME	
Type	Duplex (twin tube) .109" wall, steel tube arc welded frame
FRONT SUSPENSION	
Type	Oil damped, spring cushioned, ferrous iron bushed, telescopic forks
Trail	4.3"
Castor angle	61°
Rake angle	29°
REAR SUSPENSION	
Type	Pivoted swing arm with multi-rate springs on dual action shock absorbers. Three-way spring adjustment feature.
WHEEL RIMS	
Type	Chrome plated steel, front WM-1 width x 19", rear WM-1 width x 18". Drop centers, 36 spoke
Spokes	10 ga. spring steel
TIRES AND TUBES	
Tires	2.75 x 19" front, 3.00 x 18" rear, trials tread, 4-ply nylon cord Nitto tires
Tubes	Nitto butyl rubber tubes
Tire pressures	22 psi front, 25 psi rear (rider only) 25 psi front, 28 psi rear (rider & passenger)
BRAKES	
Type	Drum type with single leading shoe, front and rear
Shoes	Die cast aluminum with bonded friction material
Drums	110/130mm diameter full hub drums w/cast iron friction surface

(continued)

SPECIFICATIONS, ACE 100-B (continued)

DIMENSIONS AND WEIGHT

Wheelbase	50"
Overall length	74"
Height at handlebars	43.5"
Height at saddle	32"
Width at footpegs	18"
Width at handlebars	32"
Weight (dry)	183 lbs.
Weight (fuel, lubricants, tools)	201 lbs.
Ground clearance	11"

TORQUE SETTINGS

Cylinder head nuts	105 in.-lb. (1.2 kg. m.)
Flywheel nut	170 in.-lb. (2 kg. m.)
Clutch nut	250 in.-lb. (2.9 kg. m.)
8mm rear sprocket bolts	250 in.-lb. (2.9 kg. m.)

CAPACITIES

Fuel tank	2¾ U.S. gallons (10.4 liters)
Transmission	1¼ pints (581cc or .6 liters)
Front forks	5 oz. (163cc) per fork leg (Fork ass'y. #938750 and #938750A)
	6 oz. (195cc) per fork leg (Fork ass'y. #938700)

CLEARANCES

Max. allowable cyl. taper (wear)	.008" (+.2mm)
Piston to cyl. clearance	.004" (.1mm)
Piston ring end gaps:	
Top ring	.006" to .014" (.15mm to .35mm)
Bottom ring	.004" to .012" (.10mm to .30mm)
Piston ring side play:	
Top ring	.0004" to .0024" (.01mm to .06mm)
Bottom ring	.0008" to .0024" (.02mm to .06mm)
Piston pin to piston	.00008" (.002mm)
Piston pin to connecting rod bearing	.0003" to .0006" (.007mm to .014mm)
Connecting rod to crank pin	.0005" (.013mm)
Connecting rod side play	.002" to .004" (.05 to .1mm)

COMPRESSION PRESSURE

Normal compression pressure	80 to 150 lbs.

PERFORMANCE

Maximum speed	62 mph (road gear)
Climbing ability	30°
Fuel consumption	155 mpg at 31 mph (level road)

(continued)

SPECIFICATIONS, ACE 100-B (continued)

TIMING SPECIFICATIONS

ACE 100B Ignition Timing

(0.071") 19°41' B.T.D.C.
(0.075") 20°14' B.T.D.C.
(0.079") 20°50' B.T.D.C.
(0.083") 21°19' B.T.D.C.
(0.087") 21°50' B.T.D.C.
(0.091") 22°22' B.T.D.C.
(0.094") 22°52' B.T.D.C.
(0.098") 23°22' B.T.D.C.
(0.102") 23°50' B.T.D.C.
(0.106") 24°20' B.T.D.C.
(0.110") 24°47' B.T.D.C.
(0.114") 25°15' B.T.D.C. - STD.
(0.118") 25°44' B.T.D.C.
(0.122") 26°10' B.T.D.C.
(0.126") 26°36' B.T.D.C.

ACE 100B Transfer Port Timing

(1.54") 39mm 64°10' STD.
(1.50") 32mm 67°00'
(1.46") 37mm 69°44'
(1.42") 36mm 72°23'

ACE 100B Exhaust Port Timing

(1.30") 33mm 79°58'
(1.26") 32mm 82°23' STD.
(1.22") 31mm 84°46'
(1.18") 30mm 87°07'
(1.14") 29mm 89°45'

ACE 100B Inlet Port Timing

(2.80") 71mm 61°10'
(2.83") 72mm 63°28'
(2.87") 73mm 65°44' STD.
(2.91") 74mm 67°59'
(2.95") 75mm 70°13'
(2.99") 76mm 72°27'
(3.03") 77mm 74°41'
(3.07") 78mm 76°55'

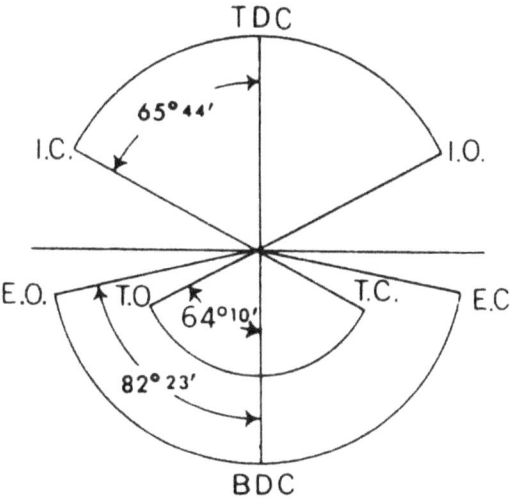

ACE 100B Stock Engine Port Timing
(total duration)

Inlet: 131°28'
Exhaust: 164°46'
Transfer: 128°20'

145

SPECIFICATIONS, 100-MX — SUPER RAT

ENGINE

Type	25° inclined single cylinder, two stroke/cycle air-cooled. Loop scavenged, piston port induction
Rated horsepower	Sufficient
Maximum torque at	6,600 rpm
Bore	50mm (1.97")
Stroke	50mm (1.97")
Piston displacement	98cc (5.99 C.I.)
Atmospheric compression ratio	5.5:1
Exhaust duration	174°
Transfer duration	134°
Inlet duration	136°
Lubrication system	Fuel/oil mix
Fuel mixture	16:1
Recommended engine lubricant	SAE 30W 2-cycle racing oil
Starting system	Kickstarter

CARBURETOR

Type	Horizontal mounted Mikuni instrument with slide throttle and needle jet system
Model	VM 24 SH
Main jet	No. 220 (std.)
Venturi	24mm
Needle jet	No. N8
Jet needle	No. 4E1
Needle clip position	3rd notch (middle) std.
Pilot jet	No. 30
Idle screw	No. 2
Idle screw adjustment	1 1/4 turns from closed
Throttle slide	No. 2.0
Float valve seat	No. 2.0
Air cleaner	Washable poly-foam double element type

MAGNETO

Type	Flywheel type Kokusan Electric Co. unit
Model	FA-87
Ignition coil:	
Primary resistance	.42 ohm
Secondary resistance	5.35 ohms
Power test	Steady fire over 6mm gap at 1,000 rpm
	Steady fire over 8mm gap at 3,000 rpm
Primary exciting coil output	8 volts at 2,500 rpm ⎫ (Measured with ignition
	15 volts at 8,000 rpm ⎭ coil in circuit)
Primary exciting coil resistance	.63 ohm
Primary exciting coil air gap	.010" (.25mm)
Spark plug	NGK B10HN (std.)
	NGK B11HN (colder)
Condenser capacitance	.25 to .27 Mf. ($\pm$ 10%)
Magneto drive	Engine crankshaft
Contact breaker gap	.012" to .014" (.3mm to .4mm)

(continued)

SPECIFICATIONS, 100-MX — SUPER RAT (continued)

MAGNETO (continued)

Spark plug gap	.0177" to .0196" (.45mm to .50mm) nonadjustable
Firing point (ignition timing)	25° (.114" or 2.90mm) B.T.D.C.
Ignition coil air gap	.010" (.25mm)

CLUTCH

Type	4-plate wet type, crankshaft mounted, spring tensioned
Clutch spring free length:	
Inner spring	.67" (17mm)
Outer spring	.79" (20mm)
Clutch lever free play	3/32" (2.4mm)
Clutch lever adjustment	By spacer
Spacers available	.2mm, .3mm, .5mm
Friction plate thickness (new)	.078" (2mm)

PRIMARY DRIVE

Type	Straight cut gears
Pinion gear	17T
Primary (mainshaft) gear	63T
Primary ratio	3.71:1
Gear tooth module	1.75

TRANSMISSION

Type	5-speed wide ratio constant mesh with foot-operated gear change. Straight cut gears. (Pat. No. 495715)
Gear ratio overall:	(15Tx50T) Standard gearing
	Low 43.26
	Second 26.45
	Third 18.54
	Fourth 14.71
	Fifth 12.36

Transmission Gears

	Mainshaft		Countershaft		Ratio
Low	10T	X	35T	=	3.5:1
Second	14T	X	30T	=	2.14:1
Third	18T	X	27T	=	1.5:1
Fourth	21T	X	25T	=	1.19:1
Fifth	23T	X	23T	=	1:1

Gear tooth module	1.75
Foot change shaft end play	.008" to .012" (.2mm to .3mm)
Foot change shaft end play adj.	By washer
Washers available	.2mm - .3mm
Shifter arm adjustment	1.382" (35.1mm) measured from shifter sliding pin to inside cover surface in third gear position

(continued)

SPECIFICATIONS, 100-MX — SUPER RAT (continued)

TRANSMISSION (continued)

Shifter arm adjustment method	Eccentric bolt
Shifter guide side play	.003" to .005" (.1mm to .15mm)
Shifter guide side play adj.	By spacer
Spacers available	.2mm - .3mm

FINAL DRIVE

Type	Chain and sprockets
Chain dimensions	½ x ¼" No. 420 Japanese Standard Chain
Rear wheel sprocket	50T
Countershaft sprocket	15T
Final drive ratios	3.33:1

KICKSTARTER

Kick gear	35T
Kick shaft end play	.002" to .004" (.05mm to .1mm)
Kick shaft end play adjustment	By spacer
Spacers available	.2mm - .3mm - .5mm

FRAME

Type	Duplex (twin tube) .109" wall, steel tube, arc welded frame

FRONT SUSPENSION

Type	Oil damped, spring cushioned, ferrous iron bushed, telescopic forks
Trail	4.3"
Castor angle	61°
Rake angle	30°

REAR SUSPENSION

Type	Pivoted swing arm with multi-rate springs on double damping hydraulic shock absorbers

WHEEL RIMS

Type	Chrome plated steel, WM1 width front, WM2 width rear. Drop center rims, 36 spoke holes
Spokes	10 ga. spring steel

TIRES AND TUBES

Tires	3.00x19" front, 3.25x18" rear, knobby tread, 4-ply Nitto nylon cord tires
Tubes	Nitto butyl rubber tubes

(continued)

SPECIFICATIONS, 100-MX — SUPER RAT (continued)

BRAKES	
Type	Drum type with single leading shoe, front and rear
Shoes	Die cast aluminum with bonded on friction material
Drums	4.3" (110mm) dia., die cast aluminum full hub drums with cast iron friction surface
Total lining area	18.9 sq. in.
DIMENSIONS AND WEIGHT	
Length (overall)	72"
Width (handlebar—tip to tip)	31"
Width (footpeg)	18.5"
Wheelbase	50"
Height (at saddle)	33"
Ground clearance	11.2"
Dry weight	169 lbs.
TORQUE SETTINGS	
Cylinder head nuts	105 in.-lb. (1.2 kg. m.)
Flywheel nut	170 in.-lb. (2 kg. m.)
Clutch nut	250 in.-lb. (2.9 kg. m.)
10mm rear sprocket bolts	250 in.-lb. (2.9 kg. m.)
CAPACITIES	
Fuel tank	2 U.S. gal.
Transmission	1¼ pints (581cc or .6 liters)
Front forks	6 oz. (195cc) per fork leg (938700 Fork ass'y)
	5 oz. (163cc) per fork leg (938750 & 938750A fork ass'ys)
CLEARANCES	
Max. allowable cyl. taper (wear)	.004" (.1mm)
Piston to cylinder clearance	.004" (.1mm)
Piston ring end gap	.006" to .014" (.15mm to .35mm)
Piston ring side clearance	.0004" to .0024" (.01mm to .06mm)
Piston pin to piston	.00008" (.002mm)
Piston pin to connecting rod bearing	.0003" to .0006" (.007mm to .014mm)
Connecting rod to crank pin	.0005" (.013mm)
Connecting rod side clearance	.006" to .008" (.15mm to .2mm)
COMPRESSION PRESSURE	
Using kickstarter—assuming at least 2 hours running time on ring	85 lbs.

(continued)

SPECIFICATONS, 100-MX — SUPER RAT (continued)

TIMING SPECIFICATIONS

100-MX Ignition Timing

(0.071") 19°41' B.T.D.C.
(0.075") 20°14' B.T.D.C.
(0.079") 20°50' B.T.D.C.
(0.083") 21°19' B.T.D.C.
(0.087") 21°50' B.T.D.C.
(0.091") 22°22' B.T.D.C.
(0.094") 22°52' B.T.D.C.
(0.098") 23°22' B.T.D.C.
(0.102") 23°50' B.T.D.C.
(0.106") 24°20' B.T.D.C.
(0.110") 24°47' B.T.D.C.
(0.114") 25°15' B.T.D.C. - STD.
(0.118") 25°44' B.T.D.C.
(0.122") 26°10' B.T.D.C.
(0.126") 26°36' B.T.D.C.

100-MX Transfer Port Timing

(1.54") 39mm   64°10'
(1.50") 38.5mm 65°35' - STD.
(1.52") 38mm   67°00'
(1.46") 37mm   69°44'
(1.42") 36mm   72°23'

100-MX Exhaust Port Timing

(1.30") 33mm 79°58'
(1.26") 32mm 82°23'
(1.22") 31mm 84°46'
(1.18") 30mm 87°07' - STD.
(1.14") 29mm 89°57'

100-MX Inlet Port Timing

(2.80") 71mm 61°10'
(2.83") 72mm 63°28'
(2.87") 73mm 65°44'
(2.91") 74mm 67°59' - STD.
(2.95") 75mm 70°13'
(2.99") 76mm 72°27'
(3.03") 77mm 74°41'
(3.07") 78mm 76°55'

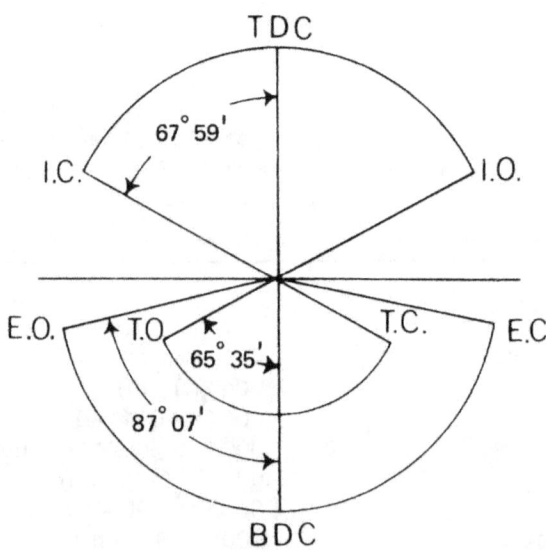

100-MX Engine Port Timing
(total duration)

Inlet: 135°58'
Exhaust: 174°14'
Transfer: 131°10'

SPECIFICATIONS, WOMBAT 125

ENGINE

Type	Loop scavenged, piston port
Model	Wombat 125/94
Rated horsepower	7,500 rpm
Maximum torque	5,900 rpm
Stroke	50mm (1.97")
Bore	56mm (2.20")
Piston displacement	123cc (7.5 cu. in.)
Compression ratio	7.2:1 atmospheric
Exhaust duration	162°
Transfer duration	128°
Inlet duration	139°
Lubrication system	Fuel/oil mix
Recommended engine lubricant	SAE 30W 2-cycle oil
Fuel mixture	16:1 first 500 miles, 20:1 thereafter
Starting system	Kickstarter

CARBURETOR

Type	Horizontal mounted Mikuni
Model	VM 24 SH-83B beginning frame No. C01701
Main jet	Std. 140
Venturi	24mm
Needle jet	O-4
Jet needle	4J6
Needle clip position	2nd notch (std.)
Pilot jet	15
Idle screw adjustment	1½ turns from closed
Throttle slide	1.5
Float valve seat	2.5
Starting carburetor jet	40
Air cleaner	Washable poly foam element type

MAGNETO / ALTERNATOR

Type	Flywheel type Kokusan Electric Co. unit with external HT coil (IG-4134)
Model	FP-6101
Lighting coil	45 watt rated
Lighting coil output	Over 6 volts at 2,500 rpm (with 45 watt circuit load); under 9 volts at 8,000 rpm
Ignition coil	
Power test	Steady fire over 7mm gap at 500 rpm Steady fire over 8mm at 5,000 rpm
Spark plug	NGK (std.) B-8HS NGK (cold) B-9HS
Condenser capacitance	.25 to .27 mf. (± 10%)
Magneto drive	Engine crankshaft
Contact breaker gap	.012" to .014" (.3mm to .4mm)
Spark plug gap	.024" to .027" (.6mm to .7mm)
Firing point (ignition timing)	.094" (2.4mm) BTDC

(continued)

SPECIFICATIONS, WOMBAT 125 (continued)

TRANSMISSION

Type: 5-speed, wide-ratio constant mesh with foot-operated gear change (Pat. No. 495715)

Gear ratio overall:
Standard gearing (56 x 14)
Low 37.84
Second 25.69
Third 18.33
Fourth 13.44
Fifth 10.45

Transmission gears

	Main shaft		Countershaft		Ratio
Low	9T	X	31T	=	3.44:1
Second	12T	X	28T	=	2.34:1
Third	15T	X	25T	=	1.67:1
Fourth	18T	X	22T	=	1.22:1
Fifth	20T	X	19T	=	0.95:1

Gear tooth module: 2.0
Foot change shaft end-play: .008" to .012" (.2mm to .3mm)
Foot change shaft end-play adj.: By washer
Washers available: .2mm-.3mm
Shifter arm adjustment: 1.382" (35.1mm) measured from shifter sliding pin to inside cover surface in third gear position
Shifter arm adjustment method: Eccentric bolt
Shifter guide side-play: .003" to .005" (.1mm to .15mm)
Shifter guide side-play adj.: By spacer
Spacers available: .2mm-.3mm

CLUTCH

Type: 4-plate wet type, crankshaft mounted
Clutch spring free length
  Inner spring: .68" (17.3mm)
  Outer spring: .66" (16.8mm)
Clutch lever free-play: 3/32" (2.4mm)
Clutch lever adjustment: By spacer
Spacers available: .2mm-.3mm-.5mm
Friction plate thickness (new): .098" (2.5mm)

PRIMARY DRIVE

Type: Helical cut gears
Pinion gear: 20T
Primary (main shaft) gear: 55T
Primary ratio: 2.75:1
Gear tooth module: 1.75

FINAL DRIVE

Type: Chain and sprockets
Chain dimensions: No. 428
Rear wheel sprocket: 56T
Countershaft sprocket: 14T
Final drive ratio: 4:1

(continued)

SPECIFICATIONS, WOMBAT 125 (continued)

KICKSTARTER	
Kick gear	29T
Kick shaft end-play	.002" to .004" (.05mm to .1mm)
Kick shaft end-play adjustment	By spacer
Spacers available	.2mm-.3mm-.5mm
LIGHTING SYSTEM EQUIPMENT	
Headlight	5" dia., dual sealed beam Stanley Electric Unit
Bulb data:	
Headlamp	6V35W/35W
High beam indicator	6V 1.5W
Speedometer lamp	6V 1.5W
Stop- and taillamp	6V 20W/5W
Dimmer switch	2 position - high, low
Main switch	3 position - off, ign., and ign./lights
Battery	6 volt, 4 ampere-hr., 3 cell, visible level, GN4-2A unit
Rectifier	Selenium type, single plate, 6 volt, 5-SH-E unit
FRAME	
Type	Duplex (twin tube), steel tube arc welded frame
FRONT SUSPENSION	
Type	Oil damped, spring cushioned, ferrous iron bushed, telescopic forks
Trail	4.92"
Castor angle	60°
Rake angle	30°
REAR SUSPENSION	
Type	Pivoted swing arm with multirate springs on single action hydraulic shock absorbers. 3-way spring and 2-position adjustment feature
WHEEL RIMS	
Type	Front 1.60A x 21", rear 1.185B x 18". Drop centers, 36 spokes
Spokes	10 ga. spring steel
TIRES AND TUBES	
Tires	2.75 x 21" front, 3.50 x 18" rear, trial tread, 4-ply nylon cord Nitto tires
Tubes	22 psi front, 25 psi rear (rider only)
Tire pressures	25 psi front, 28 psi rear (rider and passenger)

(continued)

SPECIFICATIONS, WOMBAT 125 (continued)

BRAKES

Type	Drum type with single leading shoe front and rear
Shoes	Die cast aluminum with bonded-on friction material
Drums	4.3" (110 front) 5.2" (130mm rear) dia., die cast aluminum full hub drums with cast iron friction surface

DIMENSIONS AND WEIGHT

Wheelbase	53"
Overall length	80.5"
Height at handlebars	42.70"
Height at saddle	30.74"
Width at handlebars	32.3"
Weight (dry)	208 lbs.
Ground clearance	9.5"

TORQUE SETTINGS

Cylinder head nuts	170 in.-lb. (2 mkg)
Flywheel nut	170 in.-lb. (2 mkg)
Clutch nut	250 in.-lb. (2.9 mkg)
Sprocket bolts	250 in.-lb. (2.9 mkg)

CAPACITIES

Fuel tank	2.8 U.S. gallons (10.4 liters)
Transmission	1¼ pints (581cc or .6 liters)
Front forks	5 oz. (148cc) per fork leg

CLEARANCES

Max. allowable cyl. taper (wear)	.008" (+.2mm)
Piston to cylinder clearance	.004" (.1mm)
Piston ring end gaps:	
Top ring	.006" to .014" (.15mm to .35mm)
Bottom ring	.004" to .012" (.10mm to .30mm)
Piston ring side-play:	
Top ring	.0004" to .0024" (.01mm to .06mm)
Bottom ring	.0008" to .0024" (.02mm to .06mm)
Piston pin to piston	.0008" (.02mm)
Piston pin to connecting rod bearing	.0003" to .0006" (.007mm to .014mm)
Connecting rod to crankpin	.0005" (.013mm)
Connecting rod side-play	.002" to .004" (.05mm to .1mm)

TIMING SPECIFICATIONS (STD.)

Transfer port timing			
(0.094")	2.4mm		BTDC
Transfer port timing			
(1.52")	38.5mm	64° 03'	BBDC
Exhaust port timing			
(1.26")	32mm	81° 01'	BBDC
Inlet port timing			
(3.27")	83mm	69° 27'	BTDC

SPECIFICATIONS, SUPER COMBAT 125

ENGINE

Type	2-stroke gasoline, air-cooled, 25° inclined single Alumiferric alloy cylinder. Loop scavenged, piston port/reed valve induction
Model	Hodaka 125SC97
Rated horsepower	@ 10,000 rpm
Maximum torque	@ 8,300 rpm
Bore	56mm (2.20")
Stroke	50mm (1.97")
Piston displacement	123cc (7.5 cu. in.)
Compression ratio	8.6:1 (actual)
Exhaust duration	170°
Transfer duration	133° 44'
Inlet duration	Control by reed
Lubrication system	Fuel/oil mix
Recommended engine lubricant	SAE 30W racing 2-cycle oil
Fuel/oil mixture	16:1
Starting system	Kickstarter
Induction system	Reed valve

CARBURETOR

Type	Horizontal mounted Mikuni instrument with slide throttle and needle jet system
Model	VM 32 SC
Main jet	Std. 350
Venturi	32mm
Needle jet	R9
Jet needle	6F9
Needle clip position	3rd notch (std.)
Pilot jet	35
Idle screw adjustment	1¼ turns from closed
Throttle slide	
Float valve seat	3.3
Starting carburetor jet	80
Air cleaner	Washable micronic foam, oil saturated

IGNITION SYSTEM

Type	Kokusan Denki MR2397 inner rotor capacitor discharge ignition (CDI)
Ignition coil	
Power test	Steady fire over 7mm gap at 500 rpm Steady fire over 14mm gap at 3,000 rpm
Spark plug	NGK (std.) B9HV NGK (cold) B10V
Spark plug gap	.016" to .024" (.4mm to .7mm)
Firing point (ignition timing)	Align stator reference line with center line on rotor when piston is at 3.95mm (.155") BTDC

(continued)

SPECIFICATIONS, SUPER COMBAT 125 (continued)

CLUTCH
Type	5-plate wet type, crankshaft mounted
Clutch spring free length	
Inner spring	17.3mm (.68")
Outer spring	16.9mm (.66")
Clutch lever free-play	2.4mm (.094")
Clutch lever adjustment	By spacer
Spacers available	.2mm-.3mm-.5mm
Friction plate thickness (new)	2.5mm (.098")

PRIMARY DRIVE
Type	Spur gears
Pinion gear	21T
Primary gear	59T
Primary ratio	2.81:1
Gear tooth module	1.75

TRANSMISSION
Type	5-speed, wide-ratio constant mesh with foot-operated gear change (Pat. No. 495715)
Gear ratio overall:	
Standard gearing	14 x 64
First	37.24
Second	25.68
Third	19.26
Fourth	16.62
Fifth	14.98

Transmission gears

	Main shaft		Countershaft		Ratio
First	10T	X	29T	=	2.90:1
Second	13T	X	26T	=	2.00:1
Third	16T	X	24T	=	1.50:1
Fourth	17T	X	22T	=	1.29:1
Fifth	18T	X	21T	=	1.17:1

Gear tooth module	2.0
Foot change shaft end-play	.008" to .012" (.2mm to .3mm)
Foot change shaft end-play adj.	By washer
Washers available	.2mm-.3mm
Shifter arm adjustment	1.382" (35.1mm) measured from shifter sliding pin to inside cover surface in third gear position.
Shifter arm adjustment method	Eccentric bolt
Shifter guide side-play	.003" to .005" (.1mm to .15mm)
Shifter guide side-play adj.	By spacer
Spacers available	.2mm-.3mm

FINAL DRIVE
Type	Chain and sprockets
Chain dimensions	No. 428 heavy duty Daido chain (½" x 5/16" x 0.335" roller)
Rear wheel sprocket	64T
Countershaft sprocket	14T
Final drive ratio	4.57:1

(continued)

SPECIFICATIONS, SUPER COMBAT 125 (continued)

KICKSTARTER	
Kick gear	30T
Kick shaft end-play	.002" to .004" (.05mm to .1mm)
Kick shaft end-play adjustment	By spacer
Spacers available	.2mm-.3mm-.5mm
FRAME	
Type	Duplex (twin tube), with kicker tube, steel tube arc welded frame
FRONT SUSPENSION	
Type	Improved dampening system—rebound spring removed—spring rate revised
Trail	5.00"
Castor angle	60.7°
Rake angle	29.3°
Steering angle	45°
REAR SUSPENSION	
Type	Pivoted swing arm with springs on single action hydraulic shock absorbers. 2-way spring and 2-position adjustment feature
WHEEL RIMS	
Type	
(Front)	21" shoulderless alloy rim, WM-1 wides, 9-gauge spokes
(Rear)	18" shoulderless alloy rim, WM-2 width, 9-gauge spokes
TIRES AND TUBES	
Tires	3.00 x 21" front, 3.50 x 18" rear, motocross tread, 4-ply nylon cord Nitto tires
Tubes	Nitto butyl rubber tubes
Tire pressures	22 psi front, 25 psi rear (rider only)
BRAKES	
Type	Drum type with single leading shoe front and rear
Shoes	Die cast aluminum with bonded-on friction material
Drums	4.3" (110mm front) 5.2" (130mm rear) dia., die cast aluminum full hub drums with cast iron friction surface
DIMENSIONS AND WEIGHT	
Wheelbase	52.36"
Overall length	78.74"
Height at handlebars	42.99"
Height at saddle	32.2"
Width at footpegs	17.7"
Width at handlebars	32.28"
Weight (dry)	191.63 lbs.
Ground clearance	7.48"
Width (overall)	33.85"
Height (overall)	42.99"

(continued)

SPECIFICATIONS, SUPER COMBAT 125 (continued)

TORQUE SETTINGS

Cylinder head nuts	170 in.-lb. (2 mkg)
Flywheel nut	170 in.-lb. (2 mkg)
Clutch nut	250 in.-lb. (2.9 mkg)
Sprocket bolts	250 in.-lb. (2.9 mkg)
Spark plug	200 in.-lb. (2.3 mkg)

CAPACITIES

Fuel tank	2.0 U.S. gal. (7.6 liters)
Transmission	1¼ pints (591cc or .6 liter)
Front forks	6 oz. (1775cc) per fork leg

CLEARANCES

Max. allowable cyl. taper (wear)	.008" (+.2mm)
Piston to cylinder clearance	.003" (.08mm)
Top ring end-gap	.006" to .014" (.15mm to .35mm)
Piston ring side-play	.0004" to .0024" (.01mm to .06mm)
Piston pin to piston	.0008" (.02mm)
Piston pin to connecting rod bearing	.0003" to .0006" (.007mm to .014mm)
Connecting rod to crankpin	.0005" (.013mm)
Connecting rod side-play	.002" to .004" (.05mm to .1mm)

TIMING SPECIFICATIONS (STD.)

Transfer port timing
    (1.52")   38.5mm   64° 03' std.
Exhaust port timing
    (1.02")   26mm   85° std.
Inlet port timing
    (3.27")   85mm   73° 55' std. (reed controlled)

INDEX

A

Air cleaner
  Periodic maintenance 23
  Removal and installation 65-66

B

Battery
  Charging 79-80
  Inspection and testing 79
  Installation 80-81
  Periodic maintenance 17
  Removal 75
Battery bracket 108
Brakes
  Adjustment 21-22
  Competition preparation 114
  Inspection and cleaning 89-90
  Lubrication 23
  Pedal 106
  Troubleshooting 30
Breaker points 15

C

Carburetor
  Adjustment 58
  Competition preparation, Trials 118-119
  Disassembly 63-64
  Float level adjustment 63
  Idle adjustment 61
  Inspection and reassemby 64
  Jet needle adjustment 61
  Main jet 59
  Pilot jet 59
  Throttle valve 59-61
Chain
  Adjustment 19-20
  Inspection 21
  Lubrication 20
Clutch
  Adjustment 38
  Disassembly 41
  Inspection 41-42
  Lever 40
  Reassembly and inspection 42-43
  Removal 40-41
  Slip or drag 30
Competition preparation
  Brakes, wheels, and tires 114
  Cylinder 120-122
  Frame 113-114
  Gearing 114
  Gearing and suspension 120
  Motocross 115-118
  Reed valve conversion 120
  Road racing 109-113
  Trials 118-119
Condenser (capacitor) 15
Crankshaft reassembly 52-53
Cylinder head
  Competition preparation 120-122
  Cylinder and piston scores 36
  Cylinder boring 36-37
  Cylinder rings, new 37
  Decarbonizing 35-36
  Piston and cylinder measuring 36
  Piston removal 34-35
  Piston seizure 29
  Reassembly 37-38
  Removal 34

E

Electrical system
  Battery 75, 79-81
  Breaker points 15
  Condenser (capacitor) 15
  Fuse 17-18
  General information 70
  Headlight 75
  Horn 75
  Ignition system, competition preparation .. 119
  Ignition system operation 15
  Ignition timing 16-17
  Spotlight switch 17
  Magneto 72
  Magneto and flywheel installation .. 74-75
  Spark plug 8-9, 14, 15
  Stoplight switch 22
  Taillight 75
  Troubleshooting 30
  Wiring diagrams 82-85
Engine
  Case disassembly 43, 49-50
  Case reassembly 53-54
  Competition preparation, Trials 118
  Crankshaft reassembly 52-53
  Cylinder and piston measuring 36
  Cylinder and piston scores 36
  Cylinder boring 36-37
  Cylinder head and cylinder removal .. 34-35
  Decarbonizing 35-36
  Inspection 50-52
  Lubrication 19
  Noises, unusual 29

    Operating principles 33-34
    Operating requirements 26-27
    Reassembly 37
    Removal 43
Exhaust system
    Competition preparation, Trials 118
    Pipe and muffler 66

F

Flat spots 29
Fender service 104
Flywheel
    Installation 74-75
    Removal 70
Foot pegs 106
Fork, front 100, 104
Frame
    Battery bracket 108
    Brake pedal 106
    Competition preparation 113-114, 119
    Fender 104
    Foot pegs 106
    Front forks 100-104
    Seat 104
    Service 97
    Side stand 108
    Steering head 97-100
    Tool box 108
Fuel system
    Carburetor adjustments 58-63
    Carburetor overhaul 63-64
    Fuel tank 64
    General information 58
    Manifold 64
    Throttle cable 64-65
Fuse 17-18

G

Gearing, competition preparation 111, 120
Gear selector adjustment 18
General information 1-7

H

Handling, poor 30
Headlight 18, 75
Horn 75

I

Identification numbers 7
Idling, poor 29
Ignition system operation 15
Ignition timing 16-17

L

Lubrication (see Maintenance, periodic)

M

Magneto
    Installation 74-75
    Removal, disassembly, inspection,
      and reassembly 72
Maintenance, periodic
    Air cleaner 23
    Battery 17
    Brake adjustment 21-22
    Brake lubrication 23
    Breaker points 15
    Carburetors and exhausts 24
    Chain adjustment 19-20
    Chain lubrication 20
    Condenser (capacitor) 15
    Fuse 17-18
    Gear selector adjustment 18
    Headlight 18
    Ignition system operation 15
    Ignition timing 16-17
    Lubrication 19
    Maintenance schedule, enduro models ...10-11
    Maintenance schedule, off-road models ...12-13
    Oil changes 8
    Spark plugs 8-9, 14, 15
    Stoplight switch 17, 22
    Storage, winter 24-25
Manifold 64
Manual organization 1-2
Master link 21
Misfiring 29
Motocross preparation 115-118

O

Oil changes 8
Overheating 29

P

Parts replacement 4
Pistons
    Decarbonizing 35-36
    Measuring 36
    Reassembly and installation 37-38
    Removal 34-35
    Scores 36
Power loss 29

R

Reed valve conversion 120
Road racing 109-113

S

Safety hints	3-4
Seat	104
Serial numbers	7
Service hints	2-3
Shifter assembly	54-57
Side stand	108
Spark plugs	8-9, 15

Specifications
- Ace 90 125-129
- Ace 100 130-135
- Ace 100-B 140-145
- Dirt Squirt 100 136-139
- Super Combat 125 155-158
- Wombat 125 151-154
- 100-MX (Super Rat) 146-150

Spotlight switch 17
Starting difficulties 27-29
Steering head
- Adjustment 97-99
- Disassembly, inspection, and reassembly 99-100
- Lubrication 99

Stoplight switch 22
Storage, winter 24-25
Supplies, expendable 6-7
Suspension, rear 104

T

Taillight 75
Throttle cable 64-65
Tire changing and repair 95-96
Tires, competition preparation 114, 119
Tool box 108
Tools 4-6, 8
Transmission
- Lubrication 19
- Shifter mechanism 54-57
- Troubleshooting 30

Trials 118
Troubleshooting
- Brake problems 30
- Clutch slip or drag 30
- Electrical problems 30
- Engine noises 29
- Engine operating requirements 26-27
- Flat spots 29
- General information 26
- Handling, poor 30
- Idling, poor 29
- Instruments, troubleshooting 4-6
- Misfiring 29
- Overheating 29
- Piston seizure 29
- Power loss 29
- Starting difficulties 27-29
- Transmission 30
- Troubleshooting guide 31-32
- Vibration, excessive 29

W

Waterproofing, competition preparation 118
Wheels
- Alignment 94-95
- Backing plate 39
- Balancing 94
- Bearings 91
- Competition preparation 114, 119
- Inspection, wheel and spoke 91
- Lacing 92-94
- Reassembly 90-91
- Removal 86-89
- Truing 92

Wiring diagrams
- 90 82
- 100A 83
- 100-B 84
- 100 (all off-road and competition models) 85

NOTES

VELOCEPRESS MANUALS – MOTORCYCLE BY MAKE

AJS 1932-1948 SINGLES & TWINS 250cc THRU 1000cc (BOOK OF)
AJS 1945-1960 SINGLES 350cc & 500cc MODELS 16 & 18 (BOOK OF)
AJS 1955-1965 SINGLES 350cc & 500cc (BOOK OF)
AJS 1957-1966 FACTORY WSM - ALL SINGLES & TWINS
AJS 1959-1969 FACTORY WSM G80CS G85CS & P11 OFF ROAD
ARIEL UP TO 1932 (BOOK OF)
ARIEL 1932-1939 PREWAR MODELS (BOOK OF)
ARIEL 1933-1951 (WORKSHOP MANUAL)
ARIEL 1939-1960 4 STROKE SINGLES (BOOK OF)
ARIEL 1958-1964 LEADER & ARROW FACTORY WSM & PARTS LIST
ARIEL 1958-1964 LEADER & ARROW (BOOK OF)
BMW R26 R27 (1956-1967) FACTORY WORKSHOP MANUAL
BMW R50 R50S R60 R69S (1955-1969) FACTORY WORKSHOP MANUAL
BMW R50/5 R60/5 R75/5 (1969-1973) FACTORY WORKSHOP MANUAL
BRIDGESTONE 90 SERIES FACTORY WSM & PARTS CATALOGUE
BRIDGESTONE 175 SERIES FACTORY WSM & PARTS CATALOGUE
BRIDGESTONE 350 SERIES FACTORY WSM & PARTS CATALOGUE
BSA SERVICE SHEETS MASTER CATALOGUE ALL MODELS 1945-1967
BSA BANTAM D1 TO D7 1948-1966 FACTORY SERVICE SHEETS MANUAL
BSA BANTAM ALL MODELS FROM 1948 ONWARDS (BOOK OF)
BSA BANTAM D14 FACTORY SERVICE MANUAL
BSA DANDY FACTORY WORKSHOP MANUAL (COMPILATION)
BSA SINGLES & V-TWINS UP TO 1926 inc. 1927 SUPPLEMENT (BOOK OF)
BSA SINGLES & V-TWINS UP TO 1930 (BOOK OF)
BSA SINGLES & V-TWINS UP TO 1935 (BOOK OF)
BSA SINGLES & V-TWINS 1936-1939 (BOOK OF)
BSA C10, C11 & C12 1945-1958 FACTORY SERVICE SHEETS MANUAL
BSA OHV & SV SINGLES 250-600cc 1945-1959 (BOOK OF)
BSA C15 & B40 1958-1967 FACTORY SERVICE SHEETS MANUAL
BSA OHV & SV SINGLES 250cc (ONLY) 1954-1970 (BOOK OF)
BSA B31, B32, B33 & B34 1945-60 FACTORY SERVICE SHEETS MANUAL
BSA OHV SINGLES 350 & 500cc 1955-1967 (BOOK OF)
BSA M20, M21 & M33 1945-1963 FACTORY SERVICE SHEETS MANUAL
BSA TWINS A7 & A10 1948-1962 FACTORY SERVICE SHEETS MANUAL
BSA TWINS A7 & A10 1948-1962 (BOOK OF)
BSA TWINS A50 & A65 1962-1965 FACTORY WORKSHOP MANUAL
BSA TWINS A50 & A65 1962-1969 (SECOND BOOK OF)
BULTACO 125cc to 37cc SINGLES 1968-1979 WORKSHOP MANUAL
CZ 125cc to 380cc SINGLES 1967-1974 WORKSHOP MANUAL
DOUGLAS 1929-1939 PREWAR ALL MODELS (BOOK OF)
DOUGLAS 1948-1957 POSTWAR ALL MODELS FACTORY SHOP MANUAL
DUCATI 160cc, 250cc & 350cc OHC MODELS FACTORY SHOP MANUAL
HODAKA 90cc,100cc & 125cc SINGLES 1964-1978 WORKSHOP MANUAL
HONDA 50cc ALL MODELS UP TO 1970 INC MONKEY & TRAIL (BOOK OF)
HONDA 90cc ALL MODELS UP TO 1966 (BOOK OF)
HONDA TWINS & SINGLES 50cc THRU 305cc 1960-1966 (BOOK OF)
HONDA TWINS ALL MODELS 125cc THRU 450cc UP TO 1968 (BOOK OF)
HONDA C100 50cc SUPER CUB O.H.C. 1959-1962 FACTORY WSM
HONDA C110 50cc SPORT CUB O.H.C. 1960-1962 FACTORY WSM
HONDA 50-65-70-90cc O.H.C. SINGLES 1959-1983 WSM
HONDA 100-125cc SINGLES CB/CD/CL/SL/TL 1970-1984 FACTORY WSM
HONDA 125-150cc TWINS C/CS/CB/CA 1959-1966 FACTORY WSM
HONDA 125-160-175-200cc TWINS 1965-1978 WORKSHOP MANUAL
HONDA 250-305cc TWINS CB/CS/CB 1961-1968 FACTORY WSM
HOHDA 250-350cc TWINS CB/CL/SL 1968-1973 FACTORY WSM
HONDA 250-360cc TWINS CB/CL/CJ 1974-1977 FACTORY WSM
HONDA 350F & 400F 4-CYLINDER 1972-1977 FACTORY WSM
HONDA 450cc TWINS CB/CL 1965-1974 K0 TO K7 WORKSHOP MANUAL
HONDA 500cc & 550cc 4-CYL 1971-1978 FACTORY WORKSHOP MANUAL
HONDA 750cc SHOC 4-CYL 1969-1978 K0~K8 WORKSHOP MANUAL
HUSQVARNA 125cc to 450cc SINGLES 1965-1975 WORKSHOP MANUAL
INDIAN PONYBIKE, BOY RACER & PAPOOSE ILL PARTS LIST & SALES LIT

J.A.P. ENGINES 1927-1952 & MOTORCYCLES 1934-1952 (BOOK OF)
MATCHLESS 1931-1939 ALL MODELS 250cc THRU 990cc (BOOK OF)
MATCHLESS 1945-1956 350 & 500cc SINGLES (BOOK OF)
MATCHLESS 1955-1966 350 & 500cc SINGLES (BOOK OF)
MATCHLESS 1957-1966 FACTORY WSM - ALL SINGLES & TWINS
NEW IMPERIAL ALL SV & OHV FROM 1935 ONWARDS (BOOK OF)
NORTON 1932-1939 PREWAR MODELS (BOOK OF)
NORTON 1932-1947 (BOOK OF)
NORTON 1938-1956 (BOOK OF)
NORTON 1945-1963 MODELS 16H, Big4, ES2, 19 & 50 WSM'S & PARTS
NORTON 1955-1963 MODELS 19, 50 & ES2 (BOOK OF)
NORTON 1948-1970 DOMINATOR TWINS FACTORY WSM'S & PARTS
NORTON 1955-1965 DOMINATOR TWINS (BOOK OF)
NORTON 1960-1970 TWIN CYLINDER FACTORY WORKSHOP MANUAL
NORTON 1970-1975 COMMANDO 850 & 750cc FACTORY WSM
NORTON 1975-1978 MK 3 COMMANDO 850 cc FACTORY WSM
PANTHER 1932-1958 LIGHTWEIGHT MODELS 250 & 350cc (BOOK OF)
PANTHER 1938-1966 HEAVYWEIGHT MODELS 600 & 650cc (BOOK OF)
PENTON-KTM-SACHS 1968-1975 100cc & 125cc WORKSHOP MANUAL
PENTON-KTM 1972-1975 175cc, 250cc & 400cc WSM & PARTS MANUALS
RALEIGH MOTORCYCLES 1919-1933 (BOOK OF)
ROYAL ENFIELD 1934-1946 SINGLES & V TWINS (BOOK OF)
ROYAL ENFIELD 1937-1953 SINGLES & V TWINS (BOOK OF)
ROYAL ENFIELD 1946-1962 SINGLES (BOOK OF)
ROYAL ENFIELD 1948-1962 350cc & 500cc PRE-UNIT BULLET WSM
ROYAL ENFIELD 1948-1963 500cc TWINS FACTORY WORKSHOP MANUAL
ROYAL ENFIELD 1952-1963 700cc TWINS FACTORY WORKSHOP MANUAL
ROYAL ENFIELD 1956-1966 250cc CRUSADER & 350cc NEW BULLET WSM
ROYAL ENFIELD 1958-1966 250cc & 350cc SINGLES (SECOND BOOK OF)
ROYAL ENFIELD 1962-1970 INTERCEPTOR WSM'S & PARTS (Compilation)
RUDGE 1933-1939 (BOOK OF)
SACHS 1968-1975 100cc & 125cc ENGINES WSM & M/CYCLE PARTS LIST
SUNBEAM 1928-1939 (BOOK OF)
SUNBEAM 1946-1957 S7 & S8 (BOOK OF)
SUZUKI 50cc & 80cc UP TO 1966 (BOOK OF)
SUZUKI T10 1963-1967 FACTORY WORKSHOP MANUAL
SUZUKI T20 & T200 1965-1969 FACTORY WORKSHOP MANUAL
SUZUKI TWINS 1962 ONWARDS 125-500cc WORKSHOP MANUAL
TRIUMPH 1935-1949 SINGLES & TWINS (BOOK OF)
TRIUMPH 1937-1961 SINGLES SV & OHV 250cc-600cc + TERRIER & CUB
TRIUMPH 1945-1955 PRE-UNIT 350cc, 500cc & 650cc TWINS WSM No.11
TRIUMPH 1945-1959 TWINS (BOOK OF)
TRIUMPH 1956-1969 TWINS (BOOK OF)
TRIUMPH 1956-1962 PRE-UNIT 500cc & 650cc TWINS WSM No.17
TRIUMPH 1957-1963 UNIT CONSTRUCTION 350-500cc WSM No.4
TRIUMPH 1963-1974 UNIT CONSTRUCTION 350-500cc FACTORY WSM
TRIUMPH 1963-1970 UNIT CONSTRUCTION 650cc FACTORY WSM
TRIUMPH 1968-1974 TRIDENT T150 & T150V FACTORY WSM
TRIUMPH 1971-1973 650cc OIL-IN-FRAME FACTORY WSM
TRIUMPH 1973-1978 750cc BONNEVILLE & TIGER FACTORY WSM
TRIUMPH 1979-1983 750cc T140, TR7 & TR65 FACTORY WSM
VELOCETTE 1925-1970 ALL SINGLES & TWINS (BOOK OF)
VELOCETTE 1933-1952 MOV-MAC-MSS RIGID FRAME FACTORY WSM
VELOCETTE 1953-1960 MAC SPRING FRAME WSM & ILL PARTS LIST
VELOCETTE 1954-1971 MSS-VENOM-THRUXTON-VIPER FACTORY WSM
VILLIERS ENGINE UP TO 1959 INC. 3 WHEELERS (BOOK OF)
VILLIERS ENGINE UP TO 1969 (BOOK OF)
VINCENT 1935-1955 (WORKSHOP MANUAL)
YAMAHA 1961-1967 YA5 & YA6 (WORKSHOP MANUAL & ILL PARTS LIST)
YAMAHA 1968-1971 DT1 & MX SERIES Inc. GYT WORKSHOP MANUAL
YAMAHA 1971-1972 JT1& JT2 (WORKSHOP MANUAL & ILL PARTS LIST)

VELOCEPRESS MANUALS – SCOOTERS BY MAKE

BSA SUNBEAM SCOOTER WORKSHOP MANUAL 1959-1965
BSA SUNBEAM SCOOTER 1959-1965 (BOOK OF)
LAMBRETTA 1947-1957 ALL 125 & 150cc MODELS (BOOK OF)
LAMBRETTA 1957-1970 LI & TV MODELS (SECOND BOOK OF)
NSU PRIMA 1956-1964 ALL MODELS (BOOK OF)
TRIUMPH TIGRESS SCOOTER WORKSHOP MANUAL 1959-1965
TRIUMPH TIGRESS SCOOTER (BOOK OF)
VESPA 1951-1961 (BOOK OF)
VESPA 1955-1963 125 & 150cc & GS MODELS (SECOND BOOK OF)
VESPA 1955-1968 GS & SS (BOOK OF)
VESPA 1963-1972 90, 125 & 150cc (THIRD BOOK OF)

VELOCEPRESS MANUALS – MOPEDS & MOTORIZED BICYCLES

CYCLEMOTOR (BOOK OF)
NSU QUICKLY 1953-1963 ALL MODELS (BOOK OF)
PUCH MAXI N & S MAINTENANCE & REPAIR (3 MANUAL COMPILATION)
RALEIGH MOPEDS 1960-1969 (BOOK OF)

VELOCEPRESS MANUALS - THREE WHEELER'S

BOND MINICAR THREE WHEELER 1948-1967 (BOOK OF)
BMW ISETTA FACTORY WORKSHOP MANUAL
BSA THREE WHEELER (BOOK OF)
RELIANT REGAL THREE WHEELER 1952-1973 (BOOK OF)
VINTAGE MORGAN THREE WHEELER (BOOK OF)

VELOCEPRESS TECHNICAL BOOKS – MOTORCYCLE

1930'S BRITISH MOTORCYCLE CARBS & ELEC COMPONENTS (BOOK OF)
1930'S BRITISH MOTORCYCLE ENGINES (OVERHAUL & MAINTENANCE)
1930'S BRITISH MOTORCYCLE GEARBOXES & CLUTCHES (BOOK OF)
CATALOG OF BRITISH MOTORCYCLES (1951 MODELS)
LUCAS ELECTRONICS BRITISH M/CYCLES REPAIR & PARTS (1950-1977)
MOTORCYCLE ENGINEERING (P.E. Irving)
MOTORCYCLE ROAD TESTS 1949-1953 (Motor Cycle Magazine UK)
SPEED AND HOW TO OBTAIN IT (Motor Cycle Magazine UK)
TUNING FOR SPEED (P.E. Irving)
WIPAC (COMBO) MANUAL NUMBER 3 + M/CYCLE & SCOOTER MANUAL

VELOCEPRESS MANUALS – AUTOMOBILE BY MAKE

ALFA ROMEO GIULIA WORKSHOP MANUAL 1300 TO 2000cc 1962-1975
ALFA ROMEO GIULIA TECH MANUAL CARBURETED CARS FROM 1962
ALFA ROMEO GIULIA TECH MANUAL FUEL INJECTED CARS FROM 1969
ALFA ROMEO GIULIETTA & GIULIA 750 & 101 SERIES 1955-1965 WSM
AUSTIN-HEALEY SPRITE & MG MIDGET WORKSHOP MANUAL 1958-1971
BMW 600 LIMOUSINE FACTORY WORKSHOP MANUAL
BMW 600 LIMOUSINE OWNERS HAND BOOK & SERVICE MANUAL
BMW 2000 & 2002 1966-1976 WORKSHOP MANUAL
BMW 2500, 2800, 3.0 & BARVARIA WORKSHOP MANUAL
CORVAIR 1960-1969 WORKSHOP MANUAL
CORVETTE V8 1955-1962 WORKSHOP MANUAL
FERRARI HANDBOOK ROAD & RACE CARS (SERVICE/SPECS) 1948-1958
FERRARI 250GT SERVICE & MAINTENANCE by JIM RIFF 1956-1965
FERRARI 250GT & 250GTE FACTORY PARTS AND REPAIR MANUALS
FIAT 500 FACTORY WORKSHOP MANUAL 1957-1973
FIAT 600, 600D & MULTIPLA FACTORY WORKSHOP MANUAL 1955-1969
FORD MUSTANG 1965-1973 TRANSMISSION WORKSHOP MANUAL
JAGUAR E-TYPE 3.8 & 4.2 SERIES 1 & 2 WORKSHOP MANUAL
JAGUAR MK 7, 8, 9 & XK120, 140, 150 WORKSHOP MANUAL 1948-1961
MERCEDES-BENZ 230 SERIES 1963-1968
MERCEDES-BENZ 280 SERIES 1968-1972
METROPOLITAN FACTORY WORKSHOP MANUAL
MGA & MGB OWNERS HANDBOOK & WORKSHOP MANUAL
MG MIDGET TC, TD, TF & TF1500 WORKSHOP MANUAL
PORSCHE 356 1948-1965 WORKSHOP MANUAL
PORSCHE 911 2.0, 2.2, 2.4 LITRE 1964-1973 WORKSHOP MANUAL
PORSCHE 911 2.7, 3.0, 3.2 LITRE 1973-1989 WORKSHOP MANUAL
PORSCHE 912 WORKSHOP MANUAL
PORSCHE 914/4 & 914/6 1.7, 1.8, 2.0 LITRE 1970-1976 WSM
TRIUMPH TR2, TR3, TR4 1953-1965 WORKSHOP MANUAL
VOLKSWAGEN TRANSPORTER, TRUCKS & WAGONS 1950-1979 WSM
VOLVO 1944-1968 ALL MODELS WORKSHOP MANUAL

VELOCEPRESS TECHNICAL BOOKS - AUTOMOBILE

HOW TO BUILD A FIBERGLASS CAR
HOW TO BUILD A RACING CAR
HOW TO RESTORE THE MODEL 'A' FORD
MASERATI OWNER'S HANDBOOK
PERFORMANCE TUNING THE SUNBEAM TIGER
SOUPING THE VOLKSWAGEN
SOLEX CARBURETORS (EMPHASIS ON UK & EU AUTOMOBILES)
SU CARBURETORS (EMPHASIS ON UK AUTOMOBILES)
WEBER CARBURETORS (EMPHASIS ON ALFA & FIAT)

VELOCEPRESS BOOKS & GUIDES - AUTOMOBILE

COMPLETE CATALOG OF JAPANESE MOTOR VEHICLES
FERRARI 308 SERIES BUYER'S AND OWNER'S GUIDE
FERRARI BROCHURES AND SALES LITERATURE 1968-1989
FERRARI SERIAL NUMBERS PART I - ODD NUMBERS TO 21399
FERRARI SERIAL NUMBERS PART II - EVEN NUMBERS TO 1050
HENRY'S FABULOUS MODEL "A" FORD
MASERATI BROCHURES AND SALES LITERATURE

VELOCEPRESS BOOKS – AUTO RACING

BOOK OF THE 1950 CARRERA PANAMERICANA - MEXICAN ROAD RACE
DIALED IN - THE JAN OPPERMAN STORY
VEDA ORR'S NEW REVISED HOT ROD PICTORIAL
LIFE OF TED HORN – AMERICAN RACING CHAMPION

www.VelocePress.com

www.ingramcontent.com/pod-product-compliance
Lightning Source LLC
Chambersburg PA
CBHW080739300426
44114CB00019B/2630